Since Costa Rica

A Novel

Doug E. Jones

This is a work of fiction. Names, characters, places, and incidents either are the product of the author's imagination or are used fictitiously. Any resemblance to actual persons, living or dead, events, or locales, is entirely coincidental.

@Freshguy88

ISBN: 1729608922
ISBN-13: 978-1729608920

for Angie, always

CONTENTS

What Ever Happened To Saturday Night?

Hotel, Motel, Holiday Inn

Tamarindo

Cheap Sunglasses

You Should Be Dancing, Yeah

Mi Casa Es Su Casa

Our House, In The Middle Of

Gallo Pinto

Let's Go Surfin' Now

Love And Marriage

Going To The Chapel

Blood, Sweat, & Tears

Running To Stand Still

Do You Know The Way To San Jose?

On The Road Again

Go On Take The Money And Run

Montezuma's Revenge

Free Fallin'

Been Caught Stealing

Ain't Supposed To Die On A Saturday Night

Imagine the future, woke up with a scream
I was buying some feelings from a vending machine

--The Verve

1

What Ever Happened To Saturday Night?

It's Saturday night. . .

Brian cracks open a beer.

Scarfs down some pizza.

And checks the score of the game.

Pretty soon, the couch asks him to commit, but he has energy to spare so he jumps in the shower and hops on the train. He's in the city before midnight, the guys waiting for him at a bar. No wives. No kids. No curfews. And considering how much fun they're intending to have, he has no idea where he'll sleep tonight or if sleep will even be an option. It's not as if he's working tomorrow, even though he could use the money. And yet, that's not a problem. Nothing is: *Hold on, who're those chicks over by the pool table?*

Unfortunately, that was years ago, decades even; the resulting hole in his heart filled with not only the acute awareness of the necessity for money but the belief that enough of it can cure what ails him. And it's true. Money can help send his niece to college and get him that cool sports car he's always wanted. It can probably even win him the love of a beautiful woman to sit next to him in that car.

However, the one thing money can't buy is Brian's youth. Sure, pills and plastic surgery can make him look and feel young—at the risk of doing just the opposite. And diet and exercise can do wonders in the name of self-inflicted torture. But, in reality, he'd only be prolonging the inevitable. Nothing can make him young again. Nothing can take Brian back.

Except for his oldest childhood friends. Like Jack. Just seeing that stupid grin of his takes Brian back to the reckless and sometimes painful days of his youth. A simple conversation over a beer and it's the first day of middle school, Jack laughing through an apology as he searches the playground for Brian's front tooth.

And Darryl always comes home at Christmas, usually once in the summer too. Brian can hardly look at him without thinking of Camp Echo, the night Darryl fell, or *got pushed*, and landed on Brian's leg, fracturing it in three places.

As for Neal, his contribution to Brian's memory bank left more of an emotional scar, since he was the knucklehead who didn't lock up Brian's new 10-speed at Baker Park.

And he could never forget when Robbie threw-up, clearing the porch but nailing Brian's dad's rose bushes with a peanut butter shake from Doctor Jazz, one that he mixed with half a pint of Southern Comfort; Brian was charged by his dad as an accessory and grounded for a month.

Then, of course, there was Spring Break, the year the guys went to Fort Lauderdale, when Paul was responsible for Brian catching crabs—the kind that itch uncontrollably in awkward areas.

However, for all the bumps and bugs, there was an endless string of groundbreaking Saturdays, like August 29th 1992, the summer before sophomore year of high school. That was the day all seven teenagers piled into Darryl's Cavalier, the one he *borrowed* from his aunt, and drove up to Alpine

Valley for Lollapalooza, nary a license among them.

They also didn't have tickets to the festival. And were baked beyond belief. Otherwise, they never would've followed Robbie over a fence, through a corn field, and into a dirty storm drain. . .

Miraculously popping out at the venue's second stage, just in time to catch the Jim Rose Circus Sideshow; a clan of heavily pierced and tattooed performers who employed an arsenal of darts, nails, and swords to demonstrate the body's ability to withstand pain, particularly in areas one might consider predisposed to sensitivity.

A carnival trick involving surgical tubing, a plunger, and a glass of bile beer had a granola girl in the first row blowing chunks, though Paul insisted that Neal's poorly timed joke, "Say, cheese," didn't help.

As gross and downright unappetizing as the last half hour had been, the guys huddled, set to bail for some food when, unannounced, Pearl Jam's Eddie Vedder walked out on that same stage, the one way in back, behind the hill, with Chris Cornell from Soundgarden.

Just the two lead singers.

Long hair down their backs.

Eddie's band touring *Ten*.

Chris' riding high on singles "Outshined" and "Rusty Cage."

Each brandishing a guitar to play their new rock anthem "Hunger Strike" for maybe fifty people; some thunderstruck, others completely unaware they were in the presence of soon to be grunge greatness.

Brian always considered that day, even that song, a turning point in his life.

First Eddie, singing low: *I'm goin' hun-gray. . .*

Then Chris, high: *I'm goin' hun-gray-ay!*

But the guys were in Wisconsin, so afterward they went to

find brats.

By the time most of them had graduated from college and scattered across the country for work, Saturday nights with the guys had become less and less frequent, eventually morphing into a yearly escape.

For example, to close out the 20th century, six of the guys met in Lake Tahoe for a ski weekend that somehow, *seriously honey*, ended up a gambling weekend, one in which heavy losses coddled with free drinks left them all in the local drunk tank.

It wasn't until Monday morning that the guys finally quieted down in the cell, except for a suspect sniffle or two, with Robbie, tears in his eyes, clinging to a vinyl record, Prince's *1999*.

That was the last time Robbie made an appearance on a road trip, which wasn't surprising, considering it cost him his first real job out of college.

Then, there was 2007 in Miami. Super Bowl XLI. The year they all turned thirty. Five of the guys flew down to root on the Bears.

Brian even shelled out for a three-bedroom suite in South Beach. "One of the rooms is a single with a king, has its own bathroom," he told everyone, as he unlocked the door.

"Whoever brings back a girl," tried Jack, "gets the room."

Seeing as he paid for it, Brian knew he could have taken the room for himself but graciously, or just wanting to avoid an argument, agreed to give the guys a chance to prove their mettle within the tribe.

Or not. Saturday night, Super Bowl Eve, Neal tried to get a woman up to the suite, even enticing her with money. She was really good looking, barely squeezing into a red dress, just standing there outside a hotel on Ocean Drive.

She was also an undercover cop, running a Super Bowl sting. Jack tried to convince her that his friend was joking, drunk in fact, and married, possibly gay, that he only did it for the big room, so he could have his own toilet.

Neal spent the night in jail. He did make it to the game though, just in time to see Devin Hester return the opening kickoff for a Bears touchdown. However, that was the last weekend getaway for Neal after the story leaked to his wife the next summer.

Following the football game, it was chaos outside Dolphin Stadium, what with the heavy rain and everyone running around wearing plastic ponchos; some stoked, some, like Brian, dwelling on Bear turnovers.

As a result, the guys got split up for a bit, long enough for Paul to get thrown in the back of a Dade County squad car and then fly home before anyone could figure out who he pissed off and why.

A couple of years later, Paul explained to Brian that there weren't enough taxis at the stadium and he wanted to get out of the rain. Not that he minded getting wet, just that the Bears had lost and the rain was making him sad, especially with Prince's halftime rendition of "Purple Rain" playing over and over again in his head.

That was Paul's final excursion with the guys and the second time Prince Rogers Nelson played a role in their group losing a charter member.

Needless to say, these were the guys Brian grew up with, the ones who'd shared his life's biggest hits and misses.

And, because of that, Brian felt he could be himself when he was around them.

Free.

Natural.

For better or for worse.

A kid again.

By 2017, six or seven guys was unfortunately down to three.

However, not to be deterred, Jack pitched surf camp for a week in Costa Rica for their 40th birthdays. Darryl was sold immediately. Brian, on the other hand, had to think about it. "What the fuck is there to think about?" pressed Jack. "It's surf camp. For a week. In Costa Rica."

Brian could certainly afford to take time off work. He had his own house in a well-to-do suburb and lived quite comfortably, albeit alone.

So, without much more prodding, he gave in, thinking what better way to celebrate forty years on a spinning rock than burning multiple layers of skin off his body with his best friends.

He figured they'd have a couple of laughs. A couple of wipeouts. Maybe one of them would get lucky. But murder? Never.

Yes, murder.

You see, some guys cool down with age. Others, however, usually the ones at some sort of crossroads in life, tend to take it up a notch.

Out of the three, Brian felt Jack was prime to go off in Costa Rica, a thousand pent up Saturday nights inside of him ready to be unleashed.

Recently divorced or about to be divorced or about to give his wife a damn good reason for divorce, no one knew for certain, just that Jack was looking for an apartment on the North Side and didn't want to talk about it. The divorce, not the apartment.

When Brian suggested they meet on the curb at ten in the morning out in front of Delta, Jack balked, telling him that he wanted to get to O'Hare early.

Then, without proposing a better time, he told Brian he'd be at the closest bar to the gate, that he had some paperwork to sort out before the trip.

And that's where Brian found him, in Adidas trackpants

and a Hawaiian shirt, deep into his third pint of beer, signing a deed that relinquished his house to his wife.

Brian knew that Jack had put a ton of time and money into that house, especially the front lawn, and he felt sorry for him. However, he lied and told Jack that the plane was boarding, anything to get him out of the bar.

Jack did as he was told, tipping the bartender enough to ask him to mail the document for him. Problem solved, Brian thought. Jack had survived his darkest hour.

But Brian miscalculated. It wasn't even noon.

As soon as the plane leveled off, Jack was ordering Rum & Cokes two at a time, as if he was sharing with Brian, while flirting with a stewardess who made the mistake of complimenting his new mustache.

Fortunately, for Brian and his fellow passengers, Jack began to run out of steam somewhere in the hassle to change planes in Atlanta.

That meant by the time the second plane was ready for takeoff, Jack was beginning to bungle his words. "Oh, man, come on, Trump, didya dear, hear, did you hear what he said this morning?"

"If you tell me that you voted for him," said Brian, "I'm going to unfriend you on Facebook."

Jack was able to pinch just enough hair on the end of his mustache to give it a twist. "Get this. . . He wants to send the illegals to Mars, see if it's safe, then they can come back and build a wall, in space, a space wall."

Brian shook his head, unsure if Jack was joking or not. "I can't take you seriously with that mustache."

"It's," burped Jack, "for charity."

"That was November," he felt the need to remind him. "This is February."

"Somebody has to represent."

"It looks like a porn 'stache."

"A what?"

"You know, like the mustache on a male porn star from the seventies."

"Oh," started Jack, his neck losing the ability to support his head. "I guess I'm not familiar with male porn. . ."

Brian was formulating a rebuttal when he realized Jack was out, fast asleep against his shoulder; a baby, he thought, just an older one with an abundance of hair on his upper lip.

He slowly nudged Jack's mouth shut and let him rest, studying his friend's face, a coarse shade of tanning salon orange.

Jack was the first of the three to turn forty, just that Christmas. In fact, growing up, whenever Jack did something stupid, someone would point out that he should've been in the grade ahead, mostly to his defense.

Anyway, he looked thin to Brian, almost skinny, except for a beer gut the size of a bowling ball. Still, Jack was the kind of guy you'd want by your side in a bar fight, not so much because of his strength but his ingenuity.

When Jack was little his dad made a living off of cigarette vending machines, but in the fall of 1980 he caught on quick that Pac-Man was going to sell big, becoming a primary distributor to arcades in the upper-Midwest.

Jack thought this was the coolest job ever. So, not only did he gladly inherit his dad's route after flunking out of Boulder, but he invested in ATM machines too and, in recent years, even opened up a slew of laundromats throughout Illinois and southern Wisconsin.

And though Jack wasn't the least bit stimulated by his work, it allowed him to pursue his other passions like golf, fishing, and, unfortunately, gambling.

Brian wondered how hard the divorce really hit Jack or if any potential lesson he might've gained from it was lost on him entirely.

Seriously, he couldn't tell if Jack was more upset about losing custody of his kids or his father-in-law's Bears tickets.

Brian slipped into a moment of introspection, questioning his own failed relationships with women, but he couldn't sustain it, suddenly remembering that he prepaid for in-flight WiFi.

Pleased, Brian removed his topsiders with either foot, discreetly loosened the belt on his khakis, and took one of Jack's cocktails, giving it a gentle swirl before indulging in his inaugural vacation drink.

A few sips later and Brian was setting up his *I'll be away from my desk* auto-email reply, dumping loads of tedious paperwork on a colleague who also happened to be a Packers fan.

Next, he read, okay skimmed, an article on the Blackhawks Duncan Keith visiting a children's hospital, wondering the whole time if he should check his messages on OkCupid.

Brian hoped some kind words from a woman he'd never met before about how much hair he still had on his head would raise his spirits.

But there were no *Messages*.

Or *Likes*.

Not even any *Visitors*.

He wondered if it was a bad idea to list his real age. Was turning forty going to put him out to pasture? Or worse, make him irrelevant?

Brian was just over six feet tall, with the frame of an athlete, but as cerebral as he'd always been, he gravitated toward academics, numbers in particular.

And though he wasn't necessarily out of shape, he was well aware that hitting the road with his hometown crew meant bringing his A-game.

Therefore, Brian went on a diet several weeks prior to the

trip. Actually, it began as a juice fast the day after New Year's and ended up a diet; giving up white bread and soda, which he did on occasion, but also, for the first time, meat.

Additionally, he started running, four miles at a pop, straight out of the gate, so he was fairly fit. Lost five pounds in total.

Then, a few days before they were set to leave, Brian panicked, thinking that he wouldn't be able to keep up with the guys and all their drinking; Jack being borderline alcoholic while Darryl's stomach had endless storage capacity.

So, knowing that they'd be on call to party 24/7, Brian's response was to begin pounding beers to build up his tolerance, at random times of the day, even at work. Consequently, he gained back those five pounds and added two more.

Trying to relax, he took a deep breath: In through the nose. . . Out through the mouth. . . A technique he mastered in his one and only yoga class.

He unbuttoned the top of his polo shirt and repeated the process, taking air in though his nostrils, long and slow. . . Then, *damnit*, he remembered he was on a plane and probably just inhaled every disease known to mankind.

Brian forced a series of coughs and took a swig straight from the bottle of rum, sloshing it around and gargling with it before letting it slowly drain down his throat.

He dreaded the idea of getting sick before a vacation. That would be horrible, the worst thing that could ever happen while away from home.

He tried to focus on their destination. One thing for sure, he knew an ice cold winter morning was about to turn into a toasty summer afternoon, that even though Costa Rica was north of the equator like America, it was summertime there; the amount of rain signaling a change in seasons rather than a dip in temperature.

Brian had the urge to look at a map, immediately eyeballing the in-flight magazine in the seat-back pocket in front of him. A cover story on sea turtles in Costa Rica looked interesting and of course relevant, however, before he could reach for it, he found himself googling the map on his phone, which he noted was charged to 87%.

Finding Liberia, he realized they were landing on the left side or rather the Pacific side of the country, north towards the border of Nicaragua.

In the center of the map, he located the capital, San Jose, where it was noted roughly a quarter of the country's four and a half million people lived. Good info to have, thought Brian.

Any previous knowledge of Costa Rica centered around the original Jurassic Park movies, which he later found out were shot in Hawaii for budgetary reasons.

He suddenly felt bad about blowing off the turtles, so he googled them too and found six types of turtles in Costa Rica, two of them nesting in the very town they were headed to.

Darryl, meanwhile, was flying in from Phoenix via Houston and meeting them at the hotel, presumably by the pool.

Brian could picture his friend, already there, a couple of over-tanned European women smoking cigarettes and laughing at his PG-13 jokes, while he ordered another round of shots from a bartender named Manny.

With his soft black eyes and smooth brown skin, Darryl could always attract women, but he was happily married to his childhood sweetheart and more of a wingman, claiming that though he liked to flirt, he didn't feel compelled to act on it.

Therefore, Brian knew the *Pick to Click* spotlight in Costa Rica would be on his perennially single self and the newly uncaged Jack, especially for the guys back home who would want a blow-by-blow account.

He rested his head against the window, the scene beginning to take shape below him, though none of it looked real. The trees were too green, the water too blue, the sunshine bright enough to blow a fuse, as an endless succession of waves crashed into pristine beaches bordered by giant black rocks.

As the plane began its descent over the Pacific, Brian's mind drifted to his college girlfriend, the only woman he ever truly considered marrying. She had always talked about honeymooning somewhere a little off the map, *somewhere hot.*

Brian met Jenny at Illinois during freshman orientation, both of them infatuated with each other from the start. She was the reason, and a damn good one, why he didn't rush a fraternity. Or play intramurals. Or look at other women. Ever.

He missed her at times (okay, a lot) and wondered if she ever thought of him. However, truth be told, Brian dumped her. Or, rather, he forced Jenny to dump him because he wouldn't commit to getting married after graduation.

Summer before senior year, they drove to the United Center to see Pearl Jam. Brian was pumped. Jenny said they needed to talk about a wedding date.

He told her they were too young.

He told himself the guys were all single and having a blast.

He got out of the car for the show.

She didn't.

Defiant to the end, Brian bought two beers and found their seats anyway, but then a performance of "Nothingman" hit a little close to home:

Caught a bolt 'a lightnin'
Cursed the day he let it go

--Pearl Jam

The wheels hit the ground with a jolt, snapping Brian out of 1998 to find Jack awake, already in mid-conversation about a couple of "chiquitas" he was trying to line up for them.

"You're doing what?" asked Brian.

"I'm not doing anything," said Jack. "But this guy. . ." He held up his phone. "He's a bit of a go-getter."

"Just remember," Brian warned him. "We're in a foreign country. You fuck up here, you might just stay." Brian locked eyes with Jack, which wasn't easy, to make sure he was paying attention. "And I don't mean in a cabina."

"Easy, chief." Jack put his hand on Brian's shoulder. "Don't worry so much about what could happen. The future's up for grabs."

"Oh, really?"

"Yeah, buddy, I only deal in the never ending now."

"The what?"

"The never ending now," repeated Jack. "If you commit to the present, you'll be rewarded with presents."

"That's nonsense. You're paying. They're called hookers."

"Don't be so quick to judge," said Jack. "It's just a woman I met on Instagram."

"Oh."

"Besides, Lleyton told me Facebook was for old people."

"You've got a smart kid."

"Great, what does that makes us?"

"Dinosaurs?" tried Brian.

"Exactly," laughed Jack. "And what would you tell a dinosaur if you could go back in time?"

"I know what you're getting at. We're turning forty. Show's almost over. Buh-bye." Brian shrugged, trying to muster some enthusiasm. "Time to live it up."

"Forty has nothing to do with it. Could be any age," said Jack. "We've all been given the same gift, Bri, in that we know life's a temp job. What you do with that knowledge will determine how much you enjoy the time you have left, whether it's a day, a week, or another forty years."

"I get it," Brian assured him, steering Jack off the plane. "Even if your mustache makes everything you say seem overly dramatic."

"Bri," smiled Jack. "I'm not being dramatic."

"Yes, you are."

"Okay, whatever, but as of today I am officially homeless."

"And frighteningly single."

"So are you, Bri, so let's live in the moment this week."

"That's easy for you to say."

"Of course it is," said Jack. "A moment's all we've got."

Half an hour later, they were making their way through customs . . . without Brian's suitcase. And though he certainly wasn't happy about it, he didn't complain much. That wasn't his style. He liked to think it was because he was so cool, but he knew that he'd fold in a second if anyone called him out for making a fuss, especially on foreign soil.

And if he did raise a ruckus in regard to his suitcase then, for sure, even if they did find it, they'd never give it to him. None of which really mattered; *if it ain't there, it ain't there.*

Fortunately, Brian knew better than to bring anything from his wardrobe that he was overly attached to on a guy's trip. Not after Negril in '04, when a pitcher of Jamaican sorrel got up close and personal with his Charlie Sheen bowling shirt.

From then on, Brian began packing only his second or third favorite dress shirt, in a dark color that wouldn't betray a minor mishap. He also developed the habit of bringing his oldest underwear.

Dispensables, he called them, that wouldn't be making the flight home; though he felt a tinge of guilt when he was packing, like the good news is you're going to Costa Rica, the bad news is you're staying there, *and I don't mean in a cabina.* Best of luck. Thanks for your support.

The clothes were one thing, reasoned Brian, but losing his collection of odds and ends that he'd acquired over the years for trips like these was potentially a major loss. These were the items he wanted within reach at four in the morning when he was with the guys.

He packed Band-Aids, Neosporin, a needle and thread, tweezers, Advil, Duct tape, Krazy Glue, Visine, and a combination padlock (his flashlight recently joined his camera in the vacation retirement home).

And though he carefully cut and filed his finger and toenails the night before, he brought a nail-clipper anyway in case of a hangnail. And he packed condoms. For all his insecurities, Brian still felt entitled to dream.

Meanwhile, Jack stopped to change money, waving a roll of twenties at Brian like he was ahead of the game. But Brian thought he was making a rookie travel mistake by changing money at the airport.

So, he waited at a bookstore, only to find rows of romance novels mocking his love life. That's when it dawned on him that it wasn't the exchange rate that had caught his friend's eye but the bank teller with the long black hair falling playfully over her blouse.

He listened to Jack speak to the teller in Spanish, no doubt grammatically incorrect, but it got a laugh out of her, which Jack seemed happy about. Brian suddenly realized he hadn't seen him on the prowl since the night Jack met Marcy at the Cubby Bear, almost twenty years ago.

Jack thinking with his dick again. That's scary. He watched as the teller counted out a stack of colones and handed them to Jack, who in turn told her how beautiful the new Costa Rican currency was, *hermosa*, while looking directly at her, his way of giving her a compliment off the record.

Jack thanked her and left, then stopped again, this time to buy a pack of cigarettes, a local brand, Derby Extra Suave, and a lighter. Next, he spotted a straw sun hat, like something Dean Martin might have worn on holiday in Havana.

Brian waited patiently as Jack tried it on in a mirror, this way and that, until he found the look he was after by cocking it, slightly; just like his personality, thought Brian, a little off-kilter.

Once he had what he needed, Jack made a beeline for the exit, rolling his suitcase through a crop of young surfers like he was on a mission . . . with Brian in his wake, apologizing for his friend's questionable behavior.

Still, he wished he could live more like Jack, one step toward revelry at a time, without fear of the consequences. But that was asking a lot of Brian.

Fear was something he was good at. Kept him out harm's way more than once. However, Brian's therapist told him that his obsessive worrying was preventing him from having meaningful experiences.

And those experiences, his therapist went on, were the building blocks to a sustainable relationship. A relationship? Brian liked to think that he was past defining himself through other people.

He'd done his time. Went out with Jenny for three years

(*almost* three as she was prone to point out). Loved every minute of it too. Their relationship was fun, romantic, and they did it whenever they got a chance. Plain and simple, she was awesome.

Brian assumed all relationships were this easy. In hindsight, however, he knew that he'd made a terrible mistake. Basically, he panicked. In fact, he knew something was wrong right away when he couldn't properly explain to people why they broke up.

We're too young, he told them, thinking everyone would understand. They didn't.

Pre-internet, before you could change your Facebook status to single or tweet your conscious uncoupling, he had to tell everyone he knew in person: *There is no more Bri & Jen.*

And when he got back to campus in the fall, he had to do it all over again, explaining to his stunned classmates and professors and bartenders and just about the entire staff at Papa Del's Pizza that Jen wasn't dead; he simply chose not to spend any more time with her.

Of course, Brian dated after Jenny. He just developed the habit of rushing in, something apparently fools do, highlighted by the time he proposed to a kindergarten teacher he met in the bleachers at Wrigley—in the fifth inning—completely ignoring the fact that she was rooting for the Cardinals.

Gun shy. Trigger happy. Brian never found a happy medium, eventually becoming the guy that would pull the ripcord with women just when things were getting serious, so he wouldn't have to make a real decision.

Co-workers suggested that he get a hobby. Relatives, a dog. But that's what old people did, thought Brian. He wasn't there yet. Was he?

Turning forty, he felt he could be alone without having to

answer for it, that he could be fairly happy in life instead of merely content. Brian always imagined, even hoped, that his forties would be about slowing down, not, as Jack proposed, speeding up.

Getting off the floor at the Merc. Starting a hedge fund. Less running, more biking. But when Brian told a friend at work he was putting on the brakes, he had only four words for him; *less futures, more options.*

Normally, Brian wouldn't listen to a word of advice from the nut-holes he worked with, but he felt this was more than a clever Merc farewell.

Less futures, more options.

To him, once he'd really thought about it, it meant. . . less planning, more doing. Though, he'd been through this before.

Signs, he called them, like taking up yoga, though that really was a sign, 40% off, but Brian would make excuses as to why he couldn't go and then validate them by suffocating himself with work.

Always on his laptop. Looking for an angle. Or if he stared at the screen long enough, maybe a short term play on cattle.

The guys, he was aware, blamed Brian's "Nothingman" attitude on losing his mom at such a tender age, seven in fact, that his entire life had been soaked in the tragedy.

However, even though memories of his mom were limited, most were good ones, he'd tell you, revolving around her affection for playing James Taylor records while she cooked dinner.

Still, he did miss her, especially when he wanted to ask her questions about life that he didn't think his dad was equipped to answer.

Just the week before, his therapist closed a session with a quote from Abraham Lincoln, which in the state of Illinois falls along the line of a golden rule: *Most folks are as happy as they make up their minds to be.*

Brian tried to smile and caught up to Jack outside the airport where he was lighting a cigarette in the afternoon sun. "I quit," said Jack, blowing out a stream of smoke.

"Apparently." Brian looked past him, trying to find a taxi.

"I'm serious. This is my first one in months."

"So, you're pinning this on me?"

"Nah." Jack took another drag. "I'm treating myself."

"That's great" said Brian, pointing to a *Prohibido Fumar* sign. "But since twenty twelve, the general rule on where you can smoke in Costa Rica is that you can't. I looked it up with you in mind. You can smoke in your house but not in public places, like airports. Hence, the sign."

"That's funny." Jack put on his sunglasses, a pair of Aviators straight out of *Top Gun*. "I look at that sign as more of a suggestion."

"Well, don't," said Brian. "And don't play the stupid gringo."

"But the stupid gringo always has a good time."

"Come on, Jack, no need to get in trouble doing little avoidable things."

"So, go big or go home?"

"Put. It. Out."

"What's it with you and following rules?" Jack took a final drag on his cigarette and flicked it to the pavement. "Happy now?"

But the cigarette was still burning. . . "Aren't you going to properly extinguish it?"

"Huh?"

"You could start a fire," Brian told him. "Chicagoans are known for that."

"I don't see any cows, do you, Mrs. Leary?"

"Just—"

Before the debate could continue, Jack spotted a taxi-van

and *whistled* it over, motioning behind him to the surfers, whose appreciation for Jack's random act of kindness was multiplied tenfold when they got a look at his mustache.

Then, just as the surfers finished thanking him and left, another taxi-van pulled up. . .

Jack turned to Brian, "Karma."

"Or, we're standing outside an airport."

"Hola." Jack walked into the street, around to the driver's side window to talk to an older Costa Rican man. "Cuanto es Tamarindo?"

"Tamarindo?" repeated the driver, sporting a mustache of his own. "Sixty dollars."

Brian took him for his word and climbed into the back of the van, then quickly retreated, remembering to put out Jack's cigarette, which he did, stamping on it several times, mostly for show.

But Jack wasn't paying attention to him, nor was he as enamored with the driver as he was the bank teller. "Sixty American? For the two of us?"

"Two, three, four people, it is all the same," said the driver, as a woman, his age, waited quietly in the passenger seat up front. "Tamarindo es Tamarindo. It is not going anywhere. Pretty crazy, right?"

Jack glanced at the woman. "Just Tamarindo?"

The driver smiled and got out of the van with the ease of a younger man. "My wife, she is riding with me today."

"Su esposa?" asked Jack, showing off his limited Spanish.

"Sí." He took Jack's suitcase and put it in the back of the van. "This way, me and my wife, we can talk. At home, with all the grandchildren running around, no es posible."

Jack climbed into the back seat. "Entiendo."

"Your luggage?" the driver asked Brian.

"It didn't make it." Brian joined Jack in the back, failing to mask his disappointment, then read a bumper sticker on the seat that was covering a tear in the fabric; he mouthed the words, "Pura Vida."

But Jack noticed. "Why do you always talk to yourself?"

"In case someone's listening."

"Well, I'm listening," said Jack. "Just speak the fuck up."

The driver took his place behind the wheel, finding Brian in the rearview mirror. "Your luggage, maybe it comes later. Did you tell someone where you're staying?"

"That," said Brian, looking one last time for an airport employee to run through the doors with his suitcase, "and my phone number."

The driver turned to his wife, saying something to her in Spanish, like he was asking for advice, but she didn't answer him and instead pointed to the road ahead.

"How long of a ride is this anyway?" Jack asked him.

"Tranquillo," said the driver. "You're on Tico Time now."

"Okay so how long in Tico Time?" tried Jack again.

"An hour." He turned the key in the ignition. "Más o menos."

The driver glanced at his wife and pulled out of the lot, taking them on a meandering two-lane highway; southwest toward the ocean through the outskirts of Liberia, past horse farms and sugarcane fields and dusty little towns baked brown and yellow by the relentless Central American sun.

2

Hotel, Motel, Holiday Inn

Even with 800 miles of *Rich Coast* to choose from, Tamarindo was becoming known worldwide as an ideal surf spot due to its long clean break; regularly boasting three to five foot waves, even six and seven footers, keeping new and experienced surfers craving more.

A relative secret fifty years ago due to infrequent flights from the States to San Jose, Tamarindo didn't have the need for electricity or running water until the 1970s, and even then a hard rain could render the single dirt road in and out of town inaccessible (plus, no phone lines until the '90s).

However, once the roads were paved and an international airport opened in the much closer Liberia, hordes of young tourists arrived daily from all over the globe to surf, or learn to surf, one glorious wave feeding another, which also made Tamarindo a party destination and gave it its nickname, *Tamagringo.*

Home to roughly 500 people, it was swelling at close to 5,000 tourists when the guys arrived that week. And though Tamarindo's first order of business was surf lessons, it also gave guests their pick of inland excursions; complete with three-wheelers, zip-lines, and yoga.

From the airport, it took the driver about an hour to reach the coast, Brian noting that it was greener than it was inland, but still in need of a shower.

Up ahead, he could see the ocean through the palm trees, the sun casting the water a sparkling blue, then a row of bars, restaurants, hostels, and eco-friendly hotels, even a high-end condo farther up the main road, which ran less than a mile before making a small loop, like a musical note.

The traffic slowed considerably in town due to all the cars parked along the road, not to mention the tourists avoiding the crowded sidewalks. One group cut right in front of their van, a collection of women in bathing suits heading toward the beach, surfboards balancing on their heads.

Brian knew Costa Rica had progressive environmental policies but couldn't think of a better example. He could tell Jack was frustrated though, that he couldn't just roll down his window and talk to them, maybe throw out some backhanded compliments.

In fact, Jack was reaching for the sliding door when the driver turned away from the ocean and parked the van in front of the Hotel Pasatiempo.

That's where they found Darryl, against the hotel wall, struggling to find shade for his big body under a fan of banana leaves. "There're my boys," he said, going over to greet his friends with hugs and hi-fives.

Having been back to Evanston last Fourth of July, Darryl looked the same to Brian; several pounds over his playing weight, yet fairly fit, the only real difference being now that his hairline was in full retreat, he'd finally surrendered and shaved his head.

Jack stared at him like he was making a great discovery. "You're bald."

"You're a genius," scoffed Darryl.

"What? It looks good," said Jack.

"I know. I just miss my 'fro."

"You haven't had an afro since fifth grade."

"I still miss it."

Meanwhile, Brian thanked the driver, "Gracias," and handed him $70, giving him a slight bow of reverence. "My name's Brian."

"Con mucho gusto," said the driver, shaking his hand. "Vincent. My wife is Cecilia." Then he went around the back of the van and unloaded Jack's suitcase.

Brian turned to Darryl, almost afraid to ask, "Why're you waiting out here?"

"Because he misses us," laughed Jack.

"I need a drink." Darryl wiped his face with a red hand towel he'd kept from his football days. "I'm melting in this sun."

"No kidding," said Jack, before noticing Darryl's dufflebag. "Didn't you check in?"

"They're full." Darryl looked just as confused by Jack's mustache. "Is that some kind of caterpillar on your lip?"

"A valid question considering where we are," butted in Brian, "but aren't we part of the grand number making this hotel full?"

"Nope." Darryl walked over to the wall and pulled back several large banana leaves, giving them a glimpse of the hotel grounds; a garden oasis with guests lounging about a swimming pool and bar. "In case you wanna know what we're missing."

"Damn. . . What the fuck happened?" Jack removed a cigarette from behind his ear. "I spoke to the manager on the phone. We were all good."

"The manager," Darryl told him. "He remembered you, sounded like you spoke a couple of times, said he liked you, but apparently your card bounced."

"I read him off the numbers. I remember doing it." Jack lit the cigarette and took an anxious drag. "Marcy and me, we still share that card, fuck, she must've reported it stolen or something, refuted the charges."

Darryl put his arm around Jack's shoulder, giving him a hard but sympathetic squeeze. "Don't tell me you two are divorcing over this trip."

"Nah." Jack took another quick drag. "I'm not sure she believed me when I said I was coming back though."

"We've talked about this already," said Brian.

"The divorce?" asked Darryl.

Brian shook his head. "Going back."

"Guys, I'm sorry about screwing up the hotel." Jack threw his cigarette to the ground, putting it out himself. "This is seriously fucked."

Brian glared at Jack, "Uh, yeah," then turned to Darryl, "Have you looked anywhere else?"

"The manager checked around for us," he said. "But this is a busy time of year. There's some kind of surf thing going on."

"There's probably always a surf thing," said Brian. "Get to the good part."

"I'm not sure there is a good part." Darryl pointed down the road. "He said to try a hostel until we can find something better."

"A hostel?" Brian asked. "A youth hostel?"

On previous trips, Jack might've leapt out of his shoes but instead twirled one end of his mustache. "Could be some backpacker babes."

"Beards are one thing," said Brian. "But backpacker babes aren't necessarily going to understand your mustache, you know, the humor."

"You mean the humanity," said Jack. "What about the stewardess?"

"She's going to have nightmares," replied Brian.

"Unless you two want to end up sleeping on the beach, we're better off looking for a hostel." Darryl picked up his dufflebag and began walking down the side of the road. . . "Come on, tomorrow's Sunday. Something will open up."

Brian hurried after him, making his way, "Sorry," through a wall of tourists getting off a bus. "How do you even know where we're going?"

"He said we couldn't miss it."

"Sounds vague."

"Trust me." Darryl kept walking until he found a drink stand between two parked cars, a Tico boy at the helm. "Hola."

The boy looked up and smiled. "You come back."

"I brought my amigos this time."

"Bien, bien." He wiped down a blender attached to a long extension cord that disappeared between store fronts.

"I'm ready for the tamarindo." Darryl turned to the guys. "Make that three. Tres."

Brian watched as the boy got to work, loading the blender with ice, water, and a fleshy brown pulp. "What're these?" he asked, trying to roll with the drink's dark color. "Smoothies?"

"Kind of," replied Darryl. "They call it a *refresco naturale*. It's fruit juice. I thought we'd give the tamarindo a try seeing as they named the town after the tree."

"That's cool. I didn't know that," said Brian. "You see, you learn—"

But he was interrupted by the boy's blender, then Jack. "Is there a swimming pool at this hostel?"

"I'm not sure." Darryl nodded toward a tented patio across the street. "But would you settle for a pool *table*?"

"Yeah, man." Jack rubbed his hands together, eying a group of 20-year-olds in the middle of a game. "Now you're talkin'."

"How do you know that's the place?" asked Brian.

Darryl pointed to a large plastic daisy out in front, bigger than he was. "He said to try the Daisy Hostel."

Behind the pool table there was a worn-in couch, above it, in spray paint, Brian noticed the same words from the sticker in the van: *Pura Vida.*

Darryl handed the boy some money for the drinks. "Where's your suitcase, Bri?"

"I had one," he replied. "Thought I had a place to sleep tonight too."

"Fuck sleep," said Jack.

The boy gave Darryl his change and poured three to-go cups, sticking a straw in each.

Jack took his drink and started across the street, veering toward the pool table. "I can make some money off these youngsters, pay for the room."

"Fortunately, I brought a credit card that works," said Darryl, redirecting Jack to the front desk. "Let's check in first."

Brian held up his cell phone (at 73%) and a took a picture of the hostel, then hustled after the guys. "We're gonna get busted."

"For what?" asked Darryl.

Brian lowered his voice. "Being too old."

"Huh?" Jack wasn't buying it. "Us?"

"Youth hostels," said Brian, "are for youths."

"Why're you always so negative?" asked Darryl.

"I'm just. . ." Brian rubbed his jawline for the right words. "Cautiously skeptical."

"Man," laughed Darryl. "You've got to chill the fuck out."

"We don't even know if they have a room for us here," said Brian. "How can you be so damn relaxed?"

"Because." Darryl gave him a playful push. "I'm in Costa Rica with my homeboys."

Brian stood to the side and watched the guys go to work. And work it was, trying to charm the female receptionist at the hostel into giving them three beds. She was in her early twenties, permanently tan, her long hair a mix of brown and blond, depending on where it got the most sun. And, more importantly, she looked like she'd just been woken from a nap, presumably, figured Brian, her *siesta*.

Jack tried to placate her, telling her how *hermosa* the Costa Rican woman were, which didn't go over particularly well once she told them that she was from Venezuela.

So, Darryl flashed his award caliber smile, then changed speeds and gave her the sad story about the Pasatiempo being full.

However, she didn't appear overly moved and wouldn't commit to whether or not she had any open spots. Brian couldn't blame her, though; not with the big black guy yapping away while the skinny white one poked around behind him, anxiously stroking his mustache.

Brian was happy to find Darryl in good spirits. When they were kids, Darryl was not only taller and wider than everyone else but loud, especially his laugh. And the big attitude suited him when Darryl became a star football player, earning all-state in high school and all-conference at Arizona.

He even went to training camp with the '99 Bears. Unfortunately, he didn't make the team, but a hard sack on Brett Favre during a preseason game transformed him into somewhat of a folk hero (Darryl added to his legend in a postgame interview in which he referred to the Packer quarterback as Brett *Fav-re*, just like it's spelled, instead of *Far-ve*).

Pouncing on the opportunity, Darryl turned his fifteen seconds of fame into a sports bar in Tucson; Wildcat games on a Saturday, Bear games on a Sunday, with enough transplanted Chicagoans to keep his place busy and profitable through another Blackhawks Stanley Cup run. And now that the Cubs were winning, he was even starting to draw fans out of their condos in the summer to watch baseball games.

Consequently, he was set on taking *Darryl's* into the sunset. At least, that's what he told Brian in a series of emails before the trip. He said the bar was running itself, "on cruise control." Still, Brian remembered when Darryl first opened the place, making a killing on the weekends but somehow not turning a profit.

Yet, Darryl loved sports and ribs and a good beer on tap, so he stuck with it, downsizing the menu and hiring a proper chef. Soon, he was running a successful business and, as far as Brian could tell, having a blast doing it.

Meanwhile, Brian had convinced himself that it didn't matter if he liked his job at the Merc or not. It was what he was good at. But after catching up with Darryl, he began to wonder why his job never gave him any sense of satisfaction.

And though graduating from the pit seemed like a logical career move, Brian didn't feel any differently about interest rates or equities. It was just numbers and percentages and trying to manipulate them. No more. No less.

Brian returned his focus to the front desk, where he assumed the receptionist had seen enough of the *loud* Americans and was telling them as nicely as she could bother that the hostel was full.

In reality, however, she was completely indifferent, either that or still sleepy. "Págame." She spun the ledger around so they could sign in. "Dinero."

"Dinero when?" asked Jack, stepping up to the desk.

"Ahora," she said, firmly. "Now."

"Do you have WiFi?" continued Jack, setting a pile of colones on the counter.

"Sí." She rolled her eyes over her shoulder to a chalkboard. "Username, daisy, eh, password, hostel."

"That's easy." Jack slid the money forward. "For tonight. All three of us."

"The room," she said, counting out Jack's change, "es mixto."

"There's a mix-up?" asked Darryl.

"Chicos y chicas," she said.

"Ahh, mixed." A grin grew across Jack's face. "Boys and girls, together."

Darryl turned to him and rested a hand on his shoulder. "Don't get a hard-on."

Brian thought that was good advice.

But Jack peeked over his sunglasses and gave them the bad news. "It's too late."

For fifteen dollars each, they got a bed in a co-ed dorm room. Nothing fancy, just nine or ten metal bunks with an attached bathroom, featuring a simple sink, toilet, and shower; none of which were particularly clean due to an abundance of hair in the drains.

When the guys got there the dorm was empty, just a couple of backpacks playing possum, marking their territory on the best beds.

Jack found an open bottom bunk and began to unpack, beginning with his pillow, which he fluffed up after the long flight. "Never leave home without it."

"If I had known we were bringing pillows," lamented Brian, "I would've brought mine too."

"Don't talk shit." Darryl put his dufflebag on the bunk across from Jack's. "You'd be too afraid to lose it."

"How do you lose a pillow?" asked Jack.

"I don't know," said Darryl. "Ask his suitcase."

Jack held up his passport. "Is there someplace we can put

these puppies?"

"Shouldn't we keep them on us?" suggested Brian. "For security reasons?"

"No way," said Jack. "What if we go swimming tonight?"

"Swimming? Tonight? In the dark?" asked Brian, dreading the idea. "Yeah, great."

"Check it out, a lizard." Jack pointed to the far wall. "Don't get those back home."

Darryl took a closer look at it. "I believe that's a gecko."

"Like in the commercials?" Jack asked him.

Darryl nodded his head, "Yeah."

"So what's the difference?" asked Brian. "Doesn't Darlene collect lizards?"

"Both girls do," said Darryl. "Geckos are a type of Lizard. Some chirp or make a clicking sound. Some don't have eyelids."

"Weird," said Jack, just as the gecko darted up the wall. . .

"They're good to have around," continued Darryl. "They eat insects."

"Cool." Brian didn't have any beef with geckos. Spiders maybe. Snakes definitely. He walked over to a series of lockers by the bathroom door, examining them unfavorably. "This is where I would normally say, *give me your passports*, and then proceed to lock them up. But I can't do that, can I? Not without my padlock, which by the way, I've had since we were at Haven, start of sixth grade."

The guys offered Brian their condolences, which only heightened the chances of him being mad about the loss of his suitcase. However, settling a second time for mildly upset, he went back to the girl at the front desk and bought a new lock.

"You almost ready?" Darryl asked him when he returned.

"This is all I've got." Brian lifted his arms, allowing them a good look at his one and only outfit: Polo. Khakis. Topsiders.

"Get used to it."

"We'll find you something in town," said Jack. "At least a swimsuit."

"How 'bout we start with a beer?" Darryl stepped into a pair of camo cargo shorts, then picked out a neon pink tank-top, like it was nothing. "Seriously, I'm about to pass out."

"You could drink a little water instead," Brian told him, keeping a straight face. "Hydration is important at our age."

"Especially in this heat," added Jack. "I could go for another refresco."

"Mine was sour," said Brian, "though, if I think about it, also kind of sweet."

Darryl stepped toward them, sniffing at the air. "You two find some weed?"

And though they hadn't, their eyes were simultaneously drawn stoned-like to Darryl's feet, not only purple but dwarfing his flip-flops.

"Man. . ." said Jack, bending over for a closer look. "Your feet are sunburnt."

"And swollen," added Brian.

"While I was waiting for you guys," said Darryl, "I fell asleep in the shade, at least most of me did." He wiggled his giant toes over the end of the thin rubber. "Not how I wanted to start my vacation."

"No kidding," said Jack, less concerned than amazed. "Your feet are twice the size of your flip-flops."

"It's not just my feet," said Darryl. "It's the flip-flops. They're a size ten." He took them off, slowly, since they had practically melted to his skin. "Yeah, my feet are fucked but I'm a fourteen wide on a good day."

Jack nodded his head. "You always did have big fucking feet."

"And I always will," said Darryl. "Carmela texted me between flights, asked me why I left my flip-flops by the bed.

I got these at the airport in Houston. Biggest pair they had."

"Okay, but what'd you wear on the plane?" asked Brian.

Darryl smiled like a proud papa, as he removed a brand new pair of Air Jordans from his dufflebag. "Don't wanna get them sandy."

Brian had to admit, "Those're sweet."

"Remember my Jordans?" asked Jack. "They were from ninety-one, the year we beat the Lakers. I didn't wear socks with them all summer, most of which was spent at Clark Street Beach. Destroyed that pair. They stunk so bad my mother threw them out my bedroom window rather than have me carry them through the house to the garbage."

"Your mother is hilarious," said Darryl. "How is she?"

"She's good," replied Jack. "But she's not necessarily happy about my divorce, though she says she gets it, mostly from Marcy's point of view."

"If you had kept those Jordans in good condition," said Brian, steering the conversation away from mothers out of habit, "they'd probably be worth something today."

Jack agreed. "But how're you gonna convince your parents to buy you a new pair of sneakers if you never wore the last ones?"

"Point made," laughed Darryl, returning his pair to the dufflebag. "I'm going back to the flip-flops though."

"Can't blame you." Jack adjusted his hat in the bathroom mirror, then tucked a cigarette behind his ear. "Let's boogie."

"You're smoking regularly again?" Darryl asked him.

"Nah," replied Jack. "It's just an accessory."

"Keep telling yourself that." Brian put the passports in an open locker and secured it with his new lock. But before he left, he tugged on the lock, per his ritual, three times, then once more for good measure, and finally, he stared at it intently.

With the type of bounce in their step that only the first night of a vacation can provide, the guys strutted out of the dorm, past the girl at the front desk, who managed to give them half a smile, and to the street, where a warm breeze guided them toward town. . .

"I feel like a million bucks," said Jack, flicking imaginary dust from his Hawaiian shirt.

"You do have other clothes, right?" asked Darryl.

"It's become his uniform of choice," said Brian.

"It's comfortable," reasoned Jack, "and stylish," then off his trackpants, "do you even know what Adidas stands for?"

"You told us in 8th grade," said Darryl.

Brian appeased him. "All Day I Dream About Sex."

"And I still do," smiled Jack.

"Okay, but how's Brian gonna get laid?" Darryl asked him. "They'll think you're his dad."

"You're just jealous," said Jack. "Everyone knows Carmela makes you wear those stupid sweaters at Christmas."

"I like my sweaters," said Darryl.

"Yeah, and I like my nuts in a vice," joked Jack.

"You probably do," said Darryl.

Lost in conversation, they were lured by the setting sun, skipping all the shops and restaurants and crossing the main road, just a scattering of palm trees between them and the beach.

"Guy on the plane," began Darryl. "He was blacker than me but speaking Spanish to everyone like it was nothin'."

"That happens," confirmed Brian, in case his friends weren't sure. "Think of the Cubs bullpen."

"I know that," said Jack, unconvincingly as far as Brian was concerned.

"Apparently he plays soccer for a big club in London but is out on loan," continued Darryl. "Someone said he was here to play for the national team."

"Cool," said Brian, zigzagging through palm trees.

"Yeah," said Darryl, "but I didn't know there'd be brothers down here, just Rico Suave types."

"I guess I didn't think about that," said Jack.

"You wouldn't have to," said Darryl. "So me and this soccer player get to talking and I find out that the other side of Costa Rica, the Caribbean side, is full of black people."

"I'd prefer it if you used the term African-American," said Jack. "You know, to be politically correct. Everyone gets a trophy. Sis boom bah. Kind of like Brian being a vegan or whatever."

"That's all well and good but I'm a vegetarian," Brian reminded him.

"Same thing," said Jack.

"Wait," jumped in Darryl. "Brian's a vegetarian?"

"Didn't you get the email?" asked Jack.

"Oh, shit, sorry," said Darryl. "That was real, Bri? I thought you were joking."

"More like a cry for help," snickered Jack.

"No, not exactly," said Brian. "And there's a difference between vegan and vegetarian."

"Don't worry, you'll get there," said Jack. "Being a veggie is like a gateway drug to being a vegan."

"Darryl," wondered Brian. "Are you going to finish your story?"

"Okay so the other coast isn't just black people," went on Darryl, "not at all. Costa Rica started out with Indians, like we did, but instead of fending off the British, it was the Spanish who sailed over here and made themselves at home. Of course, they brought slaves from Africa to do their dirty work."

"To be clear," said Brian, "a great, great, uncle or something of mine fought for the North, and we've got a Springfield rifle over the fireplace at my cousin's house out in

Wheeling to prove it."

Darryl thanked him and carried on. "He said slavery was abolished down here in eighteen twenty-something but more blacks, mostly Jamaicans, came from all over the Caribbean to work the railroads and eventually the banana and coffee plantations. Anyway, they weren't exactly free, seeing that the Costa Rican government made black people live in one place until 1949, in Puerto Limón on the east coast. Nowadays he said black people are everywhere in the country but with so many roots on that side, some of them don't get too far."

"That's interesting," said Brian.

"But did anybody get laid in that story?" asked Jack.

"Sorry," said Brian, apologizing out of habit for him.

"Look," went on Jack. "I'm as game as anybody for a bit of local history but if we meet some women, please don't bore them to death."

"You're still drunk." Brian sighed, then looked over at Darryl. "Jack passed out on our flight."

"I'd be worried if he didn't," laughed Darryl.

"That's a load of crap," said Jack. "I was meditating."

"Since when does meditating involve drooling?" asked Brian.

"I was into it," said Jack. "Besides, I did my Costa Rica homework."

"On drugs and hookers?" asked Darryl.

"Well, that too," said Jack, "but check this out." He cleared his throat. "I found some words that could come in handy down here."

"Why I took French in high school I'll never know," mumbled Brian to himself.

"*La cuenta* is the check and *birra*, that's beer of course," began Jack, reading from a list written down his forearm.

"Isn't it, like, officially, cer-ve-*tha*?" asked Brian.

“That’s just in Spain,” said Darryl. “None of the Latinos that come into my place say it like that. It’s cer-ve-*za*, with a *z*.”

“True story,” started Jack again. “When the ex and me—”

“You’re already calling her your ex?” asked Darryl.

“Okay,” said Jack. “When Marcy and me—”

“Marcy and I,” corrected Brian.

“Fuck off,” said Jack. “When we were in Madrid on our honeymoon, we thought the bartender had a lisp or something, so we kept ordering beers just to hear him say *cervetha*.”

“I think you sent me a postcard telling me that story,” said Brian, squinting, as if it could jar his memory. “Matter of fact, that was probably the last postcard I’ve ever received from a friend.”

“You are so gay,” said Jack.

“What? No one writes anymore,” said Brian. “You brought it up. Jeez.”

“I’m just fucking with you,” said Jack.

“With a homophobic slur?” asked Brian.

“Shit, I love gay guys,” said Jack. “More chicks for me.”

“That’s not much of a retraction,” said Brian.

“You’re both gay, okay?” Darryl gave each of them a slight smack on the back of the head and took the lead through the trees. “So, *birra, cerveza, cervetha*, any way you slice it, I’m getting some suds. What else you got?”

“*Zarpe*.” Jack looked at his arm again. “*Zarpe* means last drink.”

“*Zarpe*,” repeated Brian. “Could come in handy.”

“Yeah,” said Jack. “And *zorra*, don’t forget *zorra*.”

“The girlfriend of Zorro?” tried Darryl.

“Close,” said Jack. “A *zorra* is a woman who’s, you know, good to go.”

“You’re forty,” said Brian. “What ever happened to hello,

please, and thank you?"

"Different trip," smiled Jack.

"Your mustache," said Darryl. "I finally figured it out. You look like Greg Maddux. Didn't he have a mustache when he came up?"

"He did," said Brian. "I can picture his baseball card. Nineteen eighty-seven Topps."

"Damn, good memory, Bri." Darryl nodded his head in approval. "My kids don't have to remember shit. They just ask that lady on their cell phone."

"Don't worry. Brian's not that smart," Jack told him. "He lays his old baseball cards out on his bed and stares at them for hours."

"I do not," protested Brian.

"I caught you," said Jack.

"That happened once."

"That happened recently."

"I know, I know," admitted Brian. "But I was sorting them out. I had to. A couple of rubber bands broke. Otherwise, the cards would've got mixed up." He mimicked the receptionist, "*Mixto.*"

"Mixto?" repeated Jack, as if doubting him.

"Yeah," said Brian. "I mean, do you really want Sandberg and Grace mingling in the Mets pile?"

"Of course not," said Jack, "but—"

"Look at this place." Darryl stuck his arms out to the side, stopping his friends in their tracks.

3

Tamarindo

Clear of the palm trees, the guys stood before the beach; the incredibly long smooth waves they were promised to their right, a dazzling sunset of streaking yellows, oranges, and reds to their left. Tamarindo Beach, or *Playa Tamarindo*, was set in a bay, a couple hundred yards long, bordered by a river to the north and a rocky bluff to the south.

In between, a tropical paradise where a surfer was catching his final ride of the day. A black woman, her head shaved clean, was going through a series of formidable yoga poses on a mat in the sand. And two young Costa Rican girls in crisp blue skirts and white blouses, were selling treats from a wicker basket; all of them unaware that their lives were about to change forever with the arrival of the three Americans.

The rest of the beachgoers were just taking it all in, some bringing a long day to a close, others just emerging for the night, drinks in hand.

"Mesa?" came a pleasant voice in the native tongue. The guys turned to find a pretty woman holding a tray full of bottles and glasses, nodding toward an empty table in the sand. “Sí?”

“Perfecto,” replied Jack. “Y tres birras, por favor, something local.”

“Bien,” she said, walking away.

The guys had stumbled upon a restaurant on the beach called Nogui’s, which was situated under an umbrella of tamarindo trees; their brown pods hanging like middle-earth ornaments over colorfully painted tables and chairs, while a busy bar and kitchen sat in back toward the road.

Trying to ignore how much battery his phone had left but failing miserably (65%), Brian took a few pictures of the sunset, then plopped down in a chair and let out a big breath like he’d forgotten to for a while. “Wow. . .”

“I know.” Jack pulled up a chair next to him. “And she was digging my mustache.”

“I was talking about the sunset,” said Brian.

“Well, I was talking about the waitress,” said Jack.

“She was kind of hot,” Darryl sighed, longingly. “Age appropriate too.”

“Where do I sign up?” Jack removed the cigarette from behind his ear, then started for his lighter when he realized that no one else was smoking and stopped himself, though with difficulty. “Damnit.”

“Whatcha think?” Darryl slowly lowered his weight into a chair. “Thirty-five, thirty-six?”

“Are you guessing how old she is,” asked Jack, “or are we on to cup size?”

“Straight up,” said Darryl, “she was checking out Brian.”

That was news to him, headline news. “Me?”

“She might’ve been checking out his wallet, but these things,” said Jack, pointing to his mustache. “They’re a big hit down here. Our driver from the airport had one.”

“He was seventy,” said Brian. “You get a pass at that age.”

“Come on,” continued Jack, “the mustache is a way of

life."

"Sure, for Burt Reynolds," said Darryl, "or you're in Shalamar."

"Shalamar? Be real," said Jack. "You guys are lucky I didn't grow a beard."

Darryl looked skyward. "Amen to that."

"Whatever." Jack pulled out his lighter and lit the cigarette. "I'm just glad to be here after the year I've had."

"And we're glad to have you," said Darryl. "Look at us, this is it, all the other guys have dropped out."

"Some by choice," said Brian, "some not." He tried to ignore Jack's smoking and hone in on the blazing horizon, his mind drifting to Paul and Neal and Robbie. He hadn't seen much of them lately and wished they could've made the trip.

Then, as always in these situations, his thoughts turned to the seventh guy in their crew, the one who didn't have a choice to go to Costa Rica. Or Jamaica. Or Miami. Or even Tahoe.

It was coming up on twenty years since he'd died. Still, he was in Brian's ear tonight, telling him to live it up. Consequently, a sense of obligation to his friend, duty even, rose within Brian, a notion strong enough that he felt he could possibly act on it.

He liked to think of the guys as his teammates for life, playing for the hometown club, who saw him for who he was and who he'd become, his journey. And so, with a little help from his friends, Brian felt the day's weight, months of it really, exiting his shoulders.

The idea of having a whole week with Jack and Darryl, without anyone rushing back to the responsibilities of their everyday lives, pacified him immensely.

Tico Time, thought Brian. His chest rose deep and full as he inhaled the beach. . .

The salt of the ocean.

Fish on the grill.

A whiff of weed.

Jack's stupid cigarette.

Brian's head turned instinctively to see the waitress returning with three bottles of beer, still dripping with tiny pieces of ice. She set the beers down on the table with a smile, pleasant yet reserved, and opened them one by one.

Brian quickly, almost spastically, took a swig of his beer, trying and failing not to stare at her, as she handed out menus. "Is that an eagle?" he asked, pretending to be interested in the red and yellow label.

"En Español," she said, "Águila."

"*A-gee-la*," tried Brian.

She smiled again, slightly, like any more would make her vulnerable. "Es Imperial," she went on. "You want different?"

"No," said Brian. "Gracias."

Jack snuffed out his cigarette in the sand, smiling at her, like he was doing her a favor.

But Brian wasn't done. "This is great." And he took another gulp of his beer as evidence.

She didn't appear to be overly impressed though and left, saying something in Spanish.

"Graci-*ass*," said Jack, getting an eyeful. "I have no idea what she just said but that woman there, man, I'd be shootin' ropes."

Brian gave Jack a dirty look. "Where're your manners?"

"My what?"

Brian ignored him, turning back to watch the waitress clear a couple of plates from another table, the last of the sun casting a soft, almost angelic light on her, like her image was being projected on an old movie screen.

"You don't have dibs anymore, Bri, I'm a free agent." Jack rested his hand on his plus-size stomach, unaware of the irony. "And I'm in my prime."

"Really?" questioned Brian.

"Fuck yeah." Jack slapped Brian's knee. "Forty is the new thirty, fellas."

"Unless you're gonna tell us you're pregnant," said Darryl, "you should probably lay off the Oreos."

"Whatever." Jack sat up in his chair, full of zest. "Brian's a journeyman, bouncing around from girl to girl, never making much of an impact, but me, *put me in coach*, and by the way, if I was an Oreo, I'd be *Double Stuf*."

"You're gross and a newbie as far as being divorced," said Brian, his eyes still focused on the waitress. "You're a giant red flag to women."

"Well that woman," said Jack, "brought us ice cold beers a la fuckin' playa and I'm just thinkin' 'bout a way I can thank her."

"You can thank her by leaving her alone," said Darryl.

"So be it," said Jack. "As long as she keeps those beers coming."

"To beers on the beach." Darryl raised his bottle. "To us."

"Cheers," said Jack, waiting for Brian to follow suit. "You with us, man?"

"Yeah, of course, cheers." Brian clinked his bottle into theirs. "Um, grateful to be here."

"You should be," said Jack. "Look who we've lost in the last year, this whole generation that came before us, fuck, they wrote the soundtrack to our lives. . . Bowie. Prince. Glen Frey."

"George Michael," added Darryl.

"Gay or straight," said Jack. "That guy could get you laid."

Brian took a picture of the restaurant, lying to himself that the waitress just happened to be in the frame. "They had tons of Bowie on the jukebox at Gingerman."

"I swear. . ." Jack crossed his heart. "I swear I got better at pool when one of his songs came on."

Darryl leaned back in his chair, like he was trying to recapture a memory. "How 'bout when Gibs was deejaying at that club in Bucktown? He always played Prince when we walked in."

"*Eagles Live*," said Brian. "My dad used to play that when we'd drive up to the dunes in Michigan."

"And don't forget Lemmy!" Jack raised a fist. "He died in December."

"Who's Lemmy?" asked Darryl.

"Motörhead," said Jack, as if he didn't need to.

"Motörhead?" repeated Darryl. "What's that?"

"A band," said Jack. "A hard rock band. Lemmy was a badass. Big moles on his face. Ace of Spades."

Darryl scrunched his eyebrows, confused. "What?"

"If you want to rock out with your cock out," explained Jack, "Motörhead is a good start."

"Okay, I feel ya, so then what about Maurice White?" asked Darryl. "He died last year too."

"Last February," said Brian.

"Right." Darryl took a sip of his beer. "Without Maurice. . . There's no Earth, Wind & Fire. And without Earth, Wind & Fire, there's no 'Shining Star.' "

"Classic tune," said Jack.

"Wasn't that the first song you and Carmela danced to?" asked Brian.

"Yeah, but we weren't dancing," started Darryl. "We were—"

"Bumpin' uglies?" snuck in Jack.

"Don't make me punch you," said Darryl. "We were up at Robert Crown, ice skating."

"I remember but I wouldn't call that skating," Brian told him. "You could barely stand up."

"That was the best part, she came and sat with me." Darryl

ran his hand over his head, as if he was still expecting to find hair. "We were fourteen. She was visiting her cousins or something."

"Or something," smiled Jack.

" 'Shining Star,' " said Darryl, "that song, damn, that was the beginning of everything."

The ends of Jack's mustache rose into a mischievous grin. "What happened when you got to 'Boogie Wonderland?' "

"That was a different night," laughed Darryl. "And I told you the next day."

"I can't remember," said Jack.

"That's because you smoke too much pot." Darryl took another sip of his beer. "And seein' as she's my wife now, I'll just keep it between me and Maurice."

Jack's eyes lit up. "*Do you rememba,*" he sang, "*the twenty-first night of Semptemba?*"

"Stop that." Darryl squirmed in his chair. "What're you doing?"

But Jack kept singing, "*Love was changing the minds of pretendas.*"

"If you ruin that song for me I'm going to kill you." Darryl leaned over and elbowed Jack in the ribs, the two of them playfully poking and jabbing each other until the waitress returned.

"Listo?" she asked, planting herself away from the fisticuffs, right next to Brian.

Unfortunately, "Hi," was all he could muster with her that close to him.

He just watched, mouth agape, as she shifted her weight from one hip to the other and tried again. "Ready to order?"

"Yes, right, uh, yeah, food." He picked up the menu but couldn't come up with anything but indecision.

"Sorry, he's clueless." Jack removed his hat, placing it over his heart. "Can you bring out one of your favorites? We're gonna share. Not that I can't handle my own dish but to, you know, get us going."

"Trío de Ceviche," she said, convincingly enough. "Octopus, shrimp, y sea bass."

Jack clapped his hands approvingly. "Sold."

"Slow down," Brian told him. "We just got done talking about how I don't eat meat anymore."

"It's not our fault," said Jack.

"Yeah, doesn't mean we have to suffer," laughed Darryl.

"Besides," said Jack. "It's fish."

"I can't," explained Brian, "on moral grounds."

"Christ." Jack turned back to the waitress. "Do you have a salad for my wife? Nothing with eyes."

"Sí," she smiled, turning to Brian. "I will find special for you."

And though Brian knew Jack was making fun of him, he thanked her anyway, then added, "Your English is really good."

She smiled appreciatively. "Charmed."

"I'm sure," said Jack, butting back in.

"You know this one?" she asked. "The television show?"

"Oh, right, *Charmed*," said Brian. "The three witches."

"Sí," she said. "It is how I learn English."

"Nice," said Brian.

But Jack shook his head. "Never seen it."

"Don't lie," said Darryl. "You know, with Alyssa Milano and Holly—"

"*Ehhhhh*," moaned a white woman rather effectually, her Canadian accent in full effect. Fit, thirty-ish, yoga mat rolled up neatly at her feet, she was sitting at the table opposite them with a group of rugged looking men, all with big bushy beards.

Brian got the impression they were somehow *her* men, at least that's what he thought as he turned to see what she was going on about, catching the last golden sliver of the sun as it slipped into the Pacific. . .

With everyone's focus on the sunset, Brian stole another look at the waitress; her warm chestnut eyes matching her wavy brown hair, offset by her skin, which was the color of caramel.

However, Brian sensed there was more to her and he was curious, mustering the courage to ask her, "What's your name?"

"Lita," she told him.

"Nice to meet you," said Brian, "I'm—"

"Could we. . ." Jack held up his beer to her. "Could we get another round of Imperials while you're at it?"

Throughout dinner Brian found himself wanting to kick Jack in the shins under the table but instead made excuses to talk to the waitress. And she politely played along, getting him an extra napkin, water, no mushrooms, more salad dressing, and endless rounds of beer.

Until Darryl gave him a friendly shove. "Bri, you gotta talk to her about something real."

"I know, but what do I say?"

"When all else fails," said Jack. "Let the professionals do the heavy lifting."

"Huh?"

"Take GNR," began Jack. "Use some of their lyrics on her, but don't sing them, say them: 'Her hair reminds me of a warm safe place where as a child I'd hide.' Just replace *her* with *your* and you're in. Try any band. No chick's gonna pick up on that down here."

Brian said he'd keep that in mind, however, the restaurant was almost full now and she was clearly busy.

Meanwhile, the guys were ready to bail; Darryl pitching a walk into town to work off the meal, Jack set on getting a bunch of beer and taking it back to the hostel, perhaps playing a game or two of pool with some backpacker babes.

And since Jack was newly single, Darryl caved right away, leaving Brian no choice but to signal the waitress, imaginary pen to palm of his hand, for the check.

Jack told him that because of his excessive groveling at the waitress, he had to pay for la cuenta. And, sure enough, while he added up the check, Jack and Darryl slipped over to the bar, laughing and punching each other.

Brian figured they were waiting for him to make his move and for once he planned on giving them a decent show. He took out his wallet and counted out the cash, dollars, giving her a little extra by rounding up to the nearest twenty.

Clearly a great tip, though not excessive. Any more, he thought, might make him look creepy. And with one more opportunity to talk to the waitress, solo, he didn't want to blow it.

He remembered the turtles he'd read about on the plane. He could ask her something innocuous about them. In no way could a conversation about sea turtles be perceived as him making a move on her, even if he was.

Either way, being around the guys had emboldened him. And if he felt drawn to the waitress, he supposed he should at least go through the motions of acting on it.

Closer to the ocean, Brian noticed one of the bartenders drenching a teepee of twigs and branches in kerosene. Then, once he had everyone's attention, he lit a match, quite dramatically, and tossed it on the pile, instantly engulfing the wood in flames.

That's when the black woman they'd seen doing yoga earlier reappeared, two leather belts barely covering the required body parts, with a hula hoop slung over her shoulder, like it was something much more than that.

Brian stood up and found the waitress, waving the money

at her with a forced, borderline awkward smile. He was sure she'd spotted him, but it wasn't until the third time they made eye contact that she came over.

A lump formed in Brian's throat. He wondered if he had offended her, then immediately blamed Jack for insulting her English when he told her he'd never seen *Charmed*, a blatant lie. He just called it *Witches & Tits*.

Brian felt Jack's gaffe let him off the hook with the waitress, though. It was out of his hands. He could give up the chase. But deep down, past his own bullshit, he knew better.

He also knew that if he went for it and struck out, he'd probably never see her again. So, that was good. Of course, he wanted to see her again. She was gorgeous. And the way she talked, whether seamlessly in Spanish or stumbling in English, her words were like a new song that he wanted to listen to over and over again.

Damnit, Brian felt the urge to go for it. And now here she was, standing right in front of him. He started to say something but when he hesitated she just took the money, barely acknowledging him as she carried on to the bar.

He was left to stare at her, like a boy watching his balloon float away, as music began to fill the air from a set of speakers set strategically in a tree; a trip-hop song Brian recognized from parties back home, the summer after he graduated from Illinois.

That was when his friends from the suburbs started getting apartments in the city, like Jack who found a loft in Wicker Park.

Brian was so *high* the first time he heard the song, he thought for sure it was written about Jack, who got complaints all the time from his new neighbors for a variety of infractions, mostly involving his dog, his stereo, or someone else's parking space.

Brian shook his head out of the past and tried to concentrate on the black woman, who was soaking the wicks lining her hoop in lighter fluid, then lowering them one by one into the fire.

Her hoop completely lit, she raised it above her head and snarled at the crowd like Billy Idol, signaling one of the bartenders to turn up the music.

Moving across the sand, she began some sort of tribal dance, a mix of ballet and martial arts, while painting the night sky in swirls of light.

There is a man that live next door
In my neighborhood
In my neighborhood
And he gets me down

--Massive Attack

Brian looked over at Darryl and Jack, who were bowing and clapping, enjoying themselves, duly impressed whenever the fire dancer made an increasingly more difficult and dangerous maneuver with her hoop:

Slowly rising. . .

Around her waist. . .

Over her breasts. . .

Around her neck. . .

She ducked her head under the hoop and it showed up spinning on her wrists, her hands clasped in front of her like she was firing a giant laser gun. Made it look easy too, thought Brian, and sexy as shit.

Still, when the show was over, he couldn't shake his sour mood as he joined the guys at the bar. "That was pretty cool."

"What's up with you?" asked Darryl.

Jack answered for him with his best Harry Caray impersonation, singing, "*Cause there's one, two, three strikes you're out at the—*"

"I don't know what you're talking about." Brian started for the road. "I thought we were getting some beer."

"We are," said Jack, following after him. . .

Darryl too, after he dropped a few singles in a tip basket for the fire dancer.

"There you go," said Jack, looking back at Darryl. "Laying your groundwork."

"Because she's black?" asked Darryl.

"Well you do have the same haircut," said Jack. "Besides, she's blackalicious."

"Please don't use that word," said Darryl.

"Just giving you the same heads up I gave Brian with the waitress," he said.

"You are crazy," Brian told him.

"Not to mention a racist," said Darryl.

Jack raised his voice. "How is that racist?"

"Chill," Darryl told him, taking the lead back toward the road. "I'm messing with you."

"Anyway, drinkin', dancin', and fuckin'," Jack went on. "That's what I tell women. If you're down for any of those three, I'm game. If you want the trifecta, I'm your man."

"That's nuts," said Brian.

"That's just honest," said Jack. "Look, I never cheated on Marcy. Never. But in my head, I was fucking everybody, even her mother."

"She was kind of hot," admitted Brian.

"Really?" said Jack, like he was offended. "Anyway, there's nothing wrong with having a gander at a few backpacker babes. I've earned it."

"A gander," repeated Darryl. "Is that what they're calling it these days? Maybe you should start with *Netflix and chill.*"

"Fuck that shit," said Jack. "I'm going straight to *Hulu and hump*."

Jack and Darryl started to laugh but—

"Shoot." Brian came to a halt. "My sunglasses."

"I don't remember you wearing them," said Jack.

"I wasn't." Brian ran his fingers through his hair. "That's probably why I forgot them. I'm gonna go back to the restaurant. They were expensive."

"Really?" asked Jack. "Your Wayfarers?"

But Brian held his ground. "They have sentimental value."

"Okay, Bri." Darryl patted him on the shoulder. "Should we wait for you?"

"No, that's all right." Brian was already on his way. . . "I'll meet you guys at the hostel."

4

Cheap Sunglasses

Brian went back to the restaurant on his own, though not for his sunglasses, which despite fearing for their safety he left in the locker with the passports. Brian had lied to Darryl and Jack. And lying to people, especially his friends, was hard for him. Lying to himself, on the other hand, was easy.

So, Brian was fully prepared to turn around and drink beers at the hostel all night, *no problemo*, even if what he really wanted was another shot at the waitress. He had to go back with the guys, though. Play it cool. Tomorrow was another day.

In fact, he had all week. He would get his chance. Or not. Throwing in the towel could become a viable option. But the guys were already in his head, questioning his very manhood, some chatter about the size of his balls.

He knew they'd talk the same smack back at the hostel. Why not listen to them now and do something about it? Put up or shut up. And, for a change, Brian felt inclined to put up, even if he was unsure of what that entailed.

He pulled out his cell; thinking, *it's my phone, I'll check the battery if I want to,* and was bummed to find it down to 57%.

Still, he turned on the camera function, putting it in selfie mode. Not to take a picture but to see his reflection, check on himself, get psyched, convince his ego that he wasn't too far gone from his glory days, (though he was having a hard time pinpointing just when those days were).

Brian had shaved before leaving for the airport, his cheeks just chubby enough to come off as youthful. And he had all his hair, which he didn't have to bother with since it was curly.

His smile was intact too; after taking a scolding by his dental hygienist to heart, he'd become meticulous the last few years about brushing and flossing his teeth.

Consequently, he looked good that night, best he could. Of course, it was only day one and, unlike day five, his nose still hadn't met a tree it didn't like.

Before he could change his mind, Brian ran back to the restaurant, all the way up to the bar, not meaning to join two tourists, who he took for man and wife; over fifty, overweight, and way too tan, ripping each other about something in a foreign language.

He looked around for the waitress, trying to come up with some classic lyrics for her, something romantic.

Should he go with a line or two from Prince? Or Pearl Jam? Or a new favorite of his like Band of Horses? What about a cool couplet from Arctic Monkeys? He had to choose wisely here.

Meanwhile, he didn't dare look at the couple, not while they were still arguing, maybe in Italian, thought Brian, certain words, sure, but also the hand gesturing.

Trying ignore them, he instead focused on a string of fairy lights hanging on for dear life over the edge of the bar. It didn't work.

He was drawn back to the couple and though he had no idea what they were saying, he sensed this wasn't a standard argument for them. In fact, they seemed to agree on a number of things. Still, something was wrong, maybe even at risk.

Fortunately, the bartender was also growing weary of the bickering and turned up the music. Right away Brian knew it was Peter Tosh; the guys having gone through a reggae phase in the late '90s, which just so happened to coincide with a time when they were smoking a lot of pot.

He spotted their waitress wiping down an empty table in time to the song, swaying back and forth in the sand, ever so slightly but oh so sweetly to the melodic beat.

You never miss your water
Till your well runs dry
So tell me, tell me
Whatcha gonna do
When your well runs dry?

--Tosh/Livingston (Bell)

Brian figured his own well had run dry, yes, he went there, and wondered about hers. Was she lonely? Had she suffered heartache? Or had Brian let his imagination run untethered? Maybe it was all the book covers he'd seen at the airport gift shop, guys with square jaws and dimples sweeping overworked damsels off their feet.

What was Brian thinking anyway? At thirty-nine, he'd only been with white girls. Not by choice, though. In fact, Brian was convinced he gave off a particular vibe of vanilla that bored girls of color.

In high school, he had plenty of crushes on black girls, none apparently mutual; one going all the way back to second grade when Tramaine taught him how to jump rope properly, crossovers included. Whether or not Brian made his affection for her clear is open to debate, but she never seemed to show any interest in him beyond friendship.

Then there were the brown girls. Brian would always see them on his way to Cub games on the 'L'. And heading home, perhaps with a few Old Styles in him, he would on occasion find it in himself to say hi, however, he rarely got more than a word or two out of them in return.

He knew that Latinas in particular were too hot to handle. Spicy. Sizzling. *En Fuego*, Jack used to say. What was Brian supposed to do with that, except get burned?

He did, after all, watch *Modern Family*, and Sofia Vergara was clearly a handful. And seeing Salma Hayek in *Desperado* for the first time just about blew his mind.

Brian looked back through the crowd of palm trees toward the road. Decision time. Catch up to the guys? Or stay and risk humiliating himself? Unable to choose, he just kept gawking at the waitress.

Until she finally saw him and walked over, looking confused. “La cuenta?”

“Oh, uh, no,” he stammered, somehow caught off guard while staring right at her. “I’m Brian. I, uh, never told you my name.”

She studied him quizzically. “Do you want change?”

“What? No, uh, the turtles. Don’t they get laid . . . their eggs, sorry, don’t they lay their eggs around here?”

She held back a smile. “Sí.”

“The Leatherbacks?” continued Brian, internally praising his short-term memory.

“You know them?”

“Yeah, a little, I guess.”

“I’m. . .” she started, before changing her tone, “not interested, gracias.”

Brian gulped. “In turtles?”

"In tourists," she said plainly. "I don't date tourists."

Brian's left knee buckled as he slowly backed away from the bar. . . "Date?"

She shook her head, disapprovingly. "Tourists leave."

"I understand. I wouldn't date a tourist either." Brian steadied himself against a tamarindo tree, pretending to be interested in the bark. "You must have guys hitting on you all day."

"Hitting me?"

"No, no." Brian thought about running away, just taking off. "Hitting *on* you, asking you out. I didn't see a ring. I just wanted to, I don't know, see what you were up to after you finished work. I mean, it's Saturday night for you too, right?"

Apparently, something he said struck a note with the waitress and she gave Brian a closer look, head to toe, and she wasn't shy about it. And though she seemed reasonably impressed, she concluded, "I have tables," and started back for the bar. . .

Brian just stood there speechless, though not necessarily disappointed. Instead, a sense of relief washed over him, freeing him of any further action. He could report to the guys that he'd done all he could with the waitress, that he'd struck out swinging.

However, she stopped, like she wasn't sure if she was doing the right thing. "Pero, sí, es Sábado noche," she said, before turning around to face him. "Many people go to Monkey Bar later to dance."

Brian found the Daisy Hostel packed with twenty-somethings, glowing with youth, loads of white teeth popping like flashbulbs every time they smiled; a convergence of hipsters and hippies mixed with college students, presumably studying the rainforest. Living the *Surf, Yoga, Beer* dream.

He saw the Venezuelan girl, still at the front desk, though she'd added bartending to her list of duties. So, there was a little drinking going on and lots of laughter; highlighted by two girls pointing and shouting, one looking like a tech geek, the other more of a tree-hugger.

Brian thought they might fight, or at the very least make out, but they were only comparing the color of their armpit hair (punk pink vs. a natural brown). And why not? Grow it out! They had their whole lives ahead of them. The road was open. Possibilities endless.

Brian, in fact, preferred life when it wasn't so defined. That's why he wasn't exactly thrilled when he officially became a teenager. Didn't get his driver's license until he was almost eighteen. And moved his 21st birthday party, which was supposed to go down at a bar on Rush Street, back to his dad's basement for a game of cards, like always.

If Brian could pick an ideal age, he'd shoot for twelve, when he could climb a tree, just for the fun of it; the challenge, the view, to relax. Growing up, Brian used to climb the tall pine next door all the time. And lately, he'd been considering having another go at it, for old time's sake, plotting his ascent from branch to branch.

Though once he calculated the chances of someone along the lines of a neighbor, a cop, or even a drone shooting him out of that tree, he reconsidered.

To boisterous approval, the Venezuelan girl put on some music, a song by Future, one with Drake. Not that Brian knew. Not his music, he told himself. Not his time either.

A cloud of despair settled over him. He'd been aged out. He figured if he somehow lived to eighty then turning forty must be halftime, crunch time, the dark side of the moon.

However, he didn't have a solid plan in life other than to keep doing what he was already doing, even though, more and more lately, he kind of almost felt like it wasn't good enough.

Brian found Darryl on the outdoor patio, hunched over, loading a mini-fridge with cans and cans of Imperial, while Jack made room by removing items he believed had outstayed their welcome; a bowl of moldy strawberries, several black bananas, a leftover cheese casserole, and a carton of soy milk (just because it was soy milk).

Jack was making a mess of it too, so before anyone could complain about the Gen X geriatrics, Brian tidied up and threw the food in a nearby trash can.

That's when he realized nobody was paying attention. The three of them were ghosts in this setting. Still, it could be a blessing. Under the radar was a way of life for him. He actually preferred it.

But when the fridge was full, Darryl decided to pass out the rest of the beer to whoever wanted one, so it wouldn't go warm, turning them into instant celebrities with Generation Y (or Millennials, as Brian heard them called on NPR, in order to sound less like they questioned things to the point of complaining).

"Rack 'em, mae," came a dude's voice from over by the pool table.

Brian didn't think much of it until the girl with pink armpit hair tapped him on the shoulder. "Oye, te está llamando."

Confused, Brian didn't know what to say to her other than, "Sorry."

She frowned and pointed to a surfer dude in his mid-twenties, a pool cue in each hand. "That guy, he is calling you, mira, look."

"Oh," said Brian. "Thanks. Gracias."

The dude walked over to him, *Pura Vida* tattooed across his stomach. "Rack 'em," he said a second time, handing Brian a pool cue.

But Jack intercepted it. “Eight ball?”

“Call your shot.” The dude was barefoot, in just his board shorts, with green eyes and sun-bleached ringlets of hair dangling over his bronzed shoulders.

“Brian. . .” Jack reached for the rack under the table. “You’re gonna have to sit this one out.”

“What?” Brian wanted no part of playing pool in front of everyone but feigned disappointment anyway. “Come on, man.”

“Nope, I need Darryl on this one,” said Jack. “It’s all he does at that bar of his.”

“That was me and my friends at the airport today,” said the dude, breaking up their little pow-wow. “I remember your mustache.”

“And my mustache remembers you,” said Jack.

The dude paused, as if considering whether he was being made fun of, but Darryl handed him two beers and it was back to business. “What’re we playing for?”

“Next round,” said Jack.

“Tuanis.” The dude stood on his toes to get a better look around the patio. “But mi compa seems to have split.”

“Who?” asked Jack.

“My partner,” explained the dude.

“We got time,” said Jack, racking the balls.

The dude nodded, tapping away on his cell phone.

“How long’re you down here for?” asked Jack.

“This is home, mae.” The dude finished what he was doing on his phone and took a chug of beer.

“You’re Costa Rican?” asked Jack, perhaps suggesting otherwise.

“I was born here, so yeah, but my parents weren’t,” the dude told them. “I’ve got cousins in the States though. We just surfed from Venice Beach all the way to Boco Rio down by the Mexican border. You been?”

"Venice, once, yeah," said Jack, "the one in Italy."

"Water was cold in LA, needed a full body suit," continued the dude. "So lit, though, so lit."

Jack winked at Brian. "Don't you people say *epic* anymore?"

The dude laughed, kind of. "Only if we mean it."

Brian cringed, discreetly tugging on Jack's arm. "Why do you always have to start shit?"

"I didn't do anything," said Jack. "I'm just having fun." He patted Brian on the back and then handed the pool cue to Darryl. "You break."

"Bri, man, you're all worked up." Darryl spun the cue under a piece of chalk. "What happened with the waitress?"

"I said I was going back for my sunglasses."

"We know when you're bullshitting." Darryl lined up his shot. "Just tell us what happened."

"Nothing," said Brian, noticing how much his toes hurt. "She just said something about a bar."

Darryl was rearing back to break but stopped. "There you go."

"What exactly did she say?" asked Jack.

"Something about. . ." Brian finally realized *why* his toes hurt and took off his topsiders, emptying a pile of sand from each. "Something about people going to a place called the Monkey Bar later to dance."

"Monkey Bar is a ten minute walk through town," said the dude. "Past Witch's Rock to the Best Western."

"Witch's Rock?" asked Darryl. "Isn't that where we start surf camp Monday morning?"

"Sounds right," said Brian. "I think we—"

But Jack raised a finger, cutting them off. "She said, *later?*"

"Yeah," confirmed Brian.

"That's it!" Jack's eyes went big. "Later. Not now."

"Brace yourself everyone," said Brian, anticipating one of Jack's screwball theories.

"Hold up. She's working now. . ." Jack was thinking out loud. "If she just said people go to Monkey Bar, that could be anybody at any time, but *later*, that implies she could be one of those people, seeing as she can't go now."

"That's an invitation," said Darryl.

"Really?" Brian noticed Darryl's bald head, glistening in sweat. He hoped it was somehow responsible for his poor assessment. "An invitation?" He pointed at the surfer dude. "Maybe I should be his partner. Get this game going."

"No worries, mae." The dude finished his beer and then helped himself to the second one. "We can play threes: One through five, six to ten, eleven to fifteen."

"Fine with me," said Darryl.

"Monkey Bar, that's a cool name." Jack looked at Brian. "You should head over there."

"But this is a guys trip," tried Brian.

Jack straightened Brian's shoulders and fixed the collar on his shirt. "Seriously. Go."

"I'm not gonna split up the band."

"Well, you should," said Darryl. "You're single. She's fine. Go for it. You can't expect this woman to make all the moves. She left you a clue. Pick up on it. Get your ass over to the motherfucking monkey place and make an effort. Actually, I take that back. A big effort. And if you don't have it in you, find it. That's what we're here for."

"Jeez," sighed Brian. "You're so demanding."

"If you need us, text us," said Jack.

Brian couldn't believe it. "I'm doing this by myself?"

Jack draped his arm around Brian's shoulder. "Do you want us there when you're banging her too?"

Recalling similar circumstances, Brian answered, "No."

Darryl grabbed a beer out of the fridge and tossed it to

him. "You better going."

"I won't know what to do without you guys." Brian opened the beer and took a much needed drink. "I'm no good alone."

"You're not alone," Jack told him. "You're just riding solo."

"Riding solo," echoed Brian, trying to resign himself to it. "I guess I can do that."

"Of course you can," said Darryl.

"When you get to Sharky's," said the dude, "turn right."

Jack spun Brian in the proper direction and gave him a little shove. "Go get 'em, cowboy."

Though his insides were churning, Brian relented, walking in no particular hurry toward town, while back at the hostel, Darryl bumped knuckles with Jack and called after him, waving exaggeratedly. "And don't stay out too late!"

5

You Should Be Dancing, Yeah

His first night in Costa Rica and the guys sent him into battle on his own.

No wingman.

No drinking buddy.

No partner in crime.

Just Brian, from Evanston, Illinois.

He trudged into town anyway and came upon Sharky's, a crowded indoor/outdoor sports bar with the requisite big screen TVs; its motto, *off the gancho*, written over the bar.

What did that mean, wondered Brian? *Off the gancho?* Interested, or rather interested in excuses, Brian stopped to have a look at all the people; a mix of locals and tourists, spilling out into the street.

Cool crowd, thought Brian, but one person in particular stuck out to him, a man his dad's age, dressed all in white like he just stepped off a yacht, which, given where they were, was highly doable.

What was left of the man's thinning gray hair was slicked back into a pony-tail, his skin wrinkled but tan, and he wore a chunky gold watch, as if he still used it to tell time.

He was standing at the bar with the Italian couple he'd seen at Nogui's. They were being quiet for a change, listening to him. The Canadian woman was in on it too, sipping a cocktail in a tan jumpsuit; good, imagined Brian, for a safari or even a disco.

The man spoke to the couple in English but with a European underscore, going on and on as if he was doing them a favor, something about *them* giving *him* money.

Brian considered himself quite the people watcher. To him, it was an activity. Like watching TV in person. He thought about getting a beer, seeing if the Blackhawks game was on, maybe hanging out, killing some time.

Not so fast. He knew that even if he never ran into the waitress, the guys would want a full report on Monkey Bar, proof that he tried.

Therefore, he soldiered on . . . past the Ser Om Shanti Yoga Studio . . . and the Coral Reef Surf Hostel . . . until he reached Calle Central, already working up a serious sweat, the pits to his polo shirt being exhibit one.

But what could he do? The temperature wasn't planning to drop below seventy degrees anytime soon. And it was in single digits when he left for the airport. His body was in shock. And he'd been drinking steadily.

If it holds true that a shark that stops moving dies, then he knew if he stopped drinking, he'd fall asleep.

Nursing his beer, he moseyed along the coast road, trying to time his last sip with his arrival at the bar, a self-imposed lesson in discipline.

A few cars and motorbikes drove by but most of the traffic was on foot; tourists walking from one end of town to the other until they found the right drink, dinner, or, in Brian's case, place to dance.

Soon, he came upon their surf camp, after which he began to hear music, or rather a distant throbbing bass line:

BOOM
BOOM
BOOM

Somewhere in the night. All Brian had to do was follow the beat. . . However, blocking his path were three teenagers, Ticos, the next crop of beach boys, one of them apparently inquiring as to how he was feeling: "Todo bien, mae?"

But Brian kept walking, unsure of the right answer, well, maybe not the right answer so much as the one that would let him pass unscathed.

He scolded himself for being negative. Maybe the kid wanted to sell him some weed. Or maybe Brian looked lost, still dressed in his *home* clothes.

Paranoia was not an uncommon feeling for Brian, and he openly embraced it in the pursuit of safety. So, he crossed the street to avoid the next group of boys, unashamedly transferring his wallet to a front pocket.

Of course, now there was a dog was in his way, some kind of brown German Shepherd mix, though Brian wasn't as interested in its heritage as its lack of an owner, let alone a collar or leash.

He looked back at the boys, hoping one of them would whistle his pet over, but they were long gone. It was just the two of them, man versus dog. Brian stopped, figuring if he ran it might be worse. But the dog just trotted by, very chill, as if it had plans of its own on a Saturday night.

Brian berated himself again for being so defensive, then continued walking until he saw the Best Western and finally a red sign with a monkey holding a bottle of Imperial; officially, The Crazy Monkey Bar & Pizza.

And it was LOUD.

Two taxis pulled over, one behind the other, loads of young partiers piling out. . . Brian quickly finished his beer and followed the sign through a gated arch and up two flights of stairs along the side of a hill.

At the top, Brian took his place at the end of the line to get in, getting a glimpse of the prize; a swimming pool leading to a multilevel thatched roof bar, every deck buzzing with people, drinking and dancing themselves delirious.

A four buck cover and he was almost in. He was just waiting for someone to cut him off, tell him that he was too old. Brian would protest briefly and leave. But the bouncer broke his twenty and gave him his change in colones without saying a word; the music was that deafening.

TIMES TWO.

On one side of the bar there was a deejay spinning hip hop, while on the other side, not that far away, and without the benefit of a wall, a different deejay played Latin music.

A definite conflict of interest, thought Brian, but each of them were blasting their songs so ear-piercingly loud that whatever side he was on, that's all he heard.

He checked both dance floors, several times, looking for the waitress but it was dark and somewhat chaotic, flashing lights revealing only patches of flesh.

Brian settled on getting another beer. Unfortunately, the only place he had the slightest chance of ordering a drink was a small bar tucked between the two stages, where he had to weather the one-two punch of duel sound systems and jostle for a bartender's attention amongst the masses.

After ten minutes of raising his hand, squeezing forward, and calling out his order, he was able to buy two Imperials. Two, because if the waitress showed up, he'd have a beer waiting for her.

However, Brian always had a contingency plan. In this case, if she didn't arrive by the time he finished the first beer, he'd leave, but with a consolation prize, the second beer for the walk home.

In his mind, he was halfway out the door. Seeing her, he

reasoned, was just wishful thinking at this point.

"Hola guapo," came a female voice.

Brian turned back to the dance floor, surprised to find the waitress. "Oh, hi, Lita," he started, before realizing he needed to shout for her to hear him over the music.

She looked past him. "Your friends?"

"They're back at the hostel!"

She moved closer to him. "You stay at hostel?"

"Uh, yeah." He noticed that she had changed out of her work clothes into a tight pair of jeans and a t-shirt. Simple, he thought, yet simply amazing.

Her shirt was cut open from her collar to her cleavage, as if her breasts required air, while her jeans followed the challenging curve in her hips with aplomb.

"Here." Brian handed her a beer, convinced, almost relieved, that he was way out of his league.

"Gracias." She smiled, then reached into the crowd of people, taking someone by the hand and pulling him over to her. "Este es Julio," she said, giving him Brian's beer. "He is cook at restaurant."

Julio took a quick drink and said something to Lita in Spanish, but she shook her head and pointed to Brian, after which he gave Brian a casual salute.

As far as he could tell, Julio was younger than both of them; wiry in build with dark brown skin and thick black hair. And his back was annoyingly straight, like he taught yoga on the side, exclusively to hot women.

On top of that, Julio kept grabbing at Lita, "Ven, ven conmigo," trying to get her to dance.

"Espera," she told him. "Tengo sed."

"Sad?" asked Brian, trying to regain his footing with her. "What's wrong?"

"Nada," she said, coming close again. "I am thirsty."

"You wanna beer?" Brian held his second one out to her.

"I've barely touched it."

But she just rested her hands on her hips. "Necesito algo más fuerte."

Brian got the gist of what she wanted and jumped at the chance to prove himself. Unfortunately, his enthusiasm got the best of him, leading him to shout louder than necessary, "JUST NAME IT!"

Lita winced and backed away, even touched a corner of her eye as if Brian had hit her with a saliva bomb. "No, gracias, the bartender es mi primo." And just like that she disappeared into the crowd, leaving Brian with Julio.

Was that it, he wondered? Had he just screwed things up? Or had he been the third wheel from the start? He looked over at Julio, who was anxiously tapping his foot to the onslaught of clashing sounds.

He didn't know what to say Julio or if he even spoke English. Besides, the sheer magnitude of the music was making it hard for Brian to think, let alone talk.

Then, seemingly out of the blue, Julio motioned for Brian to join him on the dance floor. Really? Brian checked to his left, then to his right, even behind himself, to make sure the gesture was meant for him.

And though he was flattered that Julio considered him the next best thing after Lita for a dance partner, Brian was inclined to pass. In fact, he thought this would be a good time to cut his losses and go back to the hostel.

Back home, if the Cubs were down in the seventh inning or the Bears behind late in the third quarter, Brian was usually the first of the guys to head for the exit.

Jack always told him that he was a pessimist, even a jinx, however, Brian claimed it was merely math, just playing the percentages of a comeback win.

Plus, once he factored in traffic on Lake Shore Drive or getting packed in like sardines on the 'L', Brian reasoned that it was prudent to leave before everyone else did.

Even so, Brian decided to stick it out that night, to see where life would take him, even if he had to make decisions on his own, with no one to bounce them off.

On such occasions, Brian often turned to the movies for advice. Miles, from *Risky Business*, was playing the role of consigliere tonight: *Sometimes you just gotta say*—He'd heard it before though, knew it was the right approach all along.

So Brian mustered the necessary gusto, *what the fuck*, and chugged half his beer, following Julio into the swarm of people on the side blaring Latin music; an uptempo mix of rap and reggaeton, accented by horns and a parade of drums.

With the dance floor packed, Brian was being pushed and shoved by the surge of the crowd, and it didn't take long for him to realize he'd be better off if he just joined in.

However, he hadn't danced since who knows when and didn't have a clue where to start, though he knew he'd be required to bring some south-of-the-border flare.

He wondered if he'd be expected to merengue.

And he hadn't done the macarena in over twenty years.

Then there was the tango. Of course, that took two.

Brian could see people partnering up but others, like him, were alone, or *freelancing* as Jack called it. Then, mindful that his balls could retract at any moment, he started shuffling his feet back and forth, even with some sand lingering annoyingly in his socks.

Once he loosened up though, Brian added a second move, raising his shoulders, one at a time, like a seesaw, anything to catch the blistering beat.

Meanwhile, Julio was doing his own thing, most of which involved thrusting his hips at people, men and women alike, anyone who showed him the least bit of attention.

Then, as trumpets flared and drums pounded, someone in

the crowd blew a whistle, after which the music picked up tempo until it was almost frenetic.

Brian gave in.

And let loose.

Jumping up and down!

Hands reaching for the sky!

He spilled some beer on himself but was surprised that he didn't care. He just laughed, deep and full, and kept on dancing, aware that this is what he was in Costa Rica for; to feel everything and nothing at all, hyper yet somehow relaxed, practically bouncing on air, wondering if this is what Jack meant by the *never ending now. . .*

Meanwhile, thanks to hundreds of equally ambitious people, the wood dance floor was taking a beating, even beginning to sag in the middle. Normally, Brian would play out some worst-case scenario in his head, one where the deck snaps and breaks away, sliding down the hill to the street just in time to collide with a bus full of nuns, each with a cat they'd just rescued from a shelter.

But there was no turning back now, so Brian ignored his conscience and continued to move his feet, just as the crowd parted, allowing Lita to slip through holding three shot glasses.

Eager, Julio rushed over to her and leaned back, letting Lita pour a shot straight down his throat, triggering a raspy growl in which he pointed at Brian with his tongue.

Lita spotted him, dancing over to Brian until she was within mere inches of his face. "Cacique," she said, handing him the second shot.

"Cacique?" repeated Brian, for an explanation.

"Es guaro." She leaned in close to him, her breasts grazing his arm. "Burning water."

Brian's entire body tingled. "Fuck it." He drank the shot in one quick go.

Lita shouted, "Bienvenido a Costa Rica!"

"Yeah!" He figured he'd passed the test.

However, she handed him the third shot, motioning for him to drink that one too. Another? Brian considered himself more of a beer guy. Besides, he just met these two. And he'd known his vital organs for years.

Furthermore, the *burning water* was merely good, nothing special, noted Brian, and probably not gluten free, which could pose problems later for his back and, in turn, surf camp.

And yet Lita was beyond anything he could ever dream up, so he downed the shot and the rest of his beer in quick succession, then started dancing again, somehow managing to fall into a jitterbug that his grandmother taught him when he was little.

Lita laughed at him—and with him, her smile radiating sarcasm and compassion, sometimes both at once. Her brown eyes sparkled like a campfire, warm and inviting. And her hips, the way they moved, *dang*, as if they had a life of their own.

Sweating from every pore, he tried to rationalize his feelings for Lita, to bring some common sense, maybe even some math into the equation.

Not much got done, though, considering the sheer volume of the music accompanying the booze to his head. But, defenses down, Brian came clean: He liked Lita, which in his world was the highest of compliments.

In the past, sure, he lusted all the time. Settled? Often. But, *liked*, that was a whole new ballgame. However, the only way to prove it to her was to keep on dancing. . . .

6

Mi Casa Es Su Casa

Brian and Lita are walking barefoot along the shore at dawn, the air neither hot nor cold, the Costa Rican sky a grayish pink, like the inside of a sea shell. The beach is quiet, empty, as if closed down for the two of them.

Brian tries some Spanish and says something funny, unwittingly.

Lita laughs and reaches for his hand.

He meets her halfway and finds himself locking fingers with her, just as a wave crashes the beach with unexpected punch, catching them off guard and getting them wet.

Lita laughs again and pulls him closer.

And he turns to her, thinking he should go in for their first kiss.

But Brian needs to urinate. Badly.

He can't decide, though, jungle or sea? Run behind a palm tree like he's hiding from her or pretend he wants to go for a swim?

Lita tugs on his shoulder for that kiss, her eyes closed, her lips puckered in anticipation.

This is it, thinks Brian. He leans in to her but his nose

starts to itch, the inside of his nose, and he's having trouble breathing—only to wake up in the hostel with Jack next to him, a pinky finger halfway up one of Brian's nostrils.

Brian angrily elbowed him off the bed. "What the fuck?"

"Easy, chief." Jack picked himself up off the floor, as if he'd been wronged. "You were snoring. Per usual."

Brian knew all that Lita stuff was too good to be true. "I have to pee," he told him, throwing on his topsiders. "Get out of my way."

Jack let him by. "Just be careful."

Brian stopped, shy of the bathroom. "Of what?"

"You mean, of who."

"Okay, Jack, who?"

"Everyone." Jack fished a lighter out of his suitcase and lit the cigarette he kept tucked behind his ear, taking a long drawn out drag. "At least everyone in our dorm."

"You can't smoke in here," Brian told him, already fearing the worst. "We'll get kicked out."

But Jack didn't extinguish the cigarette. Instead, he took another, bigger drag, exhaling a shroud of toxins into the ceiling.

"Come on." Brian shooed the smoke away. "What did I tell you about being overly dramatic?" He understood though. "What time do they want us out by?"

"Miss Venezuela said we had until ten a.m."

"And what time is it now?"

"Noon."

Despite it being Sunday in a predominantly Roman Catholic country, a day of prayer and rest, Sharky's was nearly as full as the night before, the only difference being that most everyone was seated, pretending not to be exhausted.

However, this spattering of tourists and locals wasn't down for the count. They were just nursing their way back into the game. One drink at a time. Whatever it took. Whether an Imperial, a Diet Coke, or a glass of water. Plus, Sharky's had $4 Bloody Mary's.

Just another day in paradise.

Let the games begin?

They never stopped.

Suitcases in tow, Jack and Darryl sat on either side of Brian, chowing down on chicken wings like they hadn't eaten in years, a savage display of manhood heightened by debatable etiquette and a spicy mango sauce.

Meanwhile, Brian watched in agony, questioning the view from his moral high ground, as he nibbled on *patacones* or what Jack referred to as "fancy fried banana."

They sat at a table outside, separated from the sidewalk by just a waist-high wall, the comings and goings of Tamarindo at their fingertips.

Brian noticed a tourist with his head shaved, recently, and rather poorly, sitting on the curb, face in his hands, hungover if not still drunk. He was talking to an old Tico man in English, babbling really, since it didn't appear to be either of their first languages.

From what Brian could gather, the tourist was trying to rationalize what happened last night, something presumably bad, which bothered Brian for reasons he couldn't explain.

He zoomed in on the hockey and basketball games dotting the walls, trying to find Captain Clutch or Jimmy Buckets. But the biggest screen was reserved for a Premier League soccer match, Arsenal vs. Chelsea, in which Jack blamed the latter's losing for having a girl's name.

Still, for the truly devoted, Tamarindo Church held a ten o'clock, "Come As You Are," open-faith service, where flip-flops were the norm, and the padres gave sermons in both English and Spanish. But most of all, Sunday was a day devoted to family.

Jack held up his beer, the little that was left. “To my E-Town brothers.” Then he polished it off and belched, loud, a tad late in covering his mouth.

A couple of nearby tables looked over at him in varying degrees of shock and disgust, but Jack just smiled, slightly, like he was embarrassed or apologetic, when deep down Brian knew he was happy for the attention.

Even so, Brian would be the first to admit that there was a time in their lives when producing such noises was considered god-like.

Take lunch, freshman year at ETHS, in the final days before most of their waking (and sleeping) thoughts had shifted toward sex, when a well-timed burp or fart while one of the guys was drinking milk could be comedy gold.

Darryl finished his beer off too. “Another round?”

“I want one of those Bloody Mary’s,” said Jack.

“I’m sticking to beer.” Darryl picked up the menu. “Maybe the Libertas?”

Jack peeped around his menu, having fun. “What’s that?”

“An ale,” said Darryl, struggling to read what kind. “A golden ale.”

“You get that,” Jack told him. “And a pair of glasses.”

“I’ve got my contacts in,” said Darryl. “Besides, it’s not fair. White guy wears glasses, makes him look smart. But a brother in glasses, looks like something’s wrong with him. Even Chris Paul in those State Farm commercials looks goofy as shit.”

“A blerd,” said Jack.

Darryl gave him a funny look. “A what?”

“A black nerd,” explained Brian.

Darryl started to protest but Jack had moved on. “How ’bout Westbrook? He works it.”

“I saw him on Colbert,” said Darryl. “They’re not even prescription.”

"They're just for fashion," said Brian. "It's not like he wears them on the court."

"That's the point," said Jack. "He's Clark Kent. Then game time he takes his glasses off and *bam*, he's Superman."

Darryl dipped his fingers in his water, then flicked them at Jack. "We can talk about this after we order."

"I've been ready," said Jack. "Bloody Mary. Bri?"

Brian pushed his menu to the center of the table in protest. "Where're we gonna sleep tonight?"

"Need somewhere to do the waitress?" asked Jack, fiddling with his cell phone.

"What? No," said Brian. "I mean, I just met her."

"Just how far did you get with señorita last night?" asked Darryl.

"We danced," said Brian, "in a group. And she has a name in case you don't remember. It's Lita."

"Relax, Romeo." Jack slid the menu back over to him.

"Are you gonna see her today?" asked Darryl.

"I don't know."

Jack smacked Brian's shoulder with the back of his hand. "You don't know?"

But Brian wouldn't give in. "You guys haven't even told me why they kicked us out of the hostel."

"We were going to look for a hotel anyway," said Darryl.

"Okay, but the hostel was quiet when I got back last night," said Brian. "I don't get it."

Jack put his phone down. "First of all, you got in late."

"Shit went down early, around one, one-thirty," said Darryl.

"We did well in pool," smiled Jack, waiting, Brian knew, for him to ask how well.

Darryl laughed, hand across his belly, as if to steady it. "I don't know if those kids were tired or tired of losing all their money."

"Once surfer boy had to start paying for beers," said Jack. "He was outta there."

"We were on the table, undefeated, until the music stopped," said Darryl, "though by then most everyone had wandered off to sleep."

"Or bang," said Jack.

"Or blog." Darryl waved his hand at their waitress.

"Is there a shorter version of this story?" asked Brian.

"Yeah, smart-ass, there is," said Jack. "Basically, Darryl and me had a couple beers left, so we were last back to the dorm. And when we got there, not that much later, it was lights out. Couldn't see a thing."

"Nothing," confirmed Darryl.

"Darryl had his phone out," said Jack. "You know, to see where we were goin'."

"Jack still has his flip-phone from two-thousand six," interjected Darryl. "Can't light up shit."

"It's not that old," claimed Jack. "Besides, Captain Kirk had a flip-phone. Anyway, some bitch starts moaning about the light in god knows what language and Darryl turns his phone off."

"We were completely lost in there," said Darryl.

Jack took a swig from his glass even though it was empty. "I would've sworn some commie moved our shit."

"Commies," said Darryl. "Strange how the bad guys are all Commies again."

Jack shrugged his shoulders. "Nazis are probably happy."

"Go on," said Brian, "with the story."

"So it was dark as shit in there," said Jack. "Of course, Darryl gets in the wrong bunk, knocks some Aussie kid straight out of bed and, like a bunch of babies, everyone freaks out."

"He wasn't Australian," said Darryl. "Perry lives there but he's from Belgium."

"No im-por-tan-tay," said Jack. "The main thing was that Perry was okay. He fell, what, foot and a half? So, Darryl apologizes. All's good. Everyone goes back to bed. Meanwhile, Darryl here decides to take the bunk above Perry. Few minutes later, just as everyone settles back to sleep, Darryl apparently surprises himself and farts, shaking the whole bunk, which then, no joke, just sort of collapses, all three hundred pounds of—"

"Two eighty-three," pointed out Darryl. "I'm down to two eighty-three."

"Congratulations," said Jack, "but try telling that to Perry. He got pinned between the bunks. Broke his arm. And he came here to surf. Spent a lot of money to do so. Luckily, he's already been here a week. But he wasn't happy. So Darryl gave him money for a taxi to the hospital."

"I offered to go with him," said Darryl.

"Darryl paid his doctor bill too," said Jack. "But the Venezuelan girl asked us to leave."

"I don't think she was giving us a choice," said Darryl.

Brian squirmed. "Holy shit."

Jack nodded his head. "Yeah, it was crazy."

"No, yes, that's crazy but across the street." Brian stole a glance over Jack's shoulder. "Don't look."

Darryl turned to see, "At what?"

"More like at who," said Jack, taking a peek.

"So who?" asked Darryl.

"Who do you think?" said Jack.

Brian put on his sunglasses and slumped down in his chair. "It's Lita."

She was walking down the side of the road toward Sharky's in a sarong and a t-shirt, her hair a bit of a tangled mess, like she'd just woke up. Still, she looked so good to Brian that he thought any effort on her part would just be showing off.

Jack spoke into his phone: “You are so sexy.” Then he held it out over the table, so Brian and Darryl could hear a Spanish speaking woman translate it for him. *Usted es tan attractivo*. An eager student, Jack repeated after her: “Ooo-sted ez tan attrac-tee-vo.”

Brian found this very agitating. “What. Are. You. Doing?”

“Helping you,” replied Jack, before speaking into his phone again. “I want to kiss you.” And then the woman’s response, *Quiero basarte*. He looked lovingly at Brian. “Kee-arrow bay-sar-tay.”

“Stop.” Brian kicked Jack under the table.

While Darryl urged him to pursue other options. “Come on, Bri, go say hello to her.”

“Wait. What? Slow down.” Brian definitely wanted to talk to her, especially without being bombarded by music, but he figured last night’s positive interaction was a direct result of the guaro, dismissing the notion that he made any headway with her on his own. “I don’t know, guys.”

Leaning back in his chair, Jack caught some sun and closed his eyes. “You either ride the highway to hell. . .”

Darryl snatched Jack’s hand as it went for his mustache.

But Jack kept talking, “Or walk the stairway to heaven.”

“You’re pulling that out now?” asked Brian. “Besides, I saw that on Facebook.”

“So did I,” admitted Jack. “Makes sense though. You either go out full tilt like Bon Scott or you end up on a farm with Robert Plant and Alison Krauss.”

“Point taken,” said Brian, “but if I know my rock history, Bon choked on his own vomit in the back of a car.”

“Must’ve been a hell of a night,” said Jack.

“Actually,” said Brian. “I’d rather shuck corn with the Golden God.”

“You’re stalling,” said Jack.

“Plant’s close friends call him Percy,” Brian went on. “Did

you know that?"

"She's going to pass us." Darryl pushed Brian's chair back from the table with his big foot. "Ask her if she knows of any hotels with an open room."

"There you go." Jack smiled approvingly. "Go on. Get two rooms if you have to."

"Relax, I'm on it." Brian stood up and wiped his hands with his napkin. Then, fully aware that he was tempting fate, he walked out to the street, pretending to run into her. "Hey, Lita, good morning, uh, good afternoon, yeah, how are you? Cómo estás?"

"Hola, guapo." She air-kissed him, her smooth cheek brushing against either side of his chin.

That was a custom he could get used to. "Hola." He felt like he was in a foreign movie, then quickly remembered this movie was his life.

"Me desperté con una goma."

"Huh."

"Nada."

"Oh."

"Your clothes?" wondered Lita, off his same polo and khakis. "You meet girl?"

"What? No. I mean, I met you."

"But you do not go back to hostel?"

"I did go back, yes, but I lost my luggage," said Brian. "Not me, I didn't lose it, the airline did. Or maybe the airport. I guess if I knew, it wouldn't be lost. And, as these things happen, we kind of lost our hostel too."

"You cannot find your hostel?" She shook her head. "No entiendo."

"Sorry, we didn't exactly lose our hostel. We, uh. . ." Brian avoided eye contact, thinking if he met her gaze he might never shake it. "We need a room tonight. Something a little more private, not us, I mean the guys, we need a hotel."

She pointed back to Sharky's. "Just three?"

Brian looked over at his friends, who were waving spastically at him. "Uh, yeah."

"I understand now."

"Understand what?"

"What happened at hostel."

"I swear it was an accident."

Lita bit her lip as if contemplating what to say next, though Brian looked at it more as pure seduction. "There is a house, not far," she said, finally. "Cerca, como diez minutos."

The guys took the main road south out of town on foot, just like Lita told them to, turning left at a Spanish language school, past which the pavement eventually gave way to a kind of brown reddish clay. Farther ahead, she'd spoke of a *manglar*, or what the guys translated to be a mangrove (yes) full of mangoes (no).

Regardless, that's where she wanted them to take another increasingly narrow road, away from the ocean, despite the absence of any signs of civilization; just wild bush and a tangle of trees on either side of them, none of which were able to shade them from the leering midday sun.

The Shepherd that Brian had seen on his way to the Monkey Bar jogged by, tongue out, barely glancing at them. He was sure the dog was headed to the beach, probably for a swim. Brian felt a ceremonial dip in the ocean would signify their true arrival in Costa Rica. Besides, he was melting, the heat beginning to sear his lily-white pores.

He longed for his Hawaiian Tropic lotion, for the sun protection, of course, but he also loved the smell, a throwback to simpler times, when entire summer months were devoted to the beach.

He did, however, downgrade the need for his suitcase in general. He'd survived so far without it. In fact, Brian felt rather light, as if all the effort that went into packing for the trip had been bogging him down, and now he could just forget about it. Start fresh.

"Less is more," mumbled Brian, to himself.

"You're doing it again," said Jack.

"Hold on." Brian stopped and took off his topsiders, socks too, his tender feet greeting the warm dirt with an, "Ahh. . . Mother Nature."

"Is this an official time out?" Darryl put down his dufflebag. "And why did you take your shoes off?"

"I don't know for sure." Brian started walking again, this time barefoot. "But I suppose I gotta take them off sooner or later."

"Or," said Jack, "you could just keep your shoes on and save yourself the misery."

"I'm telling you," continued Brian. "It feels good to have my bare feet touching the earth."

"What if you step on something, Bri, cut your foot?" Darryl hoisted his dufflebag onto his shoulder. "And what if it doesn't heal properly, gets all infected and shit?"

"It could spread to your brain," said Jack. "Make you go blind."

"I suppose I can't dismiss the possibility," reasoned Brian, unsure if Jack was winding him up or not. "But that's the old me. Chicago me."

Darryl corrected him, "You mean, Evanston you."

"Okay, technically, but being down here with you guys," began Brian, "it feels like when we were kids, like it's the first day of summer break."

"I was never a kid," said Jack.

"I'm trying to be serious here," said Brian.

"Sorry." Jack wheeled his suitcase beside Brian as they ambled along the road, which was beginning to resemble more of a path. "You're right about the first day of summer, that feeling of when we were young. I felt some of that at the hostel when Darryl and me had a run on the pool table."

"See what I mean?"

"Yeah, but don't forget, it's the last day of summer too. Kind of like what you said about taking your shoes off sooner rather than later."

"Huh?"

"Take this Costa Rican chick," said Jack. "She's good looking, no doubt about it. And she hooked us up with a place to stay. So, you know, it'd be great to get to know her, court her a bit. But you're on vacation, Bri. Which means you're on vacation time. Everything's accelerated, like dog years. One day is two, a kiss becomes a squeeze, two days is five—"

"Two is five?" questioned Darryl, from behind them.

"Yep," continued Jack. "And we're here a week."

"How long's that?" asked Brian. "In vacation time?"

"A lifetime," replied Jack, nodding his head like he'd done the proper calculations. "But only if you make the necessary moves. Otherwise, a week from now, you're still on day one."

"I get it, thanks, I do," said Brian. "But I also think we should've seen that sign Lita was talking about for the house."

"Ask," said Darryl, dropping his dufflebag, "and thou shall receive." The guys looked back to see him standing next to a log; *Bamboo House* painted in white from one end to the other, with an arrow pointing—

"Through there?" asked Jack, staring at a wall of bamboo. "I don't think so."

"Were you expecting the concierge to greet us?" asked Brian.

"I think we messed up," said Jack. "It's been way longer than ten minutes."

Darryl ignored him. "Let's do this." He picked his

dufflebag back up with a grunt. "Before I change my mind."

Jack gave him a funny look. "Tired, Grandpa?"

"I'm fine," said Darryl. "But my back. . . I think football finally caught up to me."

"My kryptonite was the kids' car seats," said Jack.

"Man. . ." Darryl rubbed his knuckles over his lower back. "I hear ya."

"One time Marcy didn't wanna wake Gabby from a nap," continued Jack. "Asked me to bring her inside the house while she was still strapped to her car seat. Forget it. My back was toast. Ruined my golf game."

"You had a golf game?" joked Darryl.

Brian felt the guys were testing him, that because the house was Lita's tip he was burdened with taking charge, so he gave the bamboo a thorough once-over before deciding, "Guys, I got this."

"Got what?" asked Darryl.

Brian shook a stalk. "The bamboo."

"Damn, Bri's getting all Johnny Cargo on us," said Jack.

"*Clutch* Cargo," corrected Darryl.

"If we're going back that far I prefer Jonny Quest," said Brian.

"He was eleven," said Darryl. "In fact, he still is."

"So's Brian," quipped Jack.

"All right, jeez, I get it," said Brian. "Follow me." He led the guys one by one into the bamboo, a labyrinth of stalks shooting forty, fifty feet straight into the sky, so dense in number that it became dark and noticeably cooler.

"This is creepy," said Darryl, bringing up the rear.

"Same guy that did the voice of Jonny Quest," said Jack, trying to find his way, "boom, Otter in *Animal House*."

"Good to know," said Brian, though not convinced he needed to commit it to memory.

"I thought you might like that." Jack veered away from

Brian, just slightly, only to find himself caged in by the bamboo, like bars to a jail cell. "I'm stuck."

"What if this isn't the right way?" asked Darryl.

"Yeah," said Jack. "Someone could've spun that log around just to fuck with tourists."

"Lita would've said something." Brian took out his cell phone, 42%, and tapped on his flashlight app, noticing right away that the rocks beneath their feet were painted in either green, yellow, or blue. "Guys, check this out. Look, the rocks." Brian illuminated a line of green rocks, heading through the bamboo. "If each color represents a path, one of them must lead to the house."

"Not bad," said Darryl, patting Brian on the back.

"Why don't we each stick to a color?" suggested Brian. "If anyone makes it to the house, just call out."

"Fine by me," said Darryl, setting off on the green rocks. . .

Wheels no longer an option, Jack grudgingly picked up his suitcase. "I guess I'll take door number two." He began his way through the bamboo on the blue rocks, before looking back at Brian. "You good?"

"Yeah, see you there." Brian took a deep breath and followed the yellow rocks, twisting and turning for minutes on end. . .

He noticed his mind didn't drift to Lita, that she was already there, waiting for him, obscuring all the usual preoccupations with work and bills, the gym and eating the right foods.

He imagined being with her again, like in his dream, just the two of them, about to kiss, when he arrived at a small clearing, just enough space to erect a four-story tower made entirely of bamboo.

The floors.

The walls.

The ceilings.

Everything bamboo.

Except for a large stone sphere over six feet in diameter, just off to the side, (which Brian didn't realize was an homage to stones left by indigenous people before the Spanish conquest).

He placed his hand on the stone, which was cool to the touch, and studied the bamboo structure, a world apart from the Victorian home he grew up in.

First and foremost, it was alive; some of the bamboo support posts still in the ground, growing, making it look like the house had been carved straight out of the jungle.

"Over here!" he heard Darryl.

"Me too!" yelled Jack.

Brian took a quick picture of the house, then walked around to the front, where he got a candid shot of Jack and Darryl standing in a small courtyard. "Unbelievable, isn't it?"

"But there aren't any doors," said Jack, "or windows."

"There're windows," said Darryl. "Just not any with glass."

"Well, then, those're just square holes," said Jack.

"Guys," interjected Brian. "It's the Bamboo House. What'd you think we were gonna find except—"

"Bamboo," came a man's voice.

Startled, the guys looked over to find an older man emerging from the house in just his underwear, ashen hair falling about his face, holding a six-foot piece of bamboo by his side.

Right away Brian saw that one end of the bamboo was carved to a point. "Um, guys," he said under his breath. "What the fuck?"

The man raised the bamboo. "Fence post but, yes, you should be worried."

"We're not here to cause any trouble," said Brian.

"Lighter than steel, harder than concrete," the man continued.

"I've heard a lot of good things about bamboo," tried Darryl.

"Fastest growing plant on earth." The man set the bamboo down to put on a pair of soft cotton pants. "You are Yanks," he smiled, as if being from America was amusing to him.

"Yeah." Brian noticed his charcoal eyes, seemingly looking in different directions.

As Jack reached out to shake the man's hand. "How'd you guess?"

But he didn't take it, organizing his hair into a ponytail instead. "I wasn't guessing."

Brian tried to make sense of the tattoos on his arms and chest; some faded, some really bad and childlike, like he'd got them out of boredom in prison.

"Who told you to come here?" the man asked, suspiciously.

With the man's hair pulled back, Brian recognized him as the yacht guy from Sharky's. "Someone in town," he told him, thinking he should speak up, "said there was a place out here."

"It is true, for special guests," he replied, his Euro accent coming through again. "How long were you planning to stay?"

"Just a week," said Brian. "We leave Sunday."

"There is no electricity from midnight till six in the morning."

Brian shrugged his shoulders. "No problem."

"Good, I am Ivan. I am owner."

Brian was right about his eyes. One wandered, just slightly, though he suspected he wasn't born like that, that he might've acquired it. Still, he was pleased to have found a place to stay. "Where do we sign in?"

"You don't," Ivan said. "The house is two hundred US a night. Starting now. You can pay the rest when you leave."

7

Our House, In The Middle Of

Inside the Bamboo House there was more bamboo, including the furniture and fixtures, even the plumbing; rainwater was harvested from the roof into bamboo gutters before making its way to sinks and showers. Interesting, thought Brian, but thankfully the couches and chairs had plenty of cushions and the beds all had sheets and mattresses, as well as mosquito nets. And on the first floor, there was a 4-burner gas stove and a refrigerator connected to a generator out back. Each of the guys had a floor to themselves too, though after hearing last night's story, Brian wasn't sure how Darryl ended up on top.

Once settled, they reconvened in the middle, in Jack's room. "I don't have a toilet," he complained.

"None of us do," said Darryl. "There's an outhouse."

"Is that where you went?" asked Jack.

"Yup." Darryl smiled, caressing his stomach. "And you should wait a few minutes."

"Christ," scoffed Jack. "This is going to be a fucking adventure."

"Isn't that what we wanted?" asked Brian. "Isn't that what

all your pep talks were about?"

"Don't get me wrong, I'm up for adventure," said Jack. "I just didn't think it would involve taking a dump."

"I'm fine with the bathroom situation but I don't see any outlets." Darryl held up his phone in one hand, his charger in the other. "I've got like no battery left."

"Guys, back home that's me in a nutshell," said Brian. "I'm constantly plotting my next trip to the bathroom, number two that is, I pee all the time. Seriously, it's the same thing everyday. Find a place to charge my phone. Find a place to go to the bathroom, in peace."

"And now we can't do either," complained Jack.

"Hey, I'll be the first to admit this place is a little off the grid," continued Brian, "but so was that fort we built, the one over on Hartzell."

"Summer before eighth grade," remembered Darryl.

"That lot sat empty for years," said Brian.

Darryl sighed. "Probably worth a fortune today."

"Our fort was inspiration for homeless shelters everywhere," declared Jack.

"Except we didn't sleep in it," pointed out Darryl.

Jack grinned. "I did get a hand-job in there once."

"What?" Brian was more insulted than impressed. "You brought a girl into the fort?"

"He means by himself," said Darryl. "You know, Hans Solo."

"How would you know?" Jack asked him. "Were you watching me?"

"Guys," said Darryl. "I'm gonna need to charge my phone. I've got kids."

"Fine," said Brian. "We'll just have to roll with it, charge as we go. Shops, restaurants, banks, take what we can get. Probably piss a few people off along the way but what the fuck."

"Wow. Brian. Hey." Darryl took a closer look at him, like he'd missed something. "When did you get all sensei?"

"When he saw Rosalita," said Jack. "And who could blame him? That girl could sweep the floor with those eyelashes."

"They're very long, yes, and full," said Brian.

"And they're real," added Jack.

"Wait." Brian stroked his chin, convinced of its power to help him think. "How do you know her name is Rosalita?"

"What else would Lita be?" Jack threw his hands in the air. "That's what Springsteen went with."

"I like how you took charge with the owner," Darryl told Brian. "So sexy."

"Got me hard," said Jack. "Not really, but why didn't you tell him she sent us?"

"I don't know," admitted Brian.

"Maybe she gets a commission," said Darryl.

Brian stood at the window, staring into the bamboo forest, just a few feet away. "The owner, Ivan, I saw him at Sharky's last night. He seems a bit sketch."

"You'd seem a bit sketch too if you lived in this house," said Darryl.

"Where do you think he's from?" asked Brian.

"The way he speaks English," said Darryl, "he can't be Costa Rican."

"Sounds European, Eastern European," said Jack.

"You pick that up on *Homeland*?" cracked Darryl.

"Carrie's bat crazy," replied Jack, surely knowing Darryl wasn't expecting an answer. "But I got mad respect for her."

"Well, can you narrow his accent down to an actual country?" asked Brian.

"I could if I had my own toilet to think on," said Jack.

"Shhh. . ." Darryl held out his hand. "You hear that?"

Brian leaned out the window, trying to pick up a conversation between Ivan and a woman downstairs. Or was it an argument? Spanish seemed so *rapido* to him. Still, Ivan sounded angry, the woman a lot like Lita.

"I'm going down there," Brian told the guys. "That's gotta be her."

"Hold on," said Jack. "Obviously, they're having some kind of disagreement."

Darryl nodded his head. "He might've gypped her out of her cut for sending us here."

"Okay," said Jack, "but any beef they got most likely runs deeper than us."

"I'm going." Brian started for the hole in the floor, where a bamboo ladder waited.

But Jack grabbed him by the shoulder, friendly but firm. "If it's Lita you can't wear this shirt again." He walked over to his bed and unzipped his suitcase. "I got somethin' for ya."

"You're a man on a mission." Darryl patted Brian on the back. "I'm impressed."

"It's you guys." Brian took off his polo and tossed it recklessly over his shoulder. "I feel different when I'm around you two, like I've got a chance."

"Of course, you've got a chance," Darryl told him. "You've always got a chance, Bri."

"You two are so fucking cute." Jack's fingers ran methodically through his clothes, all rolled neat and tight. "I just follow the Jimmy Buffett credo. . . *Flip or Fly*."

"Sounds like something white people do," said Darryl, turning from Jack to Brian. "Just be careful."

Jack found what he was looking for, handing Brian a black t-shirt. "*In Utero* tour."

"Cool." Brian held it up to get a better look, noticing a few rips and what looked like a hole forged from a cigarette butt. "This shirt's done its time."

"Got it at the Aragon, probably ninety-three, the week before Halloween," said Jack. "If you can't seal the deal in that, it ain't happenin'."

"Do you really think Lita knows who Nirvana is?" asked Darryl.

"Knows of? Sure. Has all their records? Probably not," replied Jack. "But the vibe is there just the same."

Brian put it on. "Thanks." He knew how much the shirt meant to Jack. If Brian was into Pearl Jam growing up, then Jack loved Nirvana. Fit their personalities, he thought, with Jack tending to play a little closer to the fire.

When Brian climbed down the ladder to the kitchen, Ivan grumbled something under his breath, though not in English or Spanish, and walked off.

That left Lita, sitting alone at the kitchen table, her head buried in her hands. "Sorry," Brian told her. "I didn't, um, hi. Is everything okay with us staying here?"

"Sí." She got up from the table, looking the other way. "I am going now."

"Yeah, me too." Brian scrambled for a reason. "I'm, uh, heading back to town." He called upstairs, "Guys, I'm gonna pick up that beer you wanted."

"Take your time," came Jack's voice. "I need a nap."

Darryl peeked his head down into the kitchen, "They're never going to fit me," then dropped his flip-flops through the hole. "I guess it's my turn to go barefoot."

"Thanks, man." Brian gladly took off his topsiders.

Lita pointed to the, "Chancletas," as he put them on.

"Chan-clay-tuz," repeated Brian, an eager student. "Do you think you could get me to the main road in my chancletas?"

"Sí," she smiled. A forced smile, thought Brian, masking other emotions, but he took what he could get.

With his inner dialogue becoming complicated, Brian knew he had to simplify the words that came out of his mouth.

Something with Ivan was troubling Lita but he knew harping on it wouldn't be wise, especially if the guys and him were somehow responsible.

So, Brian followed behind her, taking a shortcut through the bamboo from the house to where the dirt first turned to concrete on the road into town. That and the exchange with Ivan and he assumed she'd been to the Bamboo House before, which spiked his curiosity about her relationship to him; friend, foe, girlfriend, wife?

Usually, Brian would ask twenty questions mere minutes into meeting a woman, like he was vetting them for a political run, digging for the flaw that would be his out button.

But today, with Lita, he wasn't looking for excuses to leave. Instead, he was trying desperately to hang around. In fact, she was so gorgeous in Brian's eyes that he was ready to embrace any and all imperfections.

Like webbed toes. One of his cousins had them. If he stared too long, he thought they looked like baby bats.

Brian laughed to himself—then at himself. Who was he fooling? If Lita was indeed single there had to be a legitimate, if not sobering reason.

She was the kind of beautiful that if she farted most guys would convince themselves it was cute. No doubt, he had his work cut out for him with Lita.

However, in past instances Brian had been accused of trying too hard, so he decided to play it loose for a change, carefree, a distraction to her troubles, and it seemed to be working. Of course, they hadn't said a word to each other since they started walking.

Then, once they reached town, Lita paused, pointing out a store up the road. "Puedes comprar cerveza allí."

"Oh, great, cerveza."

"Mucho brete," she said. "Gracias a Dios."

Brian realized that was most likely a sendoff but played dumb. “Does that mean you’re coming with me?”

“No.”

“Oh.” Brian turned to leave. . . “Well, thanks anyway, gracias.”

But before he got too far, Lita spoke up. “I do not work so soon.”

A crack in her defense, Brian stopped, planted, and threw a pass, albeit a wobbly one. “I also need, time permitting, um, a swimsuit would be helpful.”

“You want to buy swimsuit?”

“Yeah, mine is, you know, gone,” said Brian, brushing the wrinkles out of his khakis with the back of his hands. “That’s all right. I’ll figure it out. Worse comes to worse, I can cut these into shorts.” Brian acted it out with his hands, like he was chopping hedges.

Lita winced, suggesting that she didn’t necessarily agree with him. “Mi amigo, he has una tienda by beach. You can find swimsuit there.”

“Great, what’s it called? Can I walk there? Just, uh, steer me in the right direction.”

“La tienda. . .” Like before, she stopped and bit her lip, as if she disapproved of her own decision. “I take you.”

“Thanks.” Brian was surprised. “Thank you.”

“But beer first,” she said firmly. “And do not walk behind me. I am not your driver.”

Brian crossed the road with Lita to a small store, where a couple of old chairs sat by themselves out front, kind of a mom and pop shop. “Mercado?” he tried.

“Es pulpería, es,” she started to explain but then gave up on the idea. “Less talking.”

Brian got the point and made a beeline for a row of refrigerators in the back, immediately reaching for a 12-pack of Imperial.

But Lita tapped him on the shoulder. "Get two beers. Bavarias. Dark."

"Just two? The guys—"

"You can come back later."

"Two it is, yeah, sounds good, two." One for her, thought Brian, one for him. It almost felt like a date. He begged himself not to mess things up.

He grabbed two Bavarias, making sure they were cold, and took them to the check-out line, where he set them on a dormant conveyor belt in front of an old Costa Rican woman, her skin a seasoned brown, as if she had only recently started working indoors.

"Can we drink these in the street?" Brian asked her. "Is that allowed? Are the police okay with that? The policía? Sorry, I'm new . . . ish. Nuevo?"

She slowly cocked her head to the side, looking past him to Lita. "Quatro mil doscientos sentena y cinco."

"Four Million?" Brian couldn't believe it. "That sounds a little high."

"Mil is thousand," explained Lita, picking up the beers. "Four thousand is like seven dollars US."

"According to the rate at the airport," he said, calculating it in his head, "seven dollars and four cents." But she was halfway out the door and didn't hear him, so he fished a ₡10,000 colones note from his pocket, a green one with a monkey on it, and gave it to the lady. "Doesn't colón mean Columbus?" he asked her. "I thought I read that somewhere."

The woman looked like she wanted to answer him but didn't seem to know what he was asking, which meant she was slow with the change, giving him a ₡5,000 colones note before reaching back into the register for some coins.

Anxious to catch up to Lita though, he just left, but when he got outside he couldn't find her. He scanned the street from one end to the other and then back again. But no luck. She was gone. Just like that.

Actually, she was right next to him, lost in thought, sitting in one of the chairs in front of the pulpería. When she saw him, she handed him a beer.

Brian took it, not just relieved to see her but downright rejoiceful. "Cheers."

"Salud." She took a big drink, then patted the seat next to her for him to sit down.

Brian joined her and took a big drink of his own, letting the beer glide down his throat at a leisurely pace, not just relishing the moment but trying to savor it forever.

Again they didn't speak, but Brian didn't consider it awkward. In fact, it was almost a relief not having to come up with some cheesy line.

When they were done with their beers, Lita went back inside and bought two more for the walk across town. And as the second beer kicked in, Brian began to feel lightheaded, like he was walking on sunshine, just like the song, as if Katrina and the Waves were serenading them from the rooftops.

Accustomed to being on the sidelines, this wasn't how Brian pictured it when the guys started talking about a trip to Costa Rica. But here he was, practically on parade with Lita, the prettiest girl in town.

He didn't care if it was too good to be true, though he was getting a weird vibe from people, mostly locals, he guessed, who spoke to her in Spanish along the way; Lita responding to them in varying degrees of interest and admiration, sometimes with a few words, sometimes with just a smile.

One Tico in particular appeared to inquire about Brian, and not necessarily in a nice way, but Lita didn't seem too bothered. Still, Brian didn't know if he was seen as the good-looking, or more likely, rich American who had tamed the local beauty or some dumb foreigner.

Maybe this was merely another business transaction, with Lita getting a percentage of the swimsuit sale. He must have counted half a dozen shops he could've stumbled into on his own. Within minutes though, they had made it to the Hotel Diria and a line of stores sharing the same terracotta tiled roof, kind of a Spanish style strip mall with strategically placed monkey statues to greet customers.

At the near end was *Papaya con Leche*, a bikini store from the look of it, even as Brian translated the name to mean, papaya with milk. Inside, a young woman greeted Lita warmly. "Kata is waiting for you."

Lita turned to Brian and gave him her beer, "Un momento," and then headed up a spiral staircase.

"She's going to the fitting room," explained the woman, her accent teetering toward French. "Her bathing suit is ready."

"Ready?"

"Kata, the owner, she designs them," she said. "All of the swimsuits are handmade right here."

"Oh, cool. Must be. . ." Despite thinking he was the one getting a new swimsuit, Brian had an idea. "Has Lita paid you yet?"

"No, not yet."

Brian set his credit card on the counter. "A surprise."

"You're her friend?"

"Yeah, pretty much."

The woman held her look on him, like he would catch fire if he was lying. "I suppose that's all right."

By the time Brian had signed on the dotted line, Lita was walking down the stairs wearing a green retro one-piece with tiered ruffles fanning her hips and breasts.

As far as he was concerned, "You look, wow, uh, unbelievable."

"You are next," smiled Lita. She put her sarong and t-shirt back on over her new bathing suit and stood at the counter.

"Your friend," said the woman, nodding to Brian. "El pagó por ti."

Lita turned to him, straight-faced. "Por qué?"

He couldn't tell if she was happy with his gesture or not. "I just thought you've been very helpful. It's a gift. No strings attached."

"No strings?"

Brian handed her beer back. "It means I'm not expecting anything in return."

Lita shrugged her shoulders, "That is too bad," and took another big swig from her beer.

Brian wasn't sure if Lita was drinking because she was in a good mood, into him, upset, or just showing pity on a tourist. Or, perhaps beer was merely her beverage of choice on a Sunday.

Regardless, they bought two more Bavarias before they found her friend's tienda and a pair of swim trunks for him, long ones to his knees that he was convinced knocked five years off his age.

Lita even talked her friend into giving them the local price, pleasing Brian so much that he ditched his khakis in the changing room.

"Todo listo?" she asked, when he came out in his brand new swimsuit.

"Listo?"

"I was asking if you are ready?"

"Oh, yeah," he replied, smiling from ear to ear. "I'm totally listo."

Next thing he knew, Lita and him were wading in the ocean, breaking in their new swimwear, holding cold cans of beer just above the water on yet another sunny afternoon in

Tamarindo. Brian took in the chipper blue sky, the few snow white clouds. The beach itself was a buffet of choices: Surf? Sunbathe? Frisbee? Read? Massage? Nap? Flirt?

He pretended to take interest in two Tico boys, waist deep in the waves, teaching a handful of blond-haired girls how to get up on their surfboards.

Lita nudged him. “Are you afraid of the sun?”

“Uh, no, a little, pardon?”

“Your shirt. Are you going to take off?”

“Probably not,” said Brian. “It’s Jack’s and, well, it’s Nirvana. I can’t risk losing it. Besides, I haven’t been in the sun since Labor Day Weekend . . . since September.”

“Your skin is very white, like ghost.”

“It’s true.” He held out his pale arms. “But when I was a kid I used to get really dark in the summer, darker than you.”

She splashed him playfully. “I do not believe.”

“Seriously, you won’t recognize me by the end of the week.” Brian looked at his arms again, wondering if he could still tan at his age—not to mention ride a wave. “The guys and I, we start surf camp tomorrow.”

“I surf,” she said, matter-of-factly.

Brian was impressed but had other issues he wanted to address. “Do I need to worry about sharks?”

“No, just crocodiles.”

“Ha.”

“It is true.”

“Crocodiles?”

“Por ahí.” Lita pointed to the north end of the beach, where an innocent looking river disappeared into the jungle. “They are living there but in ocean too.”

Brian tried to appear more curious than terrified. “Why would a crocodile go into the ocean?”

“If lost or hungry.”

“Lost or hungry,” he repeated. “Hmm, that’s good to

know. So, if it feels like I've been bitten by a shark, don't panic, it might just be a crocodile, who may or may not be lost but is definitely no longer hungry."

"There were signs warning people."

"Were?"

"Someone stole them."

"Jeez." He held his beer to his forehead to try and cool off. "Why doesn't the town just get rid of the crocodiles?"

"The other side of river, it is protected area," she told him. "But the river guides, they feed the crocodiles, so tourists get good picture."

"Okay, I suppose that could make sense."

"Sí, but when you do not bring a crocodile breakfast it will go looking for lunch."

"Can we talk about something else?" Brian's head was beginning to ache. "You're kind of freaking me out."

"Lo siento."

Brian turned his back on the hot sun. "Are you from here, from Tamarindo?"

"No, I live in Montezuma before."

"Montezuma?"

"It is where I go when I first come to Costa Rica," said Lita. "Como cinco horas al sur."

Brian didn't get all of that but translated what he could. "Five hours?"

"Sí, south of here. It is beautiful place."

Brian was all ears . . . and eyes, trying not to stare, but the way her wet skin glistened in the sunlight demanded it. "Montezuma," he said again, his eyes following a droplet of water as it slid between her brown, sun-freckled breasts into the friendly confines of her swimsuit.

Perhaps sensing that Brian was distracted, Lita lowered her body in the water, so only her head was above the surface. "Montezuma is like Tamarindo," she continued, "a party town but there is also big waterfall."

Brian had never seen one in person but told her, "Waterfalls are cool." He sat down in the water, bobbing a bit, a built-in excuse for floating closer to her, his body taking the lead from his brain. "And this is, uh, where you lived?"

"Sí, it was much fun. On Saturday night, everyone would go dancing at the top of the hill. Outside. Under the stars. Far from everything."

"Nice."

"It changed me. Meeting so many people. Different countries. A different life. But also good people, bad people. I began to question things and it, how do you say, opened my world. Is that right?"

"Maybe opened *up* your world but yeah."

She smiled again.

Damn, he could get used to that. And he might have told her so if he didn't think something would get lost in translation. "So, there's lots of tourists in Montezuma?"

"Sí and many stay." Lita held up her beer and arched her back toward the sky, floating on the water's surface. "Every day people come here and fall in love with Costa Rica."

Brian felt compelled to lean back too but got a nose full of water, causing him to snort and cough. "I'm all right. Go on."

"Some do not work, some maybe open business," she said, pausing so Brian could blow his nose. "But they want a new life. They want *Pura Vida*."

"What's Pura Vida?" asked Brian, just as he accidentally bumped into Lita under water and, for a moment, was sure he knew what it meant.

Lita sat up and swung around next to him, so that they were facing the same way. "It is how we live life in Costa Rica," she said in her irresistibly mellow but still enthusiastic tone. She floated into him, bumping him back, and nodded toward shore. “Pura Vida is one with nature; surfer, farmer, todo el mundo, simple, natural, positive, a pure life.”

“Cool, um. . .” Then Brian asked her what he really wanted to know. “Where does Ivan fit in? Is he just a tourist?”

Lita’s expression changed, like a cloud had been cast over her, and she stood up out of the water. “I have to work now.” Then, practically scowling, she started for shore. . .

“I’m sorry.” Brian went after her. . . “Just, who is he to you?”

“My husband’s father,” she hissed, over her shoulder.

“Your husband’s father? Oh, I, uh, so then you have a husband? Wow.” Brian scoured the crowded beach. “And where exactly is he?”

“He died,” she said, her voice carrying more anger than remorse.

Brian stopped in his tracks, scratching his head until he couldn’t remember if it itched or he was just confused. He wasn’t expecting a husband, so he definitely wasn’t expecting him to be dead.

At work. Out of town. In the army (though he recalled reading that there hadn’t been an army in Costa Rica since 1949). Okay, so, he’s taking care of the baby. Was unfaithful. Likes to watch.

But, dead?

That was a small but powerful word with implications galore, if not gory, and a rush of sympathy and compassion infiltrated his emotions, right alongside his lust for her.

As a result, he wanted desperately to say something appropriately meaningful, to throw his hat into what must have been a ring of suitors . . . of saviors.

Yet, no words came from Brian’s mouth. He couldn’t even move. He just watched as Lita marched down the beach, amazed by how strong his feelings were for her but wondering if it came at a cost that no man could afford.

8

Gallo Pinto

"Died?" An agitated Jack got up out of bed from his nap in just his tighty-whiteys. "Old people die," he told Brian. "Young people. . . They get killed."

"Word." Darryl climbed down the ladder to Jack's room, his big bare feet leading the way, dressed and ready for a night out; same cargo shorts, different shirt, this time a *Darryl's* t-shirt from his bar. "You better get dressed, Jack, I'm starvin'."

Jack gave Darryl a discerning look, then turned his attention back to Brian. "Lita happen to mention *how* her husband died?"

"She didn't." Brian reached into a plastic bag of ice and pulled out a can of Imperial for each of them. "But I found out that Ivan's her father-in-law, though that's as far as we got."

Darryl popped open his beer. "I'd say that was far enough,"

"Yeah." Jack opened his too and took a quick sip. "Time to cut that shit off."

But Brian wasn't on board. "What do you mean?"

"Huh?" Jack looked at him all beady-eyed. "I mean find another girl."

Usually, Brian would listen to Jack, mostly to shut him up, but Lita was another story. His story. "What if I don't want to? What if I can't?"

Darryl patted him on the back, as if it was settled. "Do it anyway."

"Don't sweat it, Bri. I've got something to help you get laid." Jack scrolled through his cell phone. "My son gave me some notes."

"Notes?" asked Brian, reluctantly. "From Lleyton?"

"Has he even done it yet?" asked Darryl.

"He's trying," snapped Jack, as if sharing in his son's frustration. He sat back down on his bed, like he needed to, one hand over his heart.

"You okay?" Darryl asked him.

"It's my cholesterol," said Jack. "Welcome to the new me." He had a serious, almost frightened look on his face. "Being on my own, doc said I gotta learn to cook more than burgers and pancakes."

"You had to have a doctor tell you that?" asked Brian.

"I know, right?" Jack wiped the sweat from his forehead with the back of his thumb.

"If you have a heart attack while we're on vacation," said Darryl, jabbing Jack playfully, "I'm going to kill you."

"I'm fine," sighed Jack, "fit as a fiddle, just gotta stick to my diet and stay regular."

"We're turning forty," said Darryl, "not a hundred."

"Proper bowel movements are pivotal to longevity," explained Jack, like he'd unearthed some new finding. "It's all about how you shit, piss, and cum. If you're having trouble with any of those three, call your doctor."

"Can you talk and get dressed?" asked Darryl.

"Sure," said Jack. "My guy said if you can piss three times

a day, shit twice, and cum once, you'll live a long active life."

"Makes sense," said Darryl. "But are you going somewhere with this?"

"Yeah, it all comes full circle," said Jack, "but I'll try to keep it in a straight line." He reached for his trackpants, which were folded neatly at the end of his bed. "So, as Americans, we've got it pretty good, no matter who's president, am I right?"

Darryl shrugged his shoulders, not exactly convinced. "Ehhh."

"And no I didn't vote for Trump," said Jack. "I may be dumb but I'm not stupid."

"I'm still hungry," pointed out Darryl.

"Okay, I hear ya." Jack put on the pants. "As Americans though, we're raised to forget grandma and grandpa and the countries and culture we come from and stick to the one we've created, the one inside a TV or nowadays a fucking cell phone. Cigarettes? Cool! SeaWorld? Spectacular! Reality TV shows? Number one! Turns out all three were scripted. But, as a people, we devour that shit."

"Clearly," Brian told him. "You've thought about this."

"Maybe too much," added Darryl.

"You're probably right," said Jack, buttoning up the Hawaiian shirt for another go-around. "But we've devised this all-consuming media bubble in America that has us only looking inward, at ourselves. Our music, our religion, our sports, just about all of it comes from home. And if it doesn't, you better sing it, preach it, or play it in English . . . in American."

"Okay, but how's this gonna help me get, you know?" asked Brian.

"Take soccer," carried on Jack. "Baseball might be our national pastime but—"

"Was," interjected Darryl. "Probably football now."

"Either way, soccer is the world's game," said Jack. "And it's getting bigger and bigger in the States. In fact, Lleyton just quit baseball to focus on soccer. Still, the average guy doesn't know his Messis from his Ronaldos."

"Are you sure you're going somewhere with this?" asked Darryl.

"Oh," smiled Jack, twisting one end of his mustache, "you know where I'm going with this."

"Get to it then." Darryl pulled another beer out of Brian's bag. "And quit playing with your mustache."

"I can't help it," said Jack.

"Fine," relented Darryl. "But I'm not getting less hungry."

"Okay, simmer down." Jack carefully ran a comb through his thinning hair. "Let's say you're an American abroad, in a bar, and you get to talking with some locals, like we might tonight. Fuck politics and religion, all that shit. If you can spew out some soccer knowledge, starting by calling it football, or *futbol*, you get immediate street cred. Makes you seem worldly. And chicks love worldly."

Darryl nodded his head in agreement. "Can't argue with that."

"And worldly," said Jack, "makes them think you're evolved."

"Evolved is a good look," said Darryl.

"So Lleyton made up a list, which I will send you if we ever get WiFi again." Jack flipped the lid to his phone. "Fortunately, I took a screenshot, so . . . using their FIFA ranking, he gave me the lowdown on the best soccer players in the world from each country. For example, you meet a chick from Chile, tell her your favorite player is Alexis, that's his first name by the way. Or tell her you dig Vidal's mohawk. A hot babe from France, you're all about Griezmann. Take the girl at the hostel, she was from Venezuela. Bet she would've let us stay had I merely mentioned Rondon, their big striker."

"What about Costa Rica?" asked Brian.

"Nice try." Jack put on his hat, already an integral part of his wardrobe.

"What? You were the one pushing me on Lita."

"Were."

"Come on," pressed Darryl. "You can't give out the names of all these soccer players and not give him the one he's got the best chance with. This is Brian we're talking about."

"All right, settle down. Let's see, it's alphabetical." He checked his phone again. "He's got two here for Costa Rica. Their goalie, Navas, or this Joel Campbell guy."

"Joel," realized Darryl. "That's who I met on the plane." He started down the ladder to the kitchen. "The pilot asked for his autograph as we were getting off."

"See?" Jack followed him through the hole. "That's the kind of shit that can get you laid."

"Navas and Campbell," repeated Brian, bringing up the rear. "Navas and Campbell."

Though he intended to do otherwise, Brian went silent that night, allowing Jack to steer them away from Nogui's by talking up a restaurant he'd read about online called the Green Papaya, known not just for its tacos but its dozen or so rope swings.

The guys found neighboring swings to their liking, all three pulling up to the same table; a thick slab of wood cut along its natural curve and finished smooth.

Brian swore he could hear the roof creak every time Darryl turned in his swing but the guys ignored him, ordering Imperials just about every time the waiter so much as glanced at them.

Jack and Darryl also ate every taco on the menu, not because they were feeling adventurous but because with

Darryl at the helm, they would've cleaned the restaurant out of the beef.

That meant they also chowed down on fresh mahi-mahi and seared ahi tuna tacos, while Brian attempted to talk up a black bean burger, only to get drowned out by the more important issues of the day.

Like the Bears quarterback situation.

The Blackhawks salary cap.

And whether the Cubs would *repeat* as World Series champions.

Don't get him wrong. Normally, Brian enjoyed engaging in mindless sports chatter with the guys, considering it a valid form of escapism, a metaphor for male evolution from cave man to gladiator to middle linebacker.

But Lita had his brain on lockdown. He had so many questions for her—for himself. Was it over? Only the beginning? Was he overreacting? Being a big baby? Was he expected to go after her? Man up?

He compensated by drinking too much and the journey back to the Bamboo House, though on foot, wasn't without a few spills on the gravel road.

His body was overheating. . .

His head spinning. . .

And he never fell into a deep sleep. Instead, he was left to curse the tequila shots and impromptu karaoke that capped off the night: *Sweet Home Chicago*!

Brian found himself in the courtyard at dawn, stumbling in a half trance toward the outhouse, just enough sunlight poking through the bamboo to discern Lita blocking his path.

"Where'd you. . ." Brian rubbed his eyes, unsure if he was dreaming. "Come from?"

"Hola, guapo." She adjusted a bag of groceries on her hip. "Breakfast?"

"Uh, yes, of course, thank you. Guapo? I'm guapo? What's guapo?"

"Venga." Lita started for the house, motioning for Brian to follow her.

But Brian didn't move. "I still have to, you know, I'll catch up."

By the time Brian returned to the kitchen, Lita was already at the stove, several pans going at once, like a deejay spinning records, creating a smell good enough to transform his nausea into hunger.

He was impressed. And not, he would have you know, in a chauvinistic way. "What do we have here?"

"Gallo pinto," she replied, focusing on the food.

"Como?" he asked, trying his Spanish. "Uh, Qué?"

She smiled, flipping a corn tortilla in one pan, "Gallo pinto es un desayuno típico," then turning over a couple of eggs in another.

The last pan, Brian thought, she stirred suggestively.

"White rice, black beans, a little chile roja, cebolla, cilantro, sal." She looked over at him. "Mi abuela would kill me if I told you more."

"Your ab-way-la," he tried, not knowing what she meant. "Um—"

"My grandmother. Sit down." She pointed to the bamboo table. "There is coffee."

Brian did as he was told and took a seat, pouring himself a cup from a blue pot.

"Café con leche," she said, as he added milk to it from a miniature pitcher.

"Ca-fay cone ley-chay," repeated Brian. He stuck the cup under his nose, inhaling the aroma, his eyes never wavering from Lita as she prepared him a plate of food.

"Mi familia, we are from Managua," she went on, then stopped off Brian's puzzled look. "Nicaragua. You know,

Sandinistas?"

"Sure," replied Brian, though he was referencing the Clash album.

"Mi abuela came to Costa Rica after the revolution to look for work. She cook for a Tico family in Montezuma. They love her gallo pinto." Lita sliced a couple of pieces of avocado straight onto Brian's plate. "But she use her own recipe, from Nicaragua. And when they find out, she was fired."

"What did your grandmother, uh, your abuela, do?"

"Got a job in restaurant." She set his plate in front of him. "And the restaurant start to do a good business. Even the family that fired her came to eat there."

"Oh, cool, thank you," he said, looking over his meal.

She handed him a bottle with a green cap. "Salsa Lizano."

Having no idea what it was, or how hot it was, Brian politely poured some of the brown sauce on his plate, purposely off to the side, then spoke before giving it much thought. "So, what's your connection to Ivan?"

"You talk too much." Lita slid her coffee mug toward the center of the table.

Brian took the hint and poured her a cup. "Leche?" he tried. "Sucar?"

"Azúcar," she corrected. "Sí, both."

"I don't mean to pry."

"Yes, you do."

Brian topped off her coffee with milk and sugar, then handed her the cup. "I guess I'm just curious about you."

"Eat." She blew on her coffee, then took two quick sips.

Although he could have stared at her all day, eggs were legal in his veggie handbook. So, hungry as he was, he dug in, accidentally running the yolk into the rice and beans.

That was a first. He didn't know what to do. His rice and beans had never been in danger of his eggs before. In fact, they'd never been on the same plate.

Rice and beans weren't a breakfast option. Ever. Then again, Lita made this meal for him, so he kept eating, everything, all together.

Before he knew it, Brian's taste buds were applauding his decision. "This is fantastic."

"Somethin' smells good," came a deep voice from above. Brian turned to see Darryl, following his nose down the ladder. . .

With Jack right behind him, rubbing his extended belly. "There really is a god."

Lita motioned to the stove with the back of her hand. "There is mucho," she told them, then turned back to Brian, "Vienes conmigo."

Brian didn't necessarily understand her words, but he was sure of her body language as she gathered her things to leave—presumably with him.

Pretending his heart wasn't just shot out of a cannon, Brian took a giant gulp of coffee before rolling the rest of his breakfast into a burrito for the road. "I guess," he began, his voice cracking. "I guess this is adiós, boys."

"*Adiós, adiós*?" wondered Jack. "Like forever?"

"No, of course not," said Brian. "Don't be insane."

"So, where're you going?" asked Darryl.

"I don't know," admitted Brian, his eyes glued on Lita. "I suppose it's not where, it's with who."

"Ooh," said Jack, twisting his mustache. "I like the sound of that."

Lita headed for the bamboo forest, not checking to see if Brian was trailing behind her.

"You approve of her now?" Darryl asked Jack, when she was out of earshot.

"I approve of her ass," he said. "But if I was a betting man, and of course I am, I'd still put my money on steering clear of that woman."

"Didn't you bet against the Cubs winning the World Series?" asked Brian.

"I believe in curses," replied Jack. "What can I tell you? And women are cursed."

Darryl shook his head at Jack, then stole another look at Lita before she got too far away, apparently signing off. "Call us, Bri."

"I don't have my cell phone," he told them.

Darryl made his way over to the stove. "Well, go get it."

"I don't need it," he said, taking a bite out of his burrito.

"Says who?" asked Jack.

"Yeah, aren't you gonna take any pictures?" asked Darryl.

"It doesn't matter," replied Brian, as if he'd gone anywhere without one in the last ten years. "Battery's low." Then he hustled after Lita, who was disappearing into the bamboo.

Jack turned to Darryl. "Aren't you going to do something?"

"Yeah." He stuck a fork in the gallo pinto, calling after Brian, "Surf class is at nine!"

9

Let's Go Surfin' Now

The jungle was dry when Lita brought him to Nogui's that morning, enormous brown leaves crunching under their feet, begging for rain. Still, just walking in such an exotic land was beyond exciting for him; throw in the exotic woman and his head was about to explode from a bout of pure bliss. Brian figured he slept for an hour, maybe two, but he wasn't tired, even with all the drinking.

Gallo Pinto.

Café con leche.

A winning combination. Worked like magic. It's not the heart the woman seduces, his grandfather always told him, it's the stomach.

And Lita did come over to the Bamboo House. Twice. *Hmmm*, was it because of him? Or Ivan? Or, as usual, was Brian reading too much into too little; known in his world as not enough data to make a conclusive argument.

Except for last night's fairy lights barely flickering over the bar, the restaurant was dead. Lita, though, crept in quietly, taking Brian around back to the kitchen, where the first shimmer of sunlight revealed a row of surfboards leaning expectantly against the far wall.

She picked out two: “La mía es la roja,” a svelte seven-footer and, “Take that one, guapo,” a mammoth eleven-foot board.

Guapo. There was that damn word again. Brian didn’t know what to make of it, but from the sound of it, it certainly could’ve been a member of the *gringo* family.

Regardless, the board looked heavy, requiring his full attention. So, he took a deep breath, keeping his back straight, bending at the knees, and lifted the board with a manly grunt—directly into a light fixture hanging from the ceiling.

Lita turned around in time to see him get showered in tiny pieces of glass . . . an astonished, borderline dumbfounded look sweeping across her face.

Unaware that the board was made of a hard foam and actually quite light, Brian had overexerted himself. Needless to say, he was embarrassed, even more so when Julio woke up, his brown eyes springing to life from a cot tucked under a shelf of canned goods.

Julio spoke to Lita in Spanish, sternly, like he was scolding her, but she cut him off, telling him something that made him roll over and go back to sleep with little more to say.

Brian vowed to redeem himself. He just wasn’t sure if it should involve water sports. Then again, with the guys around, or at least nearby, everything was supposed to be easier.

So minutes later, boards under their arms, Brian went with Lita to Playa Langosta, a quiet stretch of sand away from the hustle and bustle of Tamarindo that was split down the middle by the mangrove the guys had passed the day before.

Brian wasn’t aware of it but this beach was responsible in

part for the pukka shell necklace craze of the 1970s. His focus, however, was on the handful of surfers, already in the water catching rides.

She showed him her favorite surf break, *La Piedra del Zapo*, explaining that it was best before low tide, when swells came from the west. But all Brian noticed was that the waves broke way too close to a death bed of rock and coral.

They sat in the sand and watched the surfers, Lita pointing out different moves . . . and mistakes. Luckily for him, she didn't want to risk damaging the boards on the reef and took him north around the bluff, back to Tamarindo, where he had half a chance.

Still, time to get wet meant time to perform. Brian had skateboarded a couple of summers as a kid but growing up on Lake Michigan never surfed, even on the Jamaica trip when a few of the guys gave it a go.

This time, however, he didn't flinch. Not with Lita as his instructor, rocking her green swimsuit, the new one with the ruffles, which sort of hid and accentuated her breasts. In fact, Brian was downright inspired.

Unfortunately, it didn't go well for him, highlighted by a series of disastrous wipeouts in which he took in a ton of water, seemingly in every orifice.

Forget riding his surfboard, Brian was having a hard time just holding on to it. Up close, the waves were bigger than he'd expected and he struggled each time to get out past the swell, where Lita would wait for him.

He tried to mimic what she'd done, pushing the tip of his board under the waves head on, but it usually took him a couple of tries to reach her.

Half an hour into his lesson, Brian caught up to Lita in the lull between waves, sitting on her board, her feet dangling over either side.

The ocean remained calm for a few minutes, allowing

Brian to recharge, while trying his best not to think of lost or hungry crocodiles—as if they were any other kind.

He knew, statistically, that he was more likely to get struck by lightning than eaten by a shark, yet alone a crocodile. Of course, he quickly scanned the flawlessly blue sky for storms.

Lita reminded him to put his hands underneath his shoulders before pushing up on the board, though ultimately it wasn't surfing that she wanted to talk about.

She seemed apprehensive to Brian, keeping an eye on the horizon for the next set of waves, before she got to the point. "Your friends, they are going to say things about me."

"What kind of things?"

"That I am liar."

"Huh? Why?" Brian's throat clenched. "Why would they say that?"

She looked away from him, out to sea, to the next swell moving in, and laid forward on her board. "Because it is true."

Lita began paddling with her arms, harder and harder until the wave reached her, then rose to her feet in one fluid motion, settling into a pocket of water charging toward shore. . .

He wanted answers but, *dang*, he was a captive audience, watching Lita ride her board, cool and easy like it was no big deal, yet the only thing worth living for. . .

Brian ditched his inhibitions and paddled ferociously in front of the next wave. And, without over thinking it, or doing it exactly how Lita taught him, he put his *toes on the tail* and his *hands on the rails* and popped up on his board, right in the middle of the break.

Knees bent.

Arms out.

He was stiff but standing at last.

Surfing to the beach. . .

Brian found Lita on shore, surprised to see him upright, cheering for him. He started to wave to her when he spotted Jack and Darryl in the shallow water, surfboards at their sides, staring at him in disbelief as he blew right by them, all the way in, and stepped off his board, stumbling into Lita's salty wet embrace: "Guay."

Full of pride, Brian skipped surf class with the guys without a moments hesitation to be with Lita, who, now that Playa Tamarindo was filling up, said she wanted to take him to a more secluded beach. To surf, yes, but surely to explain herself too, which he knew would require some privacy. So, the two of them ditched the guys and headed toward the river, the one with the errant crocodiles, and stopped at the water's edge.

Brian knew Lita had a plan to get them to the other side, that perhaps she was only hesitating on his behalf, thinking he might be too chicken to go through with it.

He figured it was fifty yards from one side to the other, tops; the water shallow enough where the river met the ocean that he thought about surprising her and running across.

Of course, he'd never make such a bold move in real life. However, if Lita was in a way unreal, he felt inclined to act accordingly.

"One for the money," started Brian, rocking back and forth on his feet.

Lita frowned.

"Two for the show."

"The show?"

"Three to get ready."

"Para qué?"

"Let's make a run for it across the river." He rubbed his hands together, trying to psych himself up.

"Do not be stupid."

Brian folded quickly. "Okay." He could picture the headline that everyone but himself would be reading on BuzzFeed: *Tourist Ignores Local Beauty, Gets Eaten by Croc.*

So, Brian was about to sit down when that dog, the Shepherd mix, came running up to Lita, like he knew her. And she did, introducing him, as she pet him on the head. "This is Maní."

"Ma-nee?"

"It means peanut in English."

"Because of his color?"

"Sí."

"This is your dog?"

"No," she laughed. "Maní doesn't belong to anyone."

"Oh."

"Maní is famous." She crouched down and kissed him on the nose. "He have grand-dogs in America."

"Impressive." He let Maní sniff the back of his hand and, after a nervous moment or two, apparently checked out.

That's when a small boat came whirring around the bend in the river without showing any signs of slowing down. . .

Heading right at them. . .

Teenage boy at the helm. . .

Barreling onto the sand. . .

Just as he cut and raised the engine. . .

Brian tackled Lita out of the way, prematurely, since the boat stopped just short of them. Embarrassed, he quickly helped her up, apologizing profusely as he tried to wipe the sand off of her.

He stopped, realizing he was touching her too much, so he sized up the driver; young, early teens, very dark, from the sun, sure, but also like he had some native, pre-Columbus blood in him.

Lita stepped between them and spoke to the driver in Spanish before handing him some money, after which he took stock of the busy beach for other riders.

Unable to find anyone, he put his shoulder into the bow and pushed the boat back into the water, then hopped in and yanked on a long cord, like you would an old lawnmower, starting up the outboard motor again.

Brian and Lita helped Maní into the boat, which despite a fresh slathering of white paint was rather nicked up, like it had battled a pier or two.

Then, while the dog and driver got reacquainted, Brian followed Lita to the bow, wanting to be a DiCaprio to her Winslet, only they arrived safely on the other side in under a half a minute.

Once ashore, Maní took off on his own, leaving the two of them to walk with their boards along the beach to Playa Grande, where she made a point of telling him, "las tortugas," laid their eggs.

"May to October, if I'm not mistaken," said Brian, almost sure he'd nailed the dates, and sure enough Lita smiled approvingly.

Knowledge is power, he thought, and in this case, the power to impress. Smart, never a bad look. Brian felt like he had a legitimate chance with Lita. For what? He wasn't certain. For starters though, he wanted to kiss her.

As in his dream the beach was empty, and Brian wondered what it would take to put his lips to hers. A deeper conversation than turtles though, maybe even a confession of some sorts, appeared imminent. However, any grasp Brian had on logic went straight for the jugular:

She had weeks to live.

She was sent to kill him.

She's a man, baby, a man!

Back home, he tended to ignore bad news, like when the

doctor he was dating banged a patient of hers, some bullshit about dying wishes.

True to form, Brian continued to see her for another couple of weeks after that, without bringing up her transgression again, right up until she moved in with the guy.

Today was a different story though. Different setting too. With a different girl. If only he could initiate the action for once instead of dropping back on defense.

He knew the time was ripe for romance but couldn't think of the proper approach. It can't be this hard, he thought. Just put the damn board down and kiss her.

And he'd tell you that he was just about to do it too, when they ran into some dudes with surfboards of their own, lounging about in the shade of the palms, still wet, as if they'd just been in the water.

Brian didn't like the look of them:

Young.

Tan.

And ripped.

A mix of races in gnarly dreads, burnt blond afros, and scruffy goatees.

One of them sat on a cooler, recounting a "dope" wave he caught to his friends. It was, Brian realized, the surfer dude from the airport and, of course, the pool table at the hostel.

The dude stopped talking when he spotted them, directing his attention to Brian. "Mae," he started, making sure all his friends were listening, "you two going out now?"

At first Brian thought the dude was paying him a compliment, but upon further review he left his surfboard with Lita and walked over to him, not willing to let this *dude* talk shit about them, even if it meant getting his ass kicked.

"Look, pal, what business is it of yours?" tried Brian, realizing his choice of words was perhaps dated but pleased just the same to have found some guts.

However, the dude wasn't fazed. He just looked at his friends, the grin on his face growing. "Because if you're not gonna go out and catch some waves, mae, we've got a cooler full of cold beer."

"Oh." Brian was getting used to putting his foot in it, blaming it squarely on the language barrier, even if the conversation was in English. "We, uh, yeah, might go out later."

"Just snappers now."

"Snappers?" repeated Brian. "You mean crocodiles?"

"No," laughed the dude. "Ankle busters."

"Huh?"

"The waves are too small." The dude stood to open the cooler. "Have a beer." He pulled two cans of Pilsen Gold from the ice, tossing them both to Brian, the second one high and wide. . .

But Brian whipped his arm out, snatching the can, surprised at his luck but trying not to show it.

"Bit of advice," said the dude, apparently not as impressed. "Don't try and turn shit up while you're down here."

"Excuse me."

"Lita is a friend of ours."

"Of course, we're just, I wouldn't. I get it. You can trust me."

"It's not me you have to worry about," said the dude. "My dad's been here over twenty years, still gets hassled."

Another surfer said something in Spanish, seemingly at the expense of the dude, or his dad, causing the rest of them to crack up laughing.

"There's an old saying," said the dude, doing his best to ignore them. "You don't hear it as much these days, but in English it translates to, *a gringo is a gringo no matter how many chicharrones he eats*."

"What's a chee-ka-rone-ez?" asked Brian, not that he thought it mattered.

But before he got an answer, Lita joined them, apparently having heard enough chatter. "Suave un toqué."

The dude relented, taking a swig of his beer before fiddling with the antennae on an old boombox, back and forth until he was able to tune in a song clearly; after which he finished his beer and chucked the empty can at his friends, narrowly missing one of their heads, which made them laugh even harder.

"Where's your dad from?" Brian asked him.

The dude sat back down on the cooler, like it was his throne. "Chicago."

"Chicago? Chi-Town?" Brian opened one of the beers and handed it to Lita. "You're kidding? Damn. Same here."

The dude nodded his head, not overly enthusiastic but, "Todo bien, mae."

"Actually, I'm from Evanston." Brian was ready to launch into a whole Windy City spiel; Cutler, Kane, the Bean, that kind of thing, when Lita tugged at him with her eyes to leave.

"Thanks for the beer." Brian reached out to shake the dude's hand but thought better of it, bumping knuckles with him instead. "I'm Brian."

"Kenny," he said in turn, then sort of thinking out loud, "Evanston, huh?"

"Yeah."

"Tuanis."

Brian wasn't sure what *twa-nees* meant about his hometown but before he could ask, Lita held up her beer to the surfers, "Gracias," and started up the beach, her hips rolling from side to side with each graceful stride, again not looking over her shoulder to see if Brian was coming or not.

Of course, he was coming! But not without trying to find a face amongst the surfers that might reveal something about

Lita.

A wink.

A chuckle.

Maybe a grimace.

But they gave him nothing to go on. So, he took off his chancletas and caught up to her, trying his best to hold on to the moment; the *now* of the cold beer, warm beach, and hot woman, before it vanished into thin air.

Brian sat in the sand beside Lita, weary waves falling just short of their feet, and before long she began talking to him, softly, thoughtfully, but never looking directly at him.

She came clean, admitting that Jack had contacted her on Instagram before they arrived, trying to meet her. But she felt there was something loco about him and said she wasn't interested. And, no, she wasn't for sale.

Then he said he had a friend. Nice guy. Good job. Never married. She still wasn't convinced that it was a good idea but went ahead and told Jack where she worked, mostly to get him to stop messaging her.

Needless to say, Brian was stunned. And disappointed. He couldn't believe he didn't figure any of this out sooner. Lita was just a set-up. Playing a part. Her admission, kind as it was, sliced through Brian's spirit, cutting it into tiny pieces, rendering it wounded and worthless.

However, she wasn't done; she had motives of her own in meeting a single man, the part she didn't tell Jack about. Finally, she looked at him. "I need to marry."

And her husband didn't die. He was murdered a year ago. And no one had been arrested. Brian tried to speak but, not knowing where to start, remained silent.

They walked back toward the surfers, Brian assuming this is where they would go their separate ways, preferably without making a scene.

However, Brian wasn't sure what to do about the surfboard. Was he expected to take it back to the restaurant? With her? He picked up his chancletas first, hoping to get a reaction from her and he did.

Lita grabbed his arm. "I was using you," she said, like she was angry with him, the surfers all taking notice. So, she stepped closer to Brian and lowered her voice, wiping the tears running down her cheeks with the back of her hand. "I was lying. . . But you were nice to me. Lo siento. I am sorry."

"You don't have to be sorry. Really." As noted, Brian didn't mind being lied to on occasion, didn't have to be the little white ones either. Less painful, he thought. "I'll be back in Chicago on Monday, Twenty South Wacker Drive to be exact. In a funny jacket. Trading currencies from countries I couldn't find on a map."

She looked up at him, puzzled.

"Actually, that's not true, I mean, I'll be there," he told her, "but I could probably find most of those countries, the guys I work with, not so much." He finished off the rest of his beer, stalling for the right words. "Um, yeah, you can tell me what you want. Whatever you feel comfortable with."

A thoughtful sentiment, he was sure, but was that all it was? What could he really do for her besides just listen? Marry her?

Brian knew there was more drama where that story came from and he longed for his cell phone, knowing he could pretend the guys were calling, that he had to go. But without that crutch, he had to make a decision:

Grind it out and bolt at the first chance?

Or reverse course and see things through?

Maybe even throw a Hail Mary and finally get that kiss?

Brian went to the *Man on the Make* playbook in his head but a song came on the radio, interrupting his thought process, a mid-tempo ballad that caught Lita's attention too.

She raised a finger, signaling Kenny to turn the volume up and he did so right away, giving voice to a duet between a man and a woman in Spanish.

Brian had no idea what they were singing about but they seemed quite fond of each other, perhaps, the way Lita stopped to listen, in love.

With everyone watching her, Brian thought it might be a good time to slip away but unable to shake his focus from her, he stayed.

Then she closed her eyes.

And gave in to the melody.

Hips swaying.

Hands caressing the sky.

Lita sang along softly.

As she began to dance. . .

Tú eres mi amor, mi alegría
La verdad de mi vida
Mi bebe que me calma el alma con risas
Tú eres mi refugio y mi verdad

--Maná w/Shakira

10

Love And Marriage

Brian caught up to Jack and Darryl back in Tamarindo, having a beer at a picnic table where the grass met the sand out in front of Witch's Rock Surf Camp, a lively afternoon scene complete with on-site brewery. That's basically all they drank by the way, just beer, which was fine with Brian, since it seemed to fit his even-keeled personality.

Unless, of course, he drank past his magic number, which had less to do lately with how much he'd had to eat, for example, and more with how old he was.

In college, ten, twelve cups of beer was common at parties, more if there was a drinking game involved.

That number was down to seven or eight cold ones by his late twenties, maybe a Black & Tan to start, more than enough for a night in the city with the guys at Gingerman or Smart Bar.

By his thirties, a couple of beers was about right for dinner on the town, though you could easily tack on an additional pint or two if the guys gathered to watch a sporting event on TV, a few extra if they went to a game in person.

And now, on forty's doorstep, Brian was exceeding all

expectations thanks to the surfers and their endless cooler of beer.

Even so, he made his way to the bar without his friends seeing him and bought another Pilsen, chugging half of it right away to calm his nerves.

It didn't seem to be working though—unless that was the alcohol talking, in which case you would have to take into account that he just stumbled in the sand over . . . nothing.

Still, he felt emboldened, as if what just went down with Lita had given him a power surge, a bolt of adrenaline that could ward off all toxins, even if underneath it all he was absolutely terrified.

In fact, in a gesture rooted in fear more than generosity, he ordered another three beers, pints of Witch's Rock Pale Ale, finishing the rest of his Pilsen while he paid up.

Then, Brian walked over to the guys, setting the mugs down in the center of their table with a *thud* to make sure he had their attention. He leaned in, gripping the table on either side, steadying himself, and took a deep breath as he announced: "I think I'm in love."

"Did you know Witch's Rock isn't just a surf school?" asked Jack, as if he hadn't heard him.

Brian played along and pointed to the beers: "The house pale ale."

"Okay," said Jack. "But did you know it's an actual rock, a huge fucking rock that shot straight out of a volcano into the Pacific." He mimicked the rock's trajectory with his hand, it's descent into water with a fading whistle. "North of here, not too far."

"Great surf spot," added Darryl.

"Guys, I—" started Brian again.

But Jack beat him to it. "It's in one of those *Endless Summer* movies, Bri, the surf ones, you know, the documentaries."

"Guys!" Brian pounded his fist into the table with each successive word. "I'm. In. Love."

"Love?" questioned Jack, finally letting up. "I used to know a thing or two about love."

Darryl ignored him though, focusing on Brian. "With the Costa Rican chick?"

"Lita," said Brian, picturing her in his head. "She's . . . incredible."

"Lord have mercy," sighed Darryl, making room for Brian on the bench. "Sit your crazy ass down for a minute."

Brian parked himself between his friends, the three of them gifted once again with a masterful sunset; a piece of art igniting the sky in flames, the mirror image reflecting off the shallow water.

"Did you bone her?" asked Jack.

"Bone her?" Brian punched him in the thigh, hard.

And Jack got the point, kind of. "Relax. Did you make love to her?"

"And do yoga at the same time?" asked Darryl, trying not to laugh.

"Actually," admitted Brian. "We haven't even kissed."

Jack looked confused. "Then what the fuck you do?"

"We talked," said Brian, before taking on a more serious tone. "And she told me everything. About you. About Instagram. All that shit."

"Sorry," said Jack, his remorse a four on a scale to ten. "I was only trying to help." He handed Brian a stick of sunscreen. "Your nose is red."

"So everything on this trip's been a lie?" Brian stood up and chucked the sunscreen as far as he could down the beach. "The hotel? The—"

"Not the hotel." Darryl put his hand on Brian's shoulder, guiding him back into his seat. "Jack really did fuck that up."

"Okay," continued Brian. "So we didn't really get kicked

out of the hostel and—"

"No, that's true," said Jack. "Darryl fell on the guy."

"Perry," clarified Darryl.

"Fine," said Brian. "But you set me up with Lita. For what? To make me look like an idiot?"

"No, Lita, that was all you," Jack told him. "I made sure we had dinner at Nogui's but nothing about monkey bars or bamboo houses or dead husbands or—"

"By the way," interrupted Brian, "you were right, he was killed."

"That's a deal-breaker." Darryl looked from Jack to Brian to Jack again. "Right?"

"We didn't know anything about anybody getting killed," said Jack. "That's news to us. Swear to god."

"And," Darryl reminded him, "we did tell you to cut it off with her."

"I know, but fuck." Brian tried to rub the growing knot out of his forehead. "Now I've got to help her."

"Help her?" asked Darryl. "With what?"

"Keeping her house," said Brian. "The Bamboo House, it's hers, at least it was her husband's."

"So why isn't Ivan helping her?" asked Jack.

"Because he's helping himself," explained Brian. "He's trying to bamboozle her out of the property since she's not a citizen."

"Really?" asked Jack.

"She's from Managua," he replied. "That's in Nicaragua."

"But Ivan isn't Costa Rican either," said Jack.

"He is now," said Brian. "He married a woman here, had a son, the one who was killed."

Darryl shook his head. "That doesn't sound good."

"No, it doesn't, neither does the word bamboozle," said Jack. "You're not Tom Sawyer, just say muscle, he's trying to muscle her out."

Darryl laughed. “Muscle? What’ve you been watching, *Goodfellas*? How about just, screwing her over?”

“Nope,” said Brian. “That’s what I originally wanted to say but. . .” Brian put a beer in front of each them. “You’re missing the point.”

Jack took his beer and scooted closer to Brian along the bench, trying to make his beady eyes more puppy. “Are you mad at me?”

“Yes, I’m mad at you,” said Brian, nudging him away with his elbow. “But it’s too late. There was this song and, man, she did this dance to it and it was . . . unbelievably sweet, vulnerable even, like I understood every word of this song even though it was all in Spanish. After that, we talked some things through and. . . I told you, I’m in love.”

“So where’s your girlfriend?” asked Jack. “The one you’re so in love with.”

“Oh, no,” said Brian. “She’s definitely *not* my girlfriend.”

“Thank goodness,” said Darryl, wiping his head with his towel. “You were beginning to scare me.”

“Well then be scared, be very scared.” Brian threw his head back and took a chug of his beer, aware he was being theatrical. “Because she’s my fiancé.”

The guys went straight to Sharky’s for dinner. For the comfort food, yes, as well as the boatload of TVs, but also so they could take turns charging their cell phones, thanks to a friendly manager allowing them the use an outlet under the bar.

Brian was on a mission, wanting to dig up as much information as possible on Costa Rican property rights, spousal rights too, anything that would allow Lita to hold on to her house and land (with a little Navas and Campbell research on the side).

“It’s the siren song, Bri.” Jack was serious. “She’s cast a

spell on you."

And Brian had no reason to doubt him. "I couldn't take my eyes off of her."

"I get that." Darryl was tapping away at his phone. "But what's the rush in getting married?"

"What's the point of waiting?" countered Brian.

"Maybe you've got sunstroke," said Darryl. "Remember, mostly Catholics down here. Divorce is not taken lightly."

Jack found something on his phone. "You can't even think about getting a divorce until you've been married three years and, get this, there has to be some kind of, quote unquote, spousal misconduct."

"Spousal misconduct?" repeated Brian.

"Probably," said Jack, "somewhere between taking a dump in front of each other to hiding the TV remote."

"You've done that with Marcy?" asked Brian.

"The occasional dump, sure, by accident," admitted Jack, "but I would never fuck with the remote."

"Never," agreed Darryl. "The TV is your best friend when you're fighting with your wife."

"You lose the remote," said Jack, "she can still figure out a way to watch *The Affair* on her laptop but if you wanna watch the game, you're shit out of luck."

"Unless you had a real phone," said Darryl.

"Do either of you ever pick up a book?" wondered Brian.

"Did you know," continued Darryl, off his phone, "that in Costa Rica, you have to pay extra alimony in December. They call it, *a-gwin-aldoe*, kind of a Christmas bonus."

Jack poked Brian's shoulder, good-natured but hard. "You sure you're ready for this kind of commitment?"

"I gave her my word that if it came down to it," said Brian, massaging his sore shoulder, "I'd marry her."

"And if you get a divorce after three years," Darryl went on, "and want to go back home, you have to pony up thirteen months of alimony in advance before you can leave the country or you get a, hold on, I got this, an *im-ped-imento day sal-eeda.*"

"Some kind of bad salad?" joked Jack.

"Nope." Darryl didn't appear as though he thought any of this was funny. "It means when you go to the airport to catch your plane home, you can't board. And, now that they've got you, if you don't pay your alimony right away, your ass goes straight to jail."

Despite the heat, Brian shivered. "What's it say about wills?"

Jack scrolled through his phone. "It has to be written in Spanish and notarized in front of three witnesses, two of which have to be able to read it."

"Lita obviously speaks Spanish," said Darryl, "so it's not like they could trick her."

"Unless they did," qualified Jack.

Their waitress came over and set a cheeseburger in front of Darryl, his second, to which he acted all surprised, like it was a mistake, then told her to leave it, like he was doing her a favor. "We should find out how long Ivan's been down here, see if he's tight with any locals."

"He could also have some foreign friends lurking around," said Jack.

Darryl took a big bite of his cheeseburger and held up his phone, chomping away. "This says if you get married you have to apply to be a temporary resident, blah, blah, blah, check this out, you can own a business and get paid but you can't work for yourself."

"If you assume control of The Bamboo House, Bri, you could live off it." Jack laughed, mostly to himself. "Lita could make that breakfast of hers every morning and look damn fine doing it. Meanwhile, you're out back in the shade, placing bets on your phone."

"I don't gamble," said Brian.

"What're you talking about?" Jack slapped the table. "Lita is the biggest gamble of your life."

"So the odds are against me?" he asked.

"Yeah, they are," admitted Jack. "You and Lita are a longshot but that's where the fun is, that's where you get your biggest return."

Brian tried to think it through. "I could live in the Bamboo House, I suppose, with Lita. I've got savings." He looked from Darryl to Jack. "I'll be forty in a couple of months, isn't marrying her the most in the moment thing I could possibly do?"

"If you're truly in love, sure, but it's been, what, forty-eight hours?" said Darryl. "I mean, do we even know how she feels about you?"

"No, not really," conceded Brian. "But I can't imagine leaving here until I find out."

"But we're flying home on Sunday," said Darryl.

"That's why," said Brian, sheepishly raising his beer for approval, "I'm getting married tomorrow night."

Before the guys could react, a man butted in over Brian's shoulder. "You're wasting your time."

Brian recognized the voice but didn't bother to turn around, largely out of fear.

Ivan wasn't deterred though, ordering four vodka shots from the bartender and pulling up a chair at their table. "Word around town says the Yanks are enjoying themselves."

Brian knew that he was busting their balls but sensed something was off with him. For one thing, Ivan was dressed up again in his yacht regalia but had added a noticeable stain to his shirt, one that Brian felt warranted a change of outfits.

"Am I right?" asked Ivan, sweating more than the weather called for. "Tamarindo is good time?"

But Jack wasn't holding back. "Get to the point."

"Thank you, I was hoping to skip formalities," said Ivan. "You need to be gone in the morning."

Darryl sat up in his chair. "Say what?"

Ivan was casual but firm. "You can't stay at the Bamboo House any longer."

Their waitress came over with the shots, setting one down in front of each of them, but didn't stick around long, like she knew better.

"Shall we?" Ivan wiped his nose with the back of his hand, then held up his glass. "A toast, vut is saying, when door closes, new door opens."

Brian wasn't there yet but surprised himself by vocalizing it. "How, excuse me, am I wasting my time?"

"Because with her, you can't win," replied Ivan, something catching his eye out in the street. "Ah, Roxy is here."

The guys turned to find the fire dancer, her snarl apparently permanent, sitting impatiently behind the wheel of a red '70s era Jeep, no top, which, coughing up black smoke, looked better than it sounded. She leaned an elbow into the horn, *honk*!

"She has the patience of a child," continued Ivan. He gave her a quick salute and stood up before turning his attention back to the guys. "Duty calls." And with that, he drank his shot and left, taking off with Roxy in the Jeep. . . .

Brian woke up the next morning at the Bamboo House to a symphony of birds, who, lacking a credible conductor, came off more like the haphazard *toots*, *clacks*, and *whistles* of an alarm clock factory on fire.

The local monkeys chimed in too, *howling*, gathering the tribe for a morning swing through the jungle. The bar, the currency, the statues, the howling. . . Brian put it together, relatively pleased with himself: Howler monkeys.

Then there were the tree frogs, mostly the men, making

croaking noises to attract the ladies, burping so to speak from their mouths and noses.

Brian stopped himself. He didn't want to think about what other creatures could be lying in wait outside his open window.

So, he just lay there in bed underneath the mosquito net, trying to make sense of yesterday, keenly aware of its impact on today and possibly the rest of his life, thinking about Lita, as if he couldn't, and how alive he felt when he was with her, with *Rosalita!*

He knew the Springsteen song: *Rosalita, you're my stone desire*. Though he wasn't completely sure what Bruce meant by "stone," he knew it must be along the lines of hard and steady and unbreakable. As for desire, Brian felt that was mostly hormonal.

Love, on the other hand, was something else, uncharted territory for Brian, unless you counted Jenny, which he did more and more as the years went by.

Admittedly, he didn't have much to go on. His parents seemed happy, up until his mom got sick, but he was too young to really know. And later, he never paid much attention to whoever his dad was dating.

The few times his dad talked about women, Brian shut him out, a white noise. He had to, since his dad would go from asking what movie Brian saw with a date to diagramming a woman's vagina on a post-it.

Brian drifted back to 1987, the year Fox debuted a new half-hour comedy, *Married with Children*. Brian was ten at the time, when making fun of girls was more entertaining than making out with them.

"Love and Marriage," was the opening theme song to what would become one of his favorite TV shows growing up. And in the ensuing years, Brian saw all 257 episodes of Al and Peggy's highly volatile relationship, so he knew the Sinatra song choice was meant to be funny if not ironic.

Perhaps prophetic.

Maybe even a flat-out warning.

In addition, something about the show being set in suburban Chicago like himself itched at Brian's brain, poked at him, so he tended to fret over potential long term romantic relationships. He just wasn't sure they could work. For anyone.

As a result, Brian wasn't sold on love and marriage going hand in hand. Marriage? That he could do, in his head at least, for practical reasons, though he wasn't quite sure how being Lita's husband, a foreigner no less, could help her keep the Bamboo House.

He didn't even understand what Ivan was basing his claim on, just that it was something in his son's will.

Then again, Brian's knowledge of Costa Rican law was a makeshift internet session at Sharky's over cheeseburgers and beer (Brian fought off more ridicule to have a red bean salad, which he didn't enjoy in the least).

In recent years, Brian tended to weigh the emotional risks of getting involved with a woman, breaking it down to *the road* and *the result*.

The road was how he got to her place, the result being whether or not he had a decent time. Did they have something to talk about? Did they laugh? Have sex?

Could he have sex with her again? In a different position? Was she quiet or did she make a show of it? Did she want him to finish inside or out?

Was it necessary to drive to her place? Could he walk? Take the 'L'? Would an Uber be more efficient? Or should he break a cardinal rule and invite her over to his house?

And what about his affection for sports? Would she roll with it? Complain? Cubs? Sox? Did she want kids? Have a cat?

Then he would list the answers as pros or cons and add them up to determine the least painful course of action in which he could pass for a normal human being.

As for Lita, she was clearly nice to look at and the way she separated her subjects and verbs (I am, you are, he is, etc.) when speaking was cute, but who she really was, her character, that was open to debate:

Brian's head versus his heart, with an impassioned appeal from his balls.

Unfortunately, his head was jammed.

His heart had a reputation for overreacting.

And his balls were biased.

But his stomach. That's where his truth lived. His grandfather was right. And, yes, Lita was a great cook. However, she also gave him a pang in the pit of his abdomen, that feeling, that nudge compelling him to be with her—not just butterflies but fighter jets.

Bottom line, Lita was an uncertain variable. In Vegas, they'd close the books. No odds. All bets were off. He knew he'd marry Lita, though. He had to. He told her so yesterday after returning the surfboards to Nogui's.

And she seemed very happy to hear it. Downright moved. Gave him a huge hug, her body fitting seamlessly against his like a long lost puzzle piece that made him feel complete.

Brian hugged her back, not sure how hard he should hold her, but she squeezed even tighter, like she was trying to pull him straight through her.

He couldn't go back on his word now. Not possible. Not at this time in his life. If he wasn't here on earth to help this woman, then what was he here for?

What made his life . . . a life?

His job at the Merc?

Year after year.

For a paycheck?

About six years ago, he shed tears after the final bell. It's true, he did, when pork bellies were traded for the last time; some of the older guys on the floor having worked together since livestock futures took off in the 1960s.

Really? Brian couldn't believe it either. That's what broke the dam?

Before that he hadn't cried since he was twelve, summer of '89, when Cub shortstop Shawon Dunston dug out of a long slump and began raising his batting average.

A fan in the bleachers made a sign for him, the Shawon-O-Meter; tracking Dunston's average up to the minute, from struggling to hit .200 to a season high .278.

Brian didn't understand his feelings but if there was such a thing as a good cry, that was it, probably the Merc too. Things that had nothing to do with him personally.

He didn't even cry when Jenny dumped him. Internally, sure, he was crushed, but on the outside he came off more mopey than anything.

Then there was his mom. He couldn't remember how he felt when she died. Not exactly. But he didn't cry. He was sure of that. In fact, his therapist recently told him that he had more than likely internalized his feelings, which wouldn't have allowed him to process his grief.

Brian exhaled, as if he didn't realize he'd been holding his breath, then carefully opened the netting and got out of bed, still in his swimsuit, the Nirvana shirt rolled up around his neck, collecting sweat.

He rubbed his eyes.

Scratched his armpits.

And cupped his balls.

Somewhat satisfied, he climbed up the ladder to Jack's room, where his friend was on the floor, struggling to hold a plank pose, his face a beet red.

Brian unraveled the shirt and placed it over the windowsill

to dry. "Did the trick. Thanks."

"Sure. . ." A ball of sweat ran from Jack's forehead to the end of his nose, dangling precariously over the bamboo floor.

"I suppose I'll have to wear something a little more formal tonight."

"I would." Jack collapsed to the floor, out of breath. "And a ring usually goes over well at weddings."

"The guy that's conducting the service, he's bringing rings for both of us."

"Not for free."

"No, not for free," acknowledged Brian. "I'm going to walk into town, get some money, try and find some decent clothes."

Jack sat up, his breathing still labored. "You really doing this?"

Brian gave him an annoyed look, one he'd been practicing.

"Okay, fine, I had to check," said Jack. "You're coming home with us though, right?"

"Yes, I just have to be back when this whole thing with the house goes to court."

"All right, so Darryl and me will work on a hotel, two rooms, not together, in case, you know."

"I don't but, I mean, I do–is getting married the right move here or have I lost all common sense?"

"Well, yeah, you've most definitely lost any sense you've ever had, Bri, but marriage is a crapshoot no matter how you go into it. And that's not an endorsement by the way."

"Sometimes," said Darryl, coming down the ladder from his room, "I feel like I got lucky with Carmela."

"What about you and Marcy?" Brian asked Jack. "It started so promising."

"We were young," he replied. "No kids. No mortgage."

"Cubs, Braves," remembered Darryl. "She let us watch game three during the reception."

"Maddux versus Wood," said Brian. "The Cy Young winner we let get away against our Rookie of the Year."

"Yeah," said Jack, "but, you'll remember, she purposely planned the wedding in October thinking the Cubs wouldn't be playing."

"I do remember that," said Brian. "You said if the Cubs didn't make the playoffs it would be her fault."

"Unfortunately," noted Darryl, "the game didn't turn out so well."

"Neither did the marriage," said Jack.

"But you got two great kids out of it," Darryl told him, "including my totally cool god-daughter."

"Who," said Jack, "hardly ever talks to me. Not since I announced the split."

"Maybe it was the way you said it." Brian made air quotes with his fingers. " 'I'm taking my talents to Lincoln Park.' "

"I was joking," said Jack, not so convincingly. "Anyway, I don't have any answers for you, Bri."

Darryl shrugged his big shoulders. "Me neither."

"That's it." A light went on in Brian's head. "Never forget that Greg Maddux was originally a Cub. He was twenty-six, had just won his first of four Cy Young Awards and we didn't resign him."

"A low point in Cubs history," noted Darryl.

"He got five years, twenty-eight million from the Braves," said Jack.

"Today, he'd get twenty-eight million for one year," said Darryl.

"And be worth every penny," said Brian. "Maddux and Wood together. Sure, it might've thrown off the whole Cubs timeline; draft picks, revenue, free agency, a residual effect where there's no Bryzzo or World Series title last year but it also could've meant a championship well before then."

"Bri," said Darryl, "I feel ya, but what do the Cubbies have to do with Lita?"

"Jenny was my Maddux." Brian slowly started nodding his head, resigning himself to it. "I blew it with her. I can't do that again. I can't let Lita go. She's my Kerry Wood. My second chance."

"Seriously?" wondered Jack. "Baseball analogies?"

"Yup." Brian clapped his hands together, sealing his decision. "I'm gonna marry Lita before sundown. For real."

"For real, for real?" asked Darryl.

"Look at you and Jack," he said. "One in two end up in divorce."

"That's why people shouldn't get married," said Jack, "not the other way around."

"Okay," said Brian, "but you're the one that gave me the big speech about vacation time and the hurry-up offense."

"I was winging it," said Jack.

"When aren't you?" asked Brian. "And I admire that. I want more *winging it*."

Jack threw his hands up in the air, exasperated. "All this from a guy who still lives at home."

"Yes, but I own the house," explained Brian, for the umpteenth time. "I bought my dad out. He got a place in Sarasota. You know this. Anyway, decision's made. I'm getting married."

"What about surf camp?" tried Jack.

Brian raised his voice, "Today?!"

"What?" shrugged Jack, all innocent like. "It's paid for."

"I've got to get out of here," said Brian. "Just please be at Nogui's before sunset. And I'm going to need a beer, make it two, cold ones, they have to be cold, Bavarias, and a couple of bottles of champagne if you can find something good."

"You're such a bossy groom," said Darryl, giving him a supportive pat on the back.

"At my wedding," said Jack, "I just asked for a keg of Old

Style."

"And a dozen doobies," Darryl reminded him, "when you were the only one in our group who could actually roll."

Jack grinned, as if it was a compliment instead of a complaint.

"And the blow," continued Darryl. "Don't forget you wanted an eight-ball."

"Well, yeah," said Jack. "That was a given."

"Guys," interrupted Brian, "I need you to focus. Big time. Both of you are going to be my Best Man today."

"We always have been," said Jack.

"Good, because." Brian paused to rub his forehead. "Because, I don't know, I have a feeling about the ceremony and not necessarily—"

"Bri," interjected Darryl. "We got you."

"Thanks." Brian started for the ladder. . .

"But I do have some advice," said Darryl.

Brian stopped to hear him out.

"If you end up marrying this girl, whatever you do, be nice to each other," Darryl told him. "I mean it, at the very least, just be nice."

11

Going To The Chapel

Brian climbed down the ladder to his room and began gathering his things:

Phone? Check—after a charge at Sharky's and a good night's rest it was back over 70%. Of course, he'd be nice to Lita. He knew what Darryl meant, though. It's not as simple as it sounds.

Charger? Check—an outlet still a priority. Brian was pretty easygoing with all the women he'd dated, never so much as raising his voice at any of them.

Flip-flops? Or rather, chancletas? Check—probably doing his feet more harm than good at this point. Brian had never called a girlfriend a derogatory name or in any way employed the c-word.

Wallet? Check—credit card intact but zero cash left on him. And he certainly never put a hand on a woman in an aggressive manner, even that time in New Orleans when a feisty redhead with tassels on her nipples insisted he do so.

Sunglasses? Nope—long gone, your guess was as good as his. Brian hadn't been in a fight since elementary school. And that was only when he came out on the losing end in a heated game of musical chairs (the week his mom died).

Topsiders? Check—but forced into an early retirement along with his shirt and pants. Brian ran the day through his head, one sure to tread well into the night, Lita having already told him that she was staying with him at whatever hotel the guys found. Appearances were important, she said, for legal reasons.

Passport? Nope—Ivan had it, all three of theirs. Then again, Brian couldn't help but wonder if he was expected to consummate the marriage, since the guys had made it abundantly clear that Costa Ricans take the bond seriously.

Perhaps, Lita planned on towing some Catholic line of honoring the union between man and woman. Brian pictured his suitcase in a cage at the airport, his condoms trapped inside a running shoe, desperate to help.

Would condoms even come into play, though? They'd be married after all, again maybe a religious thing for Lita. However, the drawbacks to going without protection were huge.

Kids?!

Or an STD?!

Brian wouldn't know what to do with either of those.

Back home, after Jenny (who was on the pill), he always wore a condom. He'd usually wait, however, until the woman brought it up, then act surprised to find one in his wallet.

If she didn't say anything and he was the one who had to suggest handcuffing his one-eyed flute, then that could very well mean it was a one and done encounter.

He just felt more comfortable with a condom, even if it meant constantly checking to make sure it was still on. *Oh shit.*

Brian snapped out of it, chastising himself for boiling everything down to sex, a habit that had plagued him since his early teens, thanks, as mentioned, to his dad being a little too forthcoming with his primitive drawings.

Not to mention the times his dad used to come down to the basement after a few cocktails and tell his friends that he lettered in three sports in high school. . . Girls in the fall. Girls in the winter. Girls in the spring. Which Brian thought was funny—never—but blamed on his dad's teen testosterone.

How much testosterone Brian had on the cusp of forty, he wasn't sure. He made a mental note to ask his doctor, then added a mental asterisk, knowing his doctor would want him to fill a plastic see-through cup, best he could.

A *screeching* bird swooped down just outside his window, and Brian ducked instinctively, then realized he'd completely overlooked the fact that the police still hadn't found or identified who killed Lita's husband.

To Brian, that meant the killer might still be in Tamarindo, since anyone of note leaving town would become an instant suspect.

And, because it's not unusual for people to meet their demise at the hands of friends or even family, the spotlight fell straight on Ivan and even Lita, perhaps in a concerted effort, where Brian gets played the fool, which he knew, everybody does sometime.

He grabbed the empty ice bag from the night before and turned it inside out, putting his phone and charger and wallet inside, then did his usual farewell scan of the room; checking under the sheets and behind the bed, mostly just to put off the inevitable.

Eventually, he climbed down the ladder to the kitchen, keeping an eye out for Ivan, however, Brian heard him before he saw him.

Grunting and groaning drew him to a window, one in back. And from there he could see Ivan, over by the outhouse on his hands and knees, busy digging a hole in the ground with a trowel.

Most of his hair had escaped his ponytail and his shirt was off, like he'd been at it for a while, pockets of sweat finding refuge in the folds of his stomach.

But then, distracted, he stopped and looked over at the house to find Brian staring at him. "Hey! Vut are you doing?"

Certain one of the guys had heard that, Brian didn't back down. "I'd like the passports."

"Vut about your bill?"

"You kicked us out."

"You must pay."

"I'm heading to the bank," Brian told him. "I need my passport."

"Try cash machine."

"I'll get a better rate at the bank."

"How do I know if you come back?"

"I guess you don't." Brian walked out the backdoor, right over to him. "But I plan on paying the owner in full."

"Ignorance suits you," said Ivan, meeting him halfway. "But I don't have time for your foolishness."

Brian didn't appreciate Ivan matching his aggression and looked over his shoulder, not just for the guys but for his confidence. "What happened to, uh, Tico Time?"

Ivan came right up to him, somewhere between awkward and threatening. "I don't care if you pay bill or not," he said, apparently unfazed that Brian had several inches on him. "Just go back to wherever you are coming from."

And though Brian didn't think Ivan was physically imposing, that's what he found so worrisome, like Ivan was apt to play by a different set of rules—as in none.

When in dire straits Brian often resorted to humor, regardless of its merit, though in his defense he couldn't help himself. "So if you don't believe in Tico Time, how about Taco Time?"

"Vut?"

"Your Yelp review is going to be awkward."

"Mr. Yankee Doodle Dandy Man. . ." An irritated vein darted across Ivan's forehead, like a seismograph. "I'm keeping my son's property. Claro?"

"Uh, yeah, clear." Brian wasn't ready to die, not at the hands of some commie madman in the jungle. "I'm sorry about what happened to, uh, your son."

"You know nothing about him," snarled Ivan. "Or that woman you think to marry."

"Please leave her out of it."

"Don't be ridiculous," laughed Ivan, his stray eye somehow remaining serious. "She is center of it. Of everything. Huracán Rosalita, that's what they call her. She is bad storm everywhere she goes."

"No offense, but maybe you're the problem."

Not the best choice of words, Brian admitted, as Ivan raised the trowel to strike him—then stopped halfway, perhaps thinking better of it, perhaps seeing Jack and Darryl in the window above them. Meanwhile, Brian was frozen, cowering in fear.

Without saying a word, Ivan grabbed him by the arm and led him into the kitchen, where Jack and Darryl were already heading down the ladder to meet them.

Jack, of course, twisted his mustache, "You can let go of him now," while Darryl slapped his stomach like a sumo wrestler, ready to rumble.

Outnumbered, Ivan cursed in his native language and walked over to the sink, where he knelt to open a cabinet, then moved aside a small crate of rags and cleaners to reveal a hole cut in the bamboo floor.

Ivan took a last hateful look at the guys and stuck his hand inside, coming up with a metal safe about the size and shape of a shoe box.

"We appreciate you looking after our passports." Jack walked over to have a closer look. "But don't you think you're over doing it?"

Sensing trouble between the two, Brian turned to Darryl for support, but he was scouring the fridge for something to eat. "Um, Darryl?"

"Unless, he's got some food in that safe," he replied, "I'm busy."

Jack looked back at him. "I've got this, T.C."

Brian didn't know what was more concerning; Darryl being all chill about everything or Jack playing out reruns of *Magnum, P.I.* (noting that with the Hawaiian shirt and mustache, he was already in wardrobe).

Jack was hovering over Ivan, who by his utter lack of movement made it clear that he wasn't going to open the safe until the American backed the fuck up.

Jack wasn't catching on, though. Or maybe he didn't care. So Brian tugged on his shirt, leading him away for a word in private. "Jack. . . Relax. Please. This is a prime example of a situation where we don't want to do anything stupid."

"No." Jack kicked at the floor like a six-year-old. "This is where that crazy motherfucker better not doing anything stupid."

Unsure who worried him more at that point, Brian looked past Jack to Ivan, who had set the safe on the kitchen table and was now meticulously spinning its numbered dial back and forth and back again . . . before tugging gently on the safe door, a boyish grin gaining access to his grizzled old face.

Brian saw the jewels right away, a tangled sparkling mound of them as Ivan emptied a black velvet sack:

Diamond rings.

Pearl necklaces.

Silver earrings.

Exotic gems.

Gold bracelets, stacks of them.

Even a platinum grill with shiny green emeralds for each tooth.

Not just proud of his stash but quite protective, Ivan carefully returned each piece to the sack and closed it tight with rope draw strings. “Some tourists want to extend holiday,” he said, “even when they run out of money.”

Then he reached back into the safe for the passports, reading aloud their full names and addresses as he handed them out, like he was being efficient, though Brian sensed he was just emphasizing that he knew where they lived.

When he was done, Ivan removed a false floor in the safe and beneath it a handgun, which he looked over lovingly. “Dutch man come here, wanted to stay, one more week, he tell me. But he spent more than he had. Mostly on cards. That is how I get gun. His wife? That is other story.”

“How hospitable of you,” said Jack.

Ivan ignored him, holding up the weapon. “Walther PPK. It was a German military pistol in the second war.” He checked that it was properly loaded, doing so rather convincingly. “This is the gun James Bond replaced his Beretta with in *Dr. No*.”

“We get it,” Jack told him. “You like your gun.”

“It is true,” said Ivan. “I like my gun. It is good for business.”

Darryl warned him, relaxed but to the point. “Don’t try and play us.”

Meanwhile, Brian’s balls retracted into the upper regions of his groin.

“If I’m killing you,” said Ivan, “I don’t wait for you to wake up.”

“But then who would you talk to?” Darryl found a bowl of food in the fridge, a mix of meat and potatoes, carrots and plantains. He showed it to Ivan. "What's this?"

Brian didn't understand how Darryl could think of food right now, then remembered the only time he wasn't thinking about food was when he was eating it.

"Olle de Carne," Ivan told him. "I'd heat it up for you but why bother."

Tension momentarily diffused, Brian took it as his green light and without a word to anyone slipped into the bamboo forest. . .

He was aware they had adverted any real drama, but Lita was right about Ivan; something was off with him, anger issues or maybe pure greed.

Ivan was one thing but as Brian made his way to the road, he became more and more disappointed in himself. He could've easily gotten hurt back there. Without putting up a fight. He was ashamed, really.

To make matters worse, he knew he hadn't seen the last of that crazy old man. But what could he do about it? Tell the police Ivan *almost* killed him? He didn't have a scratch on him.

Lacking options, Brian decided to move on, play it by ear, be in the moment, react, something, anything.

Brian needed clothes. He was thinking Tommy Bahama. What he got, however, was closer to Tommy Chong; a pair of used blue jeans and an orange tank-top, on it a cartoon picture of a frog with *Pura Vida* written across the top.

Brian figured Ivan had put the word out on him. In fact, one clothing store got a phone call while he was inside, the owner looking Brian up and down and nodding his head, after which he was told the place was closing, some bullshit about the cash register and bad WiFi.

Brian wanted to get in touch with Lita, tell her what was going on, half hoping she'd already called the whole thing off.

Go to surf camp, she'd tell him.

Watch sports at Sharky's with your friends.

Go home to Chicago.

Lita forbade him from contacting her, though. Said it was bad luck for the groom to see the bride prior to the wedding, that she had made that mistake with Ivan's son when she was talked into taking her wedding photos before the ceremony.

She was told it was an issue with her hair, when in truth it had more to do with the sobriety of the groom, who was nervous and only marrying her out of the kindness of his heart, so that Lita and her daughters could become Costa Rican citizens, (which never happened due to his untimely death).

Brian put on the jeans and tank-top and went to a bank, withdrawing as much as he could, two thousand dollars in colones.

Then, feeling the need to get his head straight, he walked down to the beach, only to find it emptying due to an army of dark clouds marching in. And, sure enough, it started to rain, harder and harder, cool drops of water coalescing with his sweat.

The rain was a sign from the heavens, he thought, that he should pull the plug on the wedding. Any excuse would do. He was merely waiting to call his own bluff.

Still, he remembered his sister's wedding day, how it rained as they drove down Orrington Avenue to the church, putting her in a near panic.

Their grandmother, who was riding shotgun, tried to calm her down, telling her that the rain was actually good luck.

Brian assumed *Gram* was just being nice, or senile, but read years later that in some cultures, presumably his being one of them, rain was indeed a gift on one's wedding day, a purification of sorts. And since Sue was still married, he had no further reason to doubt it.

Brian ran for shelter under a trio of palm trees. . . So did the two girls in their matching outfits; clearly sisters, barely teenagers, the girls he'd seen on his first day.

Dying to know what they had in their basket, he stood up on his toes to get a better look. "Whatcha got in there?"

Apparently, the girls didn't hear him, seeing as they were facing each other, bent over at the waist, a grip on each other's long black hair, twisting it like a wet towel to get the water out.

But Brian persisted. "Smells good, uh, bueno."

"We're taking a break," said the older one, her English good, her attitude, Brian felt, not so much.

"Oh, okay, I'll be quick, uh, just one of whatever then . . . please . . . thank you."

"We don't sell them one at a time."

"Really?"

"I'm joking." An innocent smile crossed her face. "We're just bored." She held up a sticky treat. "One dollar."

"Great." Brian hurriedly handed her a ₡5,000 colones note. "What is it?"

"Cajeta de coco," she said, "with fudge."

"I'll have two."

"We have four left . . . and it's raining."

"Four would be fantastic."

The girls looked at each other and giggled, big straight smiles, the antithesis of his niece's crooked choppers.

He took a big bite into the cajeta. "Yum, this is delicious," he began, struggling to swallow so much at once. "You wouldn't happen to have a glass of milk in that basket?"

The girls laughed, like they didn't think it was a real question, the younger one holding out his change to him, but he waved it off and kept eating.

"Gracias," she said, sticking the basket under her arm at

the edge of the palm fronds.

"You're leaving?" Brian asked her.

"We have to go."

Brian started in on his second cajeta. "In the rain?"

"Yes," confirmed the older one. "We're late for a wedding."

"Oh." Brian kept eating. "A wedding?"

But the girls were off, running down the beach in the downpour. . . .

Brian decided to wait out the storm under the palms; not wanting to get soaked before the ceremony, sure, but mostly because of all the questions bouncing around his head that still needed answering. Plus, he had two cajetas to hold him over. He just needed that cold glass of milk to go with it, his comfort food, a tip of the hat to his Midwestern upbringing.

His great-grandfather even owned a few farms in Iowa, making a small fortune in butter. But he sold out and took his money to Chicago, only to lose it all in the Great Depression. Lost his life too, when he fell asleep on the train tracks, shortly after Black Tuesday.

Brian never asked his dad how the man built a butter empire or what he had his money in when the market crashed. No, he wanted to know how he could have gone to sleep on the tracks, his life holding less interest than his death.

That's what Brian tended to dwell on, the final loss instead of the string of victories. Sue first noticed when they were kids and was constantly urging him to be more positive.

The Cubs will win tomorrow, Bri, you'll see.

Trust me little brother, you're lucky she dumped you.

Don't worry. Everyone does better on the SATs the second time.

Then, just when Brian thought she was being nice to him, she'd close with her standard sendoff: *And do everyone a favor, go choke your chicken.*

Brian shrugged his shoulders, mumbling to himself, the odd raindrop breaking through the palm fronds to plop him on his head. Tired, he sat down amongst all the fallen coconuts in a dry patch against a tree and let himself drift backwards, which he tended to do when he was with the guys.

But this vacation felt different to Brian, less like a trip down memory lane, more like his life flashing before his eyes, so he figured he should pay attention to the details.

Like Jack's Nirvana t-shirt. Brian went to September of '91, freshmen year of high school. "Smells Like Teen Spirit" had just been released; becoming the cornerstone for a whole new genre of music, *GRUNGE*, thanks in part to its video, which came complete with slam dancing and anarchistic cheerleaders.

Life was never the same—for Jack.

By the time *Nevermind* took the number one spot on Billboard from Michael Jackson's *Dangerous*, Kurt Cobain and Nirvana were the be-all and end-all to Jack.

He ate, drank, did everything to Nirvana, 24/7, even lost his virginity somewhere between "Territorial Pissings" and "Drain You."

Brian was well aware that he'd digressed again, but this time he vowed to take something from it.

For every *oh well, whatever, never mind* in the lyrics, there was revolt in Kurt's voice, rebellion in his guitar, the result being not just disenchantment but downright anger.

Pimples or not, Jack woke up freshman year and took high school by the balls, while Brian stood back and watched.

He did benefit at times, like when Jack scored with a girl from New Trier and Brian got to make out with her friend while he waited.

But, terrified of tarnishing his permanent record or

ruining his grade point average, he rarely dictated the action.

Ouch. It was as if he suddenly realized how much his feet hurt. Darryl's flip-flops had worn out their welcome. Adios to the chancletas. He would've been better off staying barefoot.

Brian warily removed them, the nylon strap playing the role of carving knife, peeling back a layer of skin from his big toes, rendering them red and raw.

Painful but Brian's thoughts volleyed back to Lita, imagining her somewhere in town, getting ready for the ceremony in a full-length mirror, talking to herself about Brian, just like they do on *The Bachelor*.

It was his daydream, so Lita was flattered to receive a note from Chris Harrison regarding the Fantasy Suite, but her accent got in the way of her words and she reverted to Spanish, leaving Brian confused.

Other than a business deal, he had no idea what this day meant to Lita. He knew what it meant to him though, a lot, even if it was as exhausting as it was exhilarating, so much so that he leaned his head back against the tree and let his eyes close, allowing himself the courtesy of floating off to sleep.

12

Blood, Sweat, & Tears

When Brian awoke he wasn't sure how much time had passed, only that the rain had let up, giving the sun one last chance to make an impression. He'd slept soundly, barely stirring, even though he'd never fallen asleep in such an unusual and unguarded setting. Again, a perk for the young, he thought, knowing full well that if he dozed off against a tree in the rain back home, some upstanding citizen would call the police.

He stood, stiff with sleep, and tried to rub the wet sand off his skin, which stuck to him like he'd bathed in glue. Bracing himself against the tree, he stretched his shoulders, his calves, nothing fancy, just enough to get the blood flowing, though he really was just procrastinating. Even he knew that.

It was as if he'd spent his entire life waiting on-deck for his chance to bat, always up next, and now he was finally getting his turn to swing for the fences.

Brian began walking toward Nogui's, slowly but presumably surely, when Jack came into focus down the shore, talking to a man in a suit.

Meanwhile, Jack was in a suit of his own for the occasion,

an all-white Puma tracksuit with gold stitching, the jacket zippered to the top, which Brian knew meant Jack was taking this seriously. And, of course, he had on his now obligatory hat.

And though Brian was fully aware that the man he was with must be the attorney Lita had mentioned (as well as the notary and the person performing their ceremony), he didn't turn around and run.

Instead, he kept on walking, partially because his throat felt like it was locking up and he might need medical attention.

A hand reached for his shoulder and spun him around. . . It was Darryl, looking slick in a pair of gray slacks and a white dress shirt with, Brian noted, his sneakers, even though they were on the beach.

"You wore the Jordans . . . for me?"

"Just for you, Bri." Darryl handed him a Bavaria from a red plastic bucket stuffed with ice and beer.

Brian put his nose to the bottle. "Why does this beer smell like fish?"

"Buckets usually have more than one job."

"Did you at least change the ice?"

"Yeah, and you know who didn't complain? Lita."

"You've seen her?"

"Lookin' good too."

"Today?"

"Of course, Bri, sun's about to bounce."

"Right."

"Oh and everyone's cool with me and Jack being witnesses, some Costa Rican's gonna be one too, Julio, said he met you."

Brian nodded, barely listening.

"You in there man, you good?"

"Does it matter?"

"Probably not."

Jack walked over with the man in the suit, arm around his shoulder, like he'd known him for years. "This is Señor Contreras, he's gonna take care of the whole thing."

"Buenos tardes," said the man. "It is a pleasure to meet you." He was a Tico, in his sixties, overweight but neatly groomed. "Are you ready to get married?"

"Pretty much," replied Brian, thinking this guy could add game show host to his list of duties.

Taking Brian's beer, Jack opened it for him with his lighter. "Partake."

"I'm fine. Really." Still, Brian did as he was told and took a drink. "I've got this."

"You do realize you're getting married?" asked Darryl.

Brian took another drink, almost a chug, which appeared to worry Señor Contreras.

"Como cuando uno se come toda la miel," he said to Brian. "Y se queda en la luna."

"Pardon." Brian wasn't sure if he was supposed to get all that. "Um, the moon?"

Señor Contreras smiled knowingly, like he didn't expect him to understand, and translated it: "As when one eats all the honey and stays on the moon."

"I'm pretty sure he's talking about your honeymoon," said Jack.

Darryl raised his hand. "I think, in the nicest way possible, he's suggesting that an excess of alcohol might prevent you from fulfilling your vows tonight."

Señor Contreras started to laugh but got serious when Brian handed him a wad of cash, which he slipped into the breast pocket of his suit without counting it. "I will perform the service in English, some Spanish. It will be short but very beautiful, very emotional, people will cry.

"That's cool but will it be legal?" asked Darryl.

Jack turned to Brian. “He had to do a little back dating on some forms.”

“He what?” asked Brian.

“Don’t worry,” said Jack. “I tipped him.”

“Please sign where it’s highlighted in yellow.” Señor Contreras removed several official looking documents from a manila envelope. “And I will need to see your passport.”

Brian exchanged his passport for the short stack of papers and a pen.

“Thank you,” said Señor Contreras, as he left. “I must have a word with Rosalita before we can proceed.”

Jack waited until the man was out of ear-shot, then turned to Brian, “I’ve seen the death certificate.”

“Whose death certificate?” asked Brian, worried it might be his own.

“Dude, easy, Lita’s husband’s,” said Jack. “He’s definitely dead. Had to be confirmed dead, like documented dead, for three hundred days before she could remarry.”

“And how long has it been?” asked Darryl.

“Don’t take it personally, Bri, but she just passed three hundred recently,” said Jack. “Saw her cédula too.”

“Her what?” asked Brian

“It’s like her identity card,” replied Jack. “Everything’s fine.”

“I was hoping it wouldn’t be,” mumbled Brian, then off Jack and Darryl’s glare, “I’m joking.”

“You better be,” Jack told him.

“What?” feigned Brian, but curious nonetheless. “Why?”

“Because you missed surf camp,” said Jack. “Again.”

“What is it with you and surf camp?” asked Brian.

“It’s why we came down here,” Jack told him.

“No, it’s not,” said Brian. “It’s just the excuse we used to get as far away from home as possible.”

Jack and Darryl looked at each other, surprised.

"Yeah, because deep down," continued Brian, "it would be too painful or awkward to talk about what we're really doing here."

"Damn, Bri." Darryl punched him the arm, hard but affectionate. "Sorting. Shit. Out."

"I don't know," said Jack. "I think we've been pretty fuckin' open."

"We have," acknowledged Brian. "But I want to go deeper. I want honesty. I—"

"You want honesty," interrupted Jack. "Well then I wanna go fishing and catch a big ass marlin for my mantel, but without you going all environmental tits on me."

Brian shook his head and took another chug of his beer, as if it was necessary.

"Bri, man," sighed Darryl, "at least he's being straight with you."

"Okay, I'm not sure what you mean by environmental tits," said Brian, "but if you have to fish, like that's what you really want to do, then catch and release seems a bit more humane, especially if you consider that marlin numbers are dwindling."

"I don't know," said Jack. "Isn't it more fucked for the fish that goes back in the water?"

"Huh?"

"The fish that goes back," began Jack, "now knows that every time it takes a bite of food it might have a hook in it. That would suck, right? But there's more. While you're choking, you remember that the hook is attached to a line, on the other end, some guy loaded on pills and beer is trying his damnedest to drag you by your throat out of the water and onto to his boat, where if you so much as flinch, he'll club you over the head with a giant hammer."

Brian thought he might have a point but was unwilling to agree with Jack out loud. "Still."

"What if we eat the day's catch?" suggested Jack. "Kurt said, 'it's okay to eat fish 'cause they don't have any feelings'."

"That's from a song," pointed out Brian.

"Exactly," said Jack. "He took time to sing it."

"He was probably being sarcastic," said Brian.

Jack shifted gears. "Look, Bri, I've told you about my divorce and yeah okay I could open up a bit more, get a little more real, but we get to hang so little nowadays you guys don't want me bitching and moaning the whole time."

Brian looked around the beach, filling up with people again. "I get it. My tendency is to do the same thing, keep it light, but at our age I don't know where that gets us anymore."

"Who knows?" Jack took off his hat and pushed his hair back. "I gotta lotta of crap swirlin' around in my head."

"I think we've had some good talks this week." Darryl rested his hand on Brian's back. "This is on you, bro, you're projecting."

"Projecting?" repeated Brian, as if he didn't understand.

"Don't play dumb," said Darryl. "I know you're in therapy."

"What?"

"Your sister told me," said Darryl. "So, yeah, we can talk about our feelings but you need to put shit into action. That's always been your problem."

"He's right," said Jack.

"Besides, I've got a house full of drama back home," said Darryl. "Nothing wrong with us having a little fun, leaving it all behind for a few days."

"I did get up on a surfboard," conceded Brian. "That was cool. You both saw me. That was something I never thought I'd do."

"That was insane," said Darryl.

"I have to admit, Bri, you've had your moments on this

trip." Jack draped his arm over Brian's shoulder. "Put a few of those together and you've got yourself a life."

That sounded good. Brian took a deep breath, then noticed even more people converging on the beach, Maní too, like he wanted in on the action. But before he could figure out what was going on, music began playing from the speakers in the tamarindo tree outside Nogui's.

What song it was he couldn't tell, not because it wasn't loud enough but because Señor Contreras was waving him over to a platform, right on the beach, one that looked like it'd been scavenged from an old pier.

"Showtime," said Darryl.

Unfazed by the timing of his question, Jack asked Brian, "What happened to getting some decent clothes?"

Darryl looked the groom over. "Is it even legal to get married without shoes?"

Brian ignored them and took his spot next to Señor Contreras, who shook his hand rather formally, then exchanged a diamond ring (and the bill for it) for the paperwork.

And now it wasn't just the sisters walking toward him that had his head spinning but how much they looked like Lita.

Shoulders straight, smiles sweet, their brown eyes full of hope and dreams, they were in identical pink dresses, dropping flower petals in the sand as they approached the platform. . .

Señor Contreras stepped closer to Brian. "Tan catrineadas, como su madre."

He hadn't a clue. "Excuse me?"

"Her daughters. . ." Señor Contreras continued in English, though Brian didn't hear another word.

Just, *daughters*. So that's why everyone had come down to the beach, to see the gringo get duped. Brian didn't know what to do or even say, only that his knees were beginning to tremor.

However, when Maní led a handful of people right past him, focusing on the sun's final encore, he realized everyone wasn't coming to see the wedding, that it wasn't about him all the time, even in his own life.

He tried to steady himself, to let his thoughts simmer long enough to make a rational decision, so he zeroed in on the sunset; a light show in the sky, a living and ever-changing painting of the day. A day, like all of them, he knew he should be grateful for.

Breathe, he begged himself. Breathe.

And as the static in his head gradually subsided, he was finally able to recognize the song that was playing, a mellow tune that he hadn't heard in years, not since he was a young boy, when his mom used to put it on: "Something In The Way She Moves."

And if I'm feeling down and blue
Or troubled by some foolish game
She always seems to make me change my mind

--James Taylor

Brian cried, balled his eyes out really, his chest heaving uncontrollably as he remembered his mom in vivid detail; her long hair, straight and brown, her eyes a searing bright blue, with a cigarette planted between her fingers, always tapping the side of an ashtray that he'd made for her in kindergarten.

"Bri, you okay? Did I pick the wrong song?" asked Jack.

"No," he replied. "It's perfect."

Darryl gave him his hand towel. "Are you sure you're up for this?"

Knowing the things that towel had seen and done, Brian gave it back and let the tears fall down his face, determined more than ever to go through with the ceremony.

And now, as the memory of his mom faded, another woman came into the picture, Lita, being escorted down the petaled path by Julio. . .

Brian noted her lavender dress; elegant, yes, though more nightclub than garden club. But still, no shoes, no make-up, just her, as Taylor kept singing:

It isn't what she's got to say
But how she thinks and where she's been
To me the words are nice the way they sound

The lyrics were resonating with him in a way they never had before, as if the stars were aligned in his favor for a change, opening a door, on the other side his future, and all he had to do was walk through it.

By the time the song ended, Julio had left Lita at the platform and was taking his place alongside her daughters, opposite Jack and Darryl.

Lita looked beyond gorgeous in Brian's eyes, and he smiled nervously, just staring at her.

She laughed at him. "Hola, guapo."

"Hola," returned Brian, as he helped her onto the platform. "Um, if you don't mind me asking, what exactly does guapo mean?"

"Handsome," she replied, as if it were obvious, keeping his hands in hers.

"Oh." Brian blushed but quickly regained his composure. "And, well?" He looked from Lita to the two girls, hopeful of an explanation.

"Mis hijas," she started, before clarifying for Brian. "My daughters, they like you."

"And I like them," Brian told her. "Their brownie things too but—"

Lita squeezed his hands. "This is my third marriage."

"Three, okay, that's good to know, third time's the charm, I suppose," said Brian, "but do you have any more surprises in store for me or is this it?"

Jack and Darryl leaned in to hear her answer.

"In what store?" she asked, as if she didn't understand.

"I mean. . ."

"You don't like surprises?" Her smile went from sweet to sexy. "That is too bad. My first husband was very old, my second preferred men."

Brian stood up straight. "Surprises are fine."

That got a good laugh out of Jack and Darryl until Señor Contreras cleared his throat, ready to begin, but before he could get started—

Kenny burst out of the jungle onto the beach, running right up to the platform. "He's found a buyer," he told Lita, catching his breath. "Para las joyas."

"Mis joyas," she clarified. "All of them?"

"Sí, for cash. Today." Kenny finally realized what he'd stumbled into on the beach. "Disculpe, I didn't know—"

"Who is he selling to?" demanded Lita. "The couple from Milan?"

"Yeah, a friend of mine works at the hotel they're staying at," said Kenny. "He texted me ten, maybe fifteen minutes ago, told me the owner took a shitload of money up to their room."

Lita turned to Brian. "Ivan has my jewels."

"We saw them," he admitted, "this morning."

"Those're all yours?" asked Jack.

"He gave them to me," she said. "He has no money, just what he takes from me by renting out the Bamboo House."

"If he flips the jewels into cash," warned Kenny, "he'll

spend it."

"Let me help," said Brian. "What can I do?"

She took her girls in her arms and held them tight. "Ivan is dangerous man."

"Where's this hotel?" asked Brian. "We have to, I don't know, stop him."

"I'm sure Ivan's not welcome there," said Kenny. "He broke a bunch of furniture in the lobby on New Year's Eve, on purpose."

"Why not do business at the Bamboo House?" asked Jack, "It's private, secluded."

"I can try to cut the Italians off before they get there," proposed Kenny.

Lita didn't object. She just looked at Julio, who nodded, holding his hand out to the girls. "This is my problem," she told everyone. Then, without further notice, she took off running up the beach. . .

And Kenny darted back into the jungle. . .

His jaw hung open, Brian watched them go, then realizing what he had to do, he put the ring in his pocket and turned to Jack and Darryl, "Fuck it," before sprinting to the road. . . .

Losing daylight, Brian knew only one way to the Bamboo House; head back to town, follow the main road south past the school until it becomes a dirt road, then turn inland at the mangrove, look for the log, step into the bamboo forest, find the yellow path, and go!

Jack and Darryl followed him but he was way ahead, *running for his life*. . . Brian always associated those words with running away from something, but presently he was just as surprised as anybody to be running toward it, as hard as he could, barefoot.

Motivated by Lita, and aided by his recent long distance training, Brian popped out of the bamboo a little too fast, accidentally slamming into Kenny in the courtyard and knocking him over. "Sorry about that."

Kenny sat up slowly, "Dude," not at all pleased.

Brian tried to make amends and helped Kenny to his feet, noting how wet and . . . red his hands were. "Are you hurt?"

"No, mae, but someone is. Someone got fucked up."

"You're not sure who?"

"Nuh-uh." Kenny shrugged his shoulders. "But there's a ton of blood in the kitchen."

That same blood now on his own hands, Brian held his palms up to his face, like they might reveal what happened, then quickly tried to rub them clean on the nearest bamboo stalk. "Where's Lita?"

"Don't know. And I didn't know you were marrying her."

"Nor did I until recently but what about the Italian couple?"

"Never found them." Kenny glanced at the house, like he was almost afraid to. "That I know of."

"Wait, what, you don't think that, really?"

"Why not?"

"Their plans could've changed," said Brian. "Ivan could've met them anywhere."

"I guess."

"The safe." Brian waited a moment for Jack and Darryl, but they were nowhere in sight, so he went straight for the kitchen. . .

Kenny followed after him. . . "Maybe we should go back to town."

Brian flipped the light switch but nothing happened.

"I already tried it," Kenny told him. "Power's out."

"Is that common?"

"Generator could be down . . . or switched off."

"Ivan's supposed to leave it on until midnight."

"I should get the police."

"What? Can't we call them?"

Kenny pulled out his cell phone. "No signal."

Brian checked his phone too. "Fuck."

"I'll go," said Kenny. "I'll go to the police."

And before Brian could suggest otherwise, Kenny vanished into the bamboo. . . .

13

Running To Stand Still

It was getting darker and darker inside the Bamboo House, like a black velvet curtain coming down all around him. His sight impaired, Brian listened to the jungle; every chirp and whistle, his heart drumming so uncontrollably that he felt the need to put his hand over his chest, just to keep it from popping out.

Fortunately, he knew Jack and Darryl would show up any second. They had to. Right? Unless. . . There was no unless. The blood on Kenny could be explained. A chicken or something could have wandered onto the property. Ivan probably caught it and merely made a mess of dinner.

Brian went for the safe, figuring he'd take the whole thing before Ivan returned. He knew the bigger problem was the house though, that perhaps Ivan was well aware he'd lose the property in a court of law and was currently operating out of desperation.

Brian opened the cupboard under the sink and moved the crate, reaching into the hole for the safe, reaching. . . But Nothing. So, he got down on all fours, sticking his arm deeper into the hole, but again he came up empty.

He pulled out his phone to illuminate the hole but his attention was drawn to the floor, smeared red with blood all the way to the back door, enough of it to pool between the bamboo slats.

Knowing he'd made a horrible mistake, his lungs stiffened, making it difficult to draw in air. Mixed up in something or someone he shouldn't be, he was shit deep and needed desperately to figure out what his next move was.

First order of business: Get his damn head straight. For starters, he tried counting to ten, to slow things down, but at six he instinctively spun around, "Hey!"

Blinded by a light, Brian stuck his arm out to block a potential blow, only to catch a glimpse of Lita, both hands over her head, one clutching a flashlight, the other a large kitchen knife, ready to filet him.

She mumbled angrily under her breath in Spanish before demanding, "What are you doing here?"

"Trying to find that Italian couple," said Brian, straightening up. "Or Ivan or both."

She set the flashlight down on the counter, the knife too, visibly upset. "You scared me."

"Sorry, Lita, I told you I would help and that's . . . that's what I'm going to do."

She grabbed Brian and hugged him tight, "Gracias," as if now that he was there everything would be okay.

No pressure, thought Brian, just save the fucking day. His arms fell limp but she held on to him. When she let go, she picked up her flashlight and showed him the open safe on the kitchen table.

"Es empty," she said.

"Which means he has his gun on him."

"And my jewels."

"Actually, I'm more concerned about the gun right now."

"Do you always say everything you are thinking?"

“Um, Lita,” started Brian, unfamiliar with being so candid. “Strange timing, I know, but do you feel anything? I mean, for me? Do you?”

“Stop.” She shined the flashlight in Brian’s face, staring at him, like she was trying to get a read on who was asking her such outlandish questions.

“Hi,” smiled Brian, rather feebly.

She turned off the flashlight and came closer to him. “Why should I tell you how I feel?”

“Because I asked . . . nicely.”

“You think you are funny.”

“No, I just. . .”

She held her hand up, stopping him. “Yes, you are funny sometime.” Then she softened. “But you are always kind to me.”

“Thank you, I—”

She came right up to him. “I will tell you what you want to know.”

And though it was dark, Brian’s eyes had adjusted to what light the moon could offer, holding Lita in a warm glow.

“At beginning,” she started, with some hesitation, “I feel nothing for you. Lo siento.”

“It’s okay.”

“Then we have a dance and a surf and when you finally stood up on the wave, I think I feel something.” She stepped on his toes, looking up at him, her brown eyes framed in a perfect white. “And now. . .” Lita took ahold of his shirt. “No sé.”

“You won’t say?”

“No, I do not know.” She twisted his shirt in her fist. “But I want to know.”

He closed his eyes and tilted his head back to await her lips, but urgent voices came from the courtyard, prompting Lita to let go of him and duck behind the kitchen table.

Brian knew it was Jack and Darryl though, trying to be quiet but failing miserably. He called out to them in a whisper. "He has his gun."

"That's not good," he heard Darryl say.

And then farther off, Jack. "What about the jewels?"

"They're weren't in the safe." Brian headed outside to meet them. "However, and this is a longshot, Ivan was digging a hole by the outhouse this morning."

"He could've been doing anything," said Jack, waiting in the courtyard with Darryl. "Probably something unsanitary."

"Maybe—" Brian stopped abruptly when he heard metal *clicking* into place against metal.

"It is true," said Ivan, "I have my gun," which he was holding to Brian's temple.

Darryl spoke up first, wary but firm. "I told you not to fuck with us."

"I can't take all the credit." Ivan looked past the guys to Roxy, who was ready to strike with a bamboo spear, sharpened on both ends. "I believe you gentlemen are fans of hers."

"Not anymore," quipped Jack.

Then Ivan nodded to another woman, above them in the window, her face just visible. "I would introduce you," he said, "but I can't imagine you will become friends."

Brian recognized her as the Canadian, which in and of itself wasn't a problem, but the gun in her hand sure was. A feeling of dread enveloped his entire body, like it could suffocate him, and he reached for Lita's hand. . . But she was gone.

"I warned you." Ivan lowered the Walther to his side. "She is dangerous."

"What do you want from us?" asked Darryl. "We found another hotel."

"I want you to leave the country."

"We can do that," Brian told him. "First plane tomorrow."

"What's the rush?" asked Jack. "I paid good money to come down here."

"You Yanks are so brave," he said. "You all think you are John Wayne."

"Come on, Ivan," goaded Jack. "You're dating yourself. You mean, The Rock."

"You need to go."

"I've got a wife and three kids," said Darryl. "I'm down with that."

Jack turned to the man of the hour. "You okay cutting our trip short, Bri?"

"He does not have choice." Ivan pointed his gun at Brian again, able to keep one eye on his target, the other on the guys.

"Jack," cautioned Darryl. "Don't get any dumb ideas."

"Yeah." Brian raised his hands in surrender, trying not to wet his pants. "Let's just go."

But Jack wouldn't let up. "He's not gonna kill us," he said. "I'm sure half the town knows we were staying here."

Ivan looked up at the Canadian woman. "Anna, get your friends." And she promptly disappeared into the house before reemerging in the courtyard.

Without breaking stride, she set down a small cooler by the front door and walked straight into the bamboo forest. . .

"If there is one thing I have learned," he continued, "no body, no crime. That's why—"

"Shhh. . ." Jack cut him off. "Listen."

After all these years, Brian was convinced Jack was finally going to get them killed.

"You hear that?" asked Jack.

Everyone went silent, trying to pick up what he was talking about.

"Sounds like help is coming," continued Jack.

"But for who?" asked Ivan, confidently.

"Praise Jesus." Darryl exhaled, as if relieved, then motioned over Roxy's shoulder. "I'd put that stick down if I were you."

She didn't though. She just turned to have a look of her own, long enough for Jack to take a swing at her, slapping the back of her head, CRACK, hard enough to knock her off her feet.

Ivan's attention diverted, Brian went for his gun, chopping at it, but was too late—*shots firing*.

BANG

BANG

Brian went down as Roxy got up; his ears ringing, his vision blurred, convinced that Ivan heading toward Jack and Darryl with his gun drawn would be the last thing he ever saw.

However, with both of them furiously trading fists and feet with Roxy's spear, Ivan couldn't get a clear shot, allowing Brian to scramble over and charge head first into his ribs, flattening him, the gun flying out of his hands.

Brian was still relishing the sack, when Ivan wrapped his arm around his throat, choking him; a vein popping, windpipe closing, blackout coming, choke.

Aware that he was seconds away from losing consciousness, Brian felt around blindly for the gun with one hand while swinging at Ivan with the other, though not connecting hard enough to alter his fate.

"Stupid Yank," growled Ivan, squeezing his throat *tighter . . . and tighter*.

Brian always thought he'd die at the Mather, the local old folks home, watching the Cubs game on a warm summer's day.

But here he was suffocating to death, heading into the hereafter in Costa Rica, when he heard Jack yell, though he couldn't tell if it was in anger or pain or—

He felt Ivan's head *snap back* . . . then again . . . and again, taking blow after blow to the face until he released his grip on Brian and collapsed to the ground, out cold.

His throat stinging, Brian looked up to find Jack, standing over Ivan, red in rage, his hat in one hand, the other still clenched in a fist, like he was committed to finishing him off.

But Brian frantically pointed toward the outhouse, where Darryl was on the defensive from Roxy, who was whipping her spear around like a baton, slicing chunks of flesh off his hands and arms.

"Come on, Darryl, get her," urged Jack, before turning to Brian, "where's his gun?"

Brian didn't know, nor did he know if he would've told him if he did.

But Jack spotted it and picked it up. "This ain't the time to be fucking polite."

Brian was in no way sold on Jack having a gun at his disposal. "What," he started, still struggling to breathe, "what're you going to do with that?"

"Keep her from killing Darryl," he said.

Darryl was determined to help himself though, swinging his arm and knocking her down with a solid blow to her shoulder.

However, before he could pounce, she got up and changed course, charging full-speed at Brian, her spear leading the way. . .

Jack aimed the gun at her with two hands, "Bitch, you better," but she didn't, "stop. . ."

Until a foot came out of the shadows and tripped her, causing Roxy to fall on her spear and impale herself, one end in the ground, the other in the center of her chest.

Lita, and her guilty foot, stepped into the open, clearly shook by what happened but not necessarily apologetic. "She was going kill you."

"I know, I know." Brian took Lita's hand but his eyes were glued on the fire dancer.

"She's dead," declared Jack.

Roxy was hunched over the spear, frozen, with a stunned look on her face.

Darryl circled her. "Pretty much, yeah."

Brian hugged Lita, truly thankful. "Gracias." He hugged her tighter. "I—"

Roxy coughed, as if choking on their display of affection, and gasped for air, keenly aware that the spear was poised to slice the rest of the way through her.

"Fuck and fuck," said Darryl.

"That's gotta be the biggest trachea of all time." Jack got a closer look at where the spear entered Roxy's sternum. "Guinness big. She's breathing through this thing."

"That's what you're thinking about right now?" asked Darryl. "Whether she's breaking any world records."

"Well," said Jack, "she's alive, isn't she?"

Brian rubbed his sore Adam's apple, thankful it was in one piece. "But for how long?"

"I suppose we could just let nature take its course," said Darryl.

"This is hardly nature," countered Brian. "She's suffering."

"So fuck it." Jack gave Brian a little push. "Put her out of her misery. Finish her off."

"That's. . ." started Brian, giving it some thought, "that's got to be the dumbest thing you've ever said."

But Jack wasn't deterred. "Darryl?"

"Black on black crime," he replied. "It's already such a big problem."

"This isn't a joke," said Brian.

"Exactly. You saw her. She was fighting us to the death." Jack pointed out the puncture wounds all over Darryl's body.

"Look at this shit."

"I'm okay," said Darryl, though clearly not.

"We'd be doing her a favor at this point." Jack knelt down beside Roxy and looked into her eyes. "Am I right?"

Roxy hissed, spraying Jack's face with blood.

"Fuck this shit." Jack stood up, wiping the blood from his eyes with the back of his hand. "I'll do it."

"Jack," tried Darryl, "this isn't for us to decide."

"Hold on." Brian hustled over to where he remembered Ivan digging by the outhouse and uncovered the velvet sack about a foot deep in the dirt, then took a peek to confirm the jewels were inside and handed it to Lita. "Kenny went to get the police. Maybe we should just wait here."

"Or leave," suggested Darryl.

"Regardless of whether or not she was trying to kill us," said Brian, trying desperately to prioritize his thoughts, "she needs to get to a hospital."

"Well, she might have to settle for a morgue," said Jack.

"What?" Brian looked to Darryl. "Why?"

"Because he's gone." Jack tugged on Brian's shoulder, casting his eyes to the empty space where Ivan had passed out. "Which means this isn't over."

Brian searched fruitlessly for Ivan in the dark. "Fuck."

"He obviously left in a hurry," said Darryl, "but the question is did he see what happened to his friend Roxy?"

"Kid," began Jack, patting Brian's back. "The next time I say let's go someplace like Bolivia, let's go someplace like Bolivia."

"Bolivia?" Darryl took his towel out of his back pocket and dabbed at his wounds. "I thought our back-up plan was Belize."

"It was," said Jack. "That's from *Butch Cassidy and the Sundance Kid*."

"You're quoting movies?" Brian bent over, like he was

going to throw up. "Now?"

"Newman tells Redford that before they jump off the cliff," said Jack, "you know, into the river."

"So this is where we jump?" Darryl asked him.

"Figuratively," replied Jack.

Roxy convulsed, causing her to fall another inch farther onto the spear.

"This is fucked up," said Brian. "We need to explain everything to the police."

"It's bad enough she has a piece of bamboo stuck in her," said Jack, "but she also has bruises from fighting us. So does Ivan. Who's to say he hasn't gone to the police and blamed everything on us?"

"We are on his property," said Darryl.

"My property," clarified Lita.

"Hopefully, yeah, but Bri you're covered in blood," continued Jack, "most of which I'm thinking isn't your own."

"There's loads of it in the kitchen," said Brian.

"Could be the Italian couple's," proposed Jack.

"No one's seen them, have they?" asked Darryl.

"Huh? What?" Brian still wasn't ready to admit that they could be dead, at least out loud. Instead, he concentrated on his head, which he turned from side to side, becoming aware that one of his ears was no longer functioning.

"Hold on, Bri." Darryl examined his ears. "Assuming you started today with two earlobes, I'd say Ivan just about blew your brains out."

"Guys. . ." Brian felt for his left ear, the one that hurt, a piece missing at the bottom. "You two could've gotten me killed just now."

"He had a gun to your head," said Jack. "So could've he."

"I was aware of that," continued Brian. "But you guys didn't hear anyone coming to help us. That was all bullshit."

"Next move wins at that point," said Jack.

"And Ivan's a nut-job," added Darryl.

"But you told Jack not to get any dumb ideas," said Brian.

"Those are words of encouragement to him," explained Darryl. "You know that as well as I do."

Brian gave up and had a look in the cooler by the door, finding neat stacks of $50 and $100 bills. "Just another reason to tell the truth."

"The truth," said Darryl, getting a look at all that money, "could be hard to explain."

"And what about Lita?" Jack asked. "You want to tell the truth about what she just did? To the cops?"

"No." Brian shook his head, looking at her. "No way. Of course not."

Darryl began stretching, like he was limbering up for a track meet. "I say we make a run for it. Straight to the airport."

"I say we stay and fucking fight." Jack proficiently checked how many bullets were left in the Walther. "It's the only way to clear ourselves of this mess."

"Since when do you know how to handle a gun?" Brian asked him.

"Since I realized if I needed one, I'd better know how to use it," replied Jack. "I've been taking lessons."

"That's it," said Brian. "Running? Fighting? I've had enough. This ends here. All of it."

"I don't see how." Darryl ripped the sleeve off his shirt, then gently wrapped it around Brian's head to cover his ear.

Jack looked over at Lita. "What do you think?"

She grabbed the cooler from Brian and began stuffing the cash into the sack with the jewels, then just as suddenly stopped, rocking her eyes from one end of the courtyard to the other. "We are not alone."

Before the guys could react, several bearded men ambushed them, fists flying from all directions. . .

Brian saw Darryl level the first one that came at him with a wild overhand right to the head, then heard gunfire, hopefully from Jack, and tore off into the bamboo forest behind Lita, with one of the men, a burly one at that, tailing them. . .

Lita was fast and knew her way, but Brian was terrified of what would happen to her if the man caught up to them, so he detoured from Lita, hoping to take their assailant with.

Brian figured if he could just make it to the road, he could outrun him. However, without a clear path, the bamboo was difficult to navigate, especially in the dark.

Stealing looks back, he couldn't even see the man, but he could hear him loud and clear, ripping through the bamboo as if it were confetti. . .

By the time he reached the road, the man was no more than ten feet behind him. Fortunately, Brian had enough strength left to make a proper run for it but at the last second, worrying Lita might be somewhere on the road too, he detoured to the mangrove.

He figured that he might frustrate the man into giving up. However, as Brian barreled through the water, stepping over and around and through a tangle of vines and branches, *that bearded fuck*, without saying a single word, kept coming after him. . .

Being ahead, Brian knew that he was aiding him, finding and clearing the quickest way through the mangrove, so that by the time they reached the beach, the man was right on his heels.

Brian ran straight toward the ocean, fully aware that if the man caught him, his last breath would most likely take place under water.

Thoughts were colliding in Brian's brain like asteroids, thoughts, he feared, that would be his final few: Sue would cry for weeks. His dad would give his baseball cards away to a kid who didn't want them. But what would happen to the guys? To Lita?

Brian discovered it was low tide, as when Lita took him there, exposing the reef, something the man apparently wasn't prepared for, and he heard him fall hard, bone on rock, followed by an agonizing yet restrained wail.

Brian just kept running and running, back to Playa Tamarindo, until he was convinced he was no longer being chased and collapsed near Nogui's, against the same tree he'd napped under so peacefully just hours before.

His breathing was heavy and labored and his ear hurt badly, but he knew his feet were a problem too. He sat cross-legged to get a look at them; bruised, bleeding, they were cut to shreds, gorged with tiny sticks and rocks.

He never would've gone barefoot had he been thinking straight, without the guys, not to mention the girl, feeding him a false sense of bravado doused in liquor and lust.

Know your limits, he always told himself. That way, no one gets hurt. Speaking of which, he had to look for Lita.

But where? What if he couldn't find her? Should he go to the police? Or worse, the hospital? Did he need to concoct a story? A lie?

Didn't matter in the end, since here came the bearded man, limping noticeably but getting closer by the second. He looked angry, at least angrier than before, like any notion of all the bad things he had planned for Brian had been multiplied.

Brian wasn't going down easy though. He'd come this far. He could scream. Actually, he couldn't. He tried. So, surrounded by all those coconuts again, he scooped up as many as he could and started throwing them at the man, even hitting him as he got closer.

Unfortunately, throwing coconuts wasn't an option when the man grabbed him, so Brian reeled back, poised to smash him with one, when a coconut fell from the tree, nailing Brian square on his head.

Brian collapsed in the sand, slipping into unconsciousness for a second time that night, fighting it with all his might, knowing that if he closed his eyes now he might never open them again.

Laying in the sand, his skull pounding, Brian could see the man laughing, as if the ordeal with the American was etched in stone, that he'd won.

However, with what little strength he had left, Brian picked himself up and began running again to the end of the beach. . .

Though fumes and fear hadn't gotten him very far, when, *fuck*, he realized he was heading toward that damn monster infested river.

Then again, maybe the bearded man wouldn't follow him. Maybe he'd think better of it and give up the chase once and for all.

But the man never slowed down, so Brian just kept on running, stumbling really, until he hit the water, barely staying upright.

Regaining his footing, Brian tried to hurdle the knee-deep water all the way across, when he heard the man enter the river, still laughing, getting closer and closer, pushing the water out of his way.

Brian thought the shore would never come, that he'd hit a spiteful undercurrent keeping him from the other side.

It was too late though. He could see the man's hand reaching for his shoulder, just a couple of strides back. . .

But his arm dropped abruptly and Brian heard the man go down with a splash, followed by another more violent splash and a struggle of some sort, most of which seemed to be taking place beneath the river's surface.

And though his head was full of noise, Brian noticed the

river go quiet. Still, he didn't look back. Didn't even stop. He just kept running until he reached land. . . And then he ran some more, fully aware that the bearded man had met his match with one of Costa Rica's more infamous reptiles.

14

Do You Know The Way To San Jose?

Brian cautiously opened his eyes, one at a time, afraid of what he might find, mostly because he wasn't sure when last night ended and today began. Then again, maybe his eyes had been open the whole time and it was merely getting light outside. He was that scared, shocked really, so much so that he couldn't recall much after the river, just someone handing him a shot of liquor—after he'd thrown up.

It should be noted, however, that Brian didn't necessarily get sick because of what happened to the bearded man. Or even the fire dancer. Truth be told, he was more concerned with what could happen, namely a long prison sentence for him and his friends. *That*, he imagined, would be too far off the grid.

From the rattle and hum of the engine, Brian knew he was in a car, surely on some crappy road due to all the jostling about but moving at a persistent pace.

Someone was licking his ear, his bloody ear, then stopped when he turned to see who it was. And there was Maní in the backseat with him, acting all innocent. And Lita, thank god, was there too, fast asleep against the opposite door, her face pressed to the window, which was lit by the morning sun.

Brian knew instinctively that Jack and Darryl weren't with him but rubbed last night's gunk from his eyes and checked the row of seats behind him anyway.

Another van. He remembered the warning he gave Jack at the airport, about smoking of all things. Man, he'd give anything to see Jack light up a cigarette right now. And what about Darryl? His body was littered with nasty gashes—before they rumbled with those beards.

He took a closer look at Lita. Even with her dress muddied and torn and her hair a knotted bush, Brian couldn't get over how beautiful she looked as she slept; clutching the sack, like it was a bag full of dreams, not in a naive way but with an innocence peppered in hope.

His throat felt tight and it hurt to swallow, as if Ivan still had his hands around it. And his ear hurt too, at least what was left of it. Actually, his whole head ached, similar to a bowling ball being dropped repeatedly on the pavement.

He remembered the coconut and was drawn to the back of his head, where his index finger outlined a golf ball size lump, warm to the touch, like an egg cooking on a stove, one whose yoke could still break.

It was certainly hot enough in the van to cook an egg, stifling really, especially with the windows shut, presumably because of all the dust being kicked up along the dirt road and nothing personal.

"The air-conditioner broke down just after Samara," came a man's voice, a familiar one.

Brian checked beneath him, finding the *Pura Vida* bumper sticker on the seat. "Vincent?" he tried, his voice hoarse and barely audible. "Cecilia?"

"I hope so," laughed Vincent, "or she's going to kill me."

Brian rubbed his eyes again, trying to get a clear look at the couple. His big mustache. Her hair in a long white braid down her back.

"How are you feeling?" asked Vincent.

"I, uh—"

Cecilia spoke up, saying something to her husband in Spanish, something about, "Muchos problemas."

Those were words Brian could understand. He sat back in his seat, inadvertently locating himself in the rearview mirror; his face plastered with dirt and sand, his head still wrapped in Darryl's sleeve, one side of it crusty with blood, which he realized was responsible for the tinny taste in his mouth.

Vincent held up a plastic water bottle. "Drink."

"Thanks." Brian took the bottle and drank, slowly, allowing his throat time to open up. "I had a feeling I was going to see you again."

"We have your suitcase," said Vincent.

"My suitcase? How?"

"We checked the airport."

"Jeez, thank you. I really appreciate that."

"We went to the Pasatiempo but no luck," explained Vincent, "so we asked around town and found your friend Kenny. Or he found us. Pretty crazy, right?"

"Yeah. . . Um, my other friends. . ." Brian was almost afraid to ask. "They're okay?"

"Sí." Vincent looked over at his wife, as if measuring her concern. "Your black friend. He needs a hospital."

Brian was glad to hear they'd survived, ecstatic really, but it didn't feel like a victory. He draped his arms over the front seat, exhausted but anxious for answers. "Where're we going?"

"Mal Pais." Lita was awake, stretching her arms over her head. "We had to leave. It was not safe for us."

"I get that." Wanting to hug her, he instead rubbed Maní's back, which the dog clearly appreciated. "So where's this

Mal-pie-eece?"

"South, near the park."

"The park?"

"Cabo Blanco," she said, as if Brian should know. "The nature reserve."

"What about the airport?" Brian was trying to be patient with her, but if he wasn't going to the hospital then he better be going home. "It's, uh, isn't it north of Tamarindo?"

"Different airport," she said, checking her phone, presumably for something important.

"Oh, okay, thanks." Brian couldn't tell if Lita was really relaxed about everything or, like him, scared shitless.

But when she stopped fiddling with her phone, she traded places with Maní, resting her hand on Brian's knee. "They will be expecting you in Liberia."

"Me?" he asked as evenly as he could. "What about Jack and Darryl?"

"They are with Kenny," she told him. "They go to find Señor Contreras first. He has our passports." She squeezed his thigh, reassuringly, Brian noticing that she was wearing his wedding band on her thumb.

Brian patted down his pockets, finding her diamond ring. "And how far is this town from Tamarindo?"

"We take the big road, four hours," she replied. "But we take coast."

"We've been driving all night," said Vincent.

"Thank you, I, uh, thank you." Brian backed off asking any more questions for a while: Airports. Hospitals. Passports. Wedding rings. And head wounds! He had enough to fret over. Thinking, not talking, seemed more than reasonable for the time being.

Mal Pais, located at the southwestern tip of the Peninsula de Nicoya, got its name, *bad lands*, due to its harsh dry summers; making cattle, not crops, the most profitable form of farming. And, despite, if not because of its remote location, it also flourished as a fishing village.

However, by the time Brian showed up one winter's morning, tourism was king, in part because the secret was out on its white sand coves and jungle covered hills and, of course, superb surf breaks.

When they reached town, Kenny was waiting outside Mary's Restaurant. "Grab your stuff," he said, opening the van door. "Follow me."

Brian let Lita out before him, then left the door open for Maní: "Vamos."

But the dog didn't budge, in fact, he curled up on the seat and closed his eyes, like he was tired.

"Dogs," said Vincent. "They sense trouble."

Brian gave him a final pat on the back, "Thanks, Maní," then turned to Vincent, "I guess this is goodbye."

"Más o menos." He handed Brian his suitcase. "My wife and I, we wish you two luck."

"Thank you, gracias." Brian knew the danger they had put themselves in to help and reached into his pocket to pay him.

Vincent waved it off though. "You might need it."

But Brian gave him all his damp, smelly, stuck together colones anyway. "For gas. I'm sure I owe you more than that. For everything." Brian placed his arm across the old man's shoulder, awkward but sincere.

Meanwhile, Cecilia rolled down her window and squeezed Lita's hand, reassuringly. "Vaya con dios."

There's a line Brian never thought he'd hear in person, not him, not in this lifetime, and not since Keanu Reeves was doing his best Johnny Utah in *Point Break*.

"Gracias, señora," said Lita. "Gracias, señor."

"We will find your girls," Vincent told her, "and make sure they are okay." Then he got back in the van with his wife and drove off, Maní staring pensively out the back window. . .

Brian just stood there on the side of the road, waving goodbye, all sad eyes and droopy shoulders.

"Mae." Kenny didn't appear to be moved. "Nos juimos."

Brian had to get used to lugging a suitcase around again, especially since its wheels were useless on the uneven dirt. However, before he got more than a few feet, he came to a decision. He was ditching it. It wasn't that kind of vacation anymore. *Fuck*, it wasn't any kind of vacation.

"Hold on." Brian stopped. "I can't take this thing another foot. I don't need it."

Kenny shook his head. "No, not here. You don't want to leave anything that can trace back to you."

"Really?"

"Yeah." Kenny waited to make sure Brian did as he was told. "And you're gonna need to change into some clean clothes before you get to the airport, something normal."

Normal. Brian yearned for normal. He looked at what he was wearing, blood soaked remnants of his jeans and tank-top.

Kenny tugged on Brian's shoulder. "Let's keep movin'."

They followed Kenny past the restaurant on foot to Cabuya Road, a major intersection as far as Brian could tell, even though it lacked any current traffic, then headed inland for a bit before turning into a short driveway impeded by a gate, which blocked nothing but jungle.

Brian dropped his suitcase with a thud. "Now what?"

"We're here," replied Kenny. "This is mi chante, mi casa, where I grew up." He took Brian's suitcase and walked around the gate, leading them on a narrow jungle path up and around a hill so dense in foliage it seemed to paw at them.

Soon, Brian could hear music and laughter coming from the top of a huge volcanic boulder. The loud hearty laugh he knew belonged to Darryl and surely Jack coaxed the host to play Sublime. What he couldn't figure out, the festive mood.

Well, life's too short, so love the one you got
'Cause you might get run over or you might get shot

-- Sublime

He didn't doubt that Jack picked out that song, but there was no way he could've known they'd be walking in at the time; the lyrics being so fitting to Brian's life, though he had to admit that every song he heard lately somehow carried a deeper meaning.

Then again, maybe that was true of everyone who pushed their limits. Maybe that's why certain songs always got Jack so fired up, because he was living them.

Lovin', is what I got, I said remember that
Lovin', is what I got, now remember that

Perched atop the boulder, Brian thought Kenny's family home resembled more of a fort; half Frank Lloyd Wright prairie house in harmony with its environment and half hobo hut, the wood beams and planks being all mismatched scraps.

He was expecting to discover the guys huddled in a basement, cursing and crying; not drinking beer with Kenny's dad on the back porch, which was built into the side of the rock about twenty-five feet above the ground.

Jack and Darryl gave Brian extra-long hugs as Kenny's dad stood up to greet him. "There he is, the hero of our story," he smiled, all mischief and mayhem. "And another Evanston kid like me."

"Wait. You're from Evanston too? Kenny didn't say that. I'm Brian and—"

"The woman he falls for." Kenny's dad walked right over to her in just his Thai fisherman pants, orange ones that gave off a religious air.

"Lita," she said, introducing herself, tired but guarded. "Thank you for—"

"De nada," he said. "No worries. I'm Mike." A few years older than the guys, his once blond hair was now sheer white and longer than his son's, his body leaner, every muscle and vein jumping out of his skin. Then, as if he'd been debating what to do next, he clapped his hands, "fuck it," and removed a long bamboo stalk from part of the wall.

Brian was preparing to defend himself from an imminent attack, when a woman, earthy yet regal, joined them outside. She eyed the bamboo and smiled uneasily, her accent betraying her British upbringing. "Bit early to be smoking, innit Mike?"

"Hey, everyone," he began. "This is my better half, the lovely and talented Sam."

Sam was tall, pretty, thought Brian, close to fifty, thin but healthy, the tropical life obviously suiting her. And she was dressed similar to most people he'd met in Costa Rica, as if headed to the beach.

Mike set the bamboo bong down on a coffee table, one made from an old wooden door, the knob still attached. "It's gotta be four-twenty somewhere."

Sam frowned. "Somewhere you're not."

Mike laughed. "These cats are from my hometown, Sam. Can you believe it? Same high school and everything."

Sam seemed indifferent and turned to address their visitors. "We just said goodbye to mates of his from back home five minutes ago. Surprised you didn't see them on your way up the hill."

"Don't worry. They're not staying," Mike assured her. "In fact, they're in a hurry to get out of here."

"No rush," she said, failing to hide her relief. "Would anyone like another beer?"

As all the guys shot up their hands, Mike roared his approval, motioning for them to sit around the table, where piles of pillows beckoned them.

Then he walked over to a shelf of worn books and picked out *I Am The Messenger* by Markus Zusak, removing a small baggie from between the pages, inside which there was a green bud, flat but big, about the size of his thumb. "Mota," he announced.

Sam shook her head, smiling at him, then turned to Lita. "Come with me."

Brian couldn't figure out what Kenny's dad was so excited about; his preliminary read suggesting that he was either genuinely happy to welcome fellow Evanstonians into his home or, in musical terms, *one step over the line sweet Jesus*.

Still, despite ripples of fear and anxiety, a ruinous combo if there ever was one, Brian tried to roll with it when Mike put on some more music.

Meanwhile, the bong made its way around the table, while the guys told Mike what happened with Ivan in snippets of conversations; some gaining traction, some not, beginning with Jack commenting on the current song.

"This singer," he said. "She reminds me of Sade."

"That's a stretch," chuckled Darryl. "Sade was coast to coast, you know that, LA to Chicago."

High as he was, Brian felt compelled to interject, if for no other reason than to make sure he could string together his thoughts. "Don't forget Western Maine."

Darryl slapped his knee laughing. "It's western *male*."

Brian couldn't believe it. "What?"

"Yeah, rhymes with *love for sale.*"

"If it ain't Maine," said Jack, taking Brian's side, "then she ain't coast to coast."

"Just so you know. . ." Brian turned his head to the side, cracking his neck. "I only smoke pot when I'm with you guys."

"And I only smoke pot when I'm without you guys," said Jack.

"So then you smoke all the time," laughed Darryl, even louder.

"Someone's gotta take a hit for the team," said Jack, clearly admiring his choice of words.

"Fellas. . ." interrupted Mike. "I don't wanna burst any bubbles but this *is* Sade."

"Really?" asked Jack

"From *Soldier of Love,*" Mike went on. "Five, six years ago."

"I don't think I've done Sade this century," said Brian.

Darryl started to say something but upon review just shook his head, whispering. "I am so fucking high."

"You're also still bleeding in about twenty different places," pointed out Jack.

Brian opened his suitcase and got out the Neosporin from his toiletry kit, which he newly dubbed his survival kit. "Sit still," he told Darryl. "I'm going to clean you up."

"If Ivan doesn't kill us," said Darryl. "I'm sure Carmela will."

"For now though, you needs stitches." Brian applied some ointment to one of Darryl's cuts.

"Like stitch city," added Jack.

Brian ignored him, digging through the kit until he found a needle and thread. "Can anyone sew?"

When no one stepped up, Jack asked, "Didn't you bring

your Crazy Glue, Bri?"

Brian hesitated before admitting, "Yeah."

"Great," continued Jack. "I read on the internet we can use it instead of stitches."

"It's possible," smiled Mike, apparently digging the idea.

But Darryl wasn't as enthusiastic. "Just so you know, reading something on the internet don't mean shit what it used to. Besides, I read that too and you're only supposed to glue together an open wound if you're desperate and can't get to a hospital." He wiped his scalp with his towel, a mix of blood and sweat running red down his face. "There is a hospital in town, right?"

"Sí, mae, close, a police station too." Kenny walked in with a round of beers, giving the first one to their patient. "In case you guys didn't notice, Darryl sticks out down here."

"Boy's right," said Mike, helping himself to a beer on his way to the record player. "You know, in the eighties these guys made a comeback with a couple of ballads. But that's not who they were. Not really. They were a jam band from the sixties. A rock n roll orchestra." He carefully removed a record from a double album and held up the cover. "*Chicago Transit Authority*, came out in 1969."

Mike put on side one and turned up the volume, presumably counter-intuitive to his pontificating but nonetheless adding a certain ambiance. "Saw them in concert last time I went home and they were killing it, just like when they first started, not exactly the original band but the horns and the main keyboard dude were all there." He took a chug of his beer. "And when I woke up the next morning, it hit me: When you're young you do crazy shit because you think you're gonna live forever. But when you're old you do it because you know you're gonna die."

Darryl nodded, "Exactly."

"That's a good one," said Jack. "Where'd you hear that?"

Mike tapped his head. “The man cave.”

“So Chicago had a midlife crisis in the eighties,” suggested Jack.

“Pretty much,” confirmed Mike.

“Where’s that leave us?” asked Brian.

Mike pointed to one of the speakers, just as Chicago’s horn section ripped into gear. “Well, for one, rock n roll is on life support.” He stopped, regarding Darryl, “funk too,” then continued, “so our generation, you get some confused cats because when you’re somewhere in the middle of your life, you don’t always know what to do, especially when music used to point you in the right direction.” He laughed, tilting his head back, as if picturing it. “Like when you’re sixteen and every song seems to be about fast cars and faster girls.”

The guys all laughed in agreement: “Damn skippy.” “What else is there?” “True dat.”

“That’s why I’m stoked I went to India when I was young,” said Mike. “Not sure I could do it now. My twin brother came too. Had to, I guess. But, hey, that’s where I met Sam.”

“I’d heard about twins going to India while we were in high school.” Jack cracked open his beer. “A few years ahead of us.”

“Scotty and I were class of ninety,” said Mike.

“The story goes,” continued Jack, “that *after* one of them spent time in an Indian jail, he got rich on some drug deal and ran off to Central America somewhere, which I’m now thinking must’ve been Costa Rica.”

“Sounds right,” smiled Mike, all stoney-eyed.

“Sounds crazy,” laughed Darryl, until he came to an abrupt halt. “Am I the only one who’s hungry?”

Jack ignored him, focusing on Mike’s story. “How’d you settle on Mal Pais?”

“Because it wasn’t easy to get to.” Mike tapped bowl to the bong against the table, emptying the remaining ashes.

Meanwhile, Brian wasn't sure if he could put the right words to the rumblings between his ears. So, content to just listen, he concentrated on his bare feet, which were numb with pain, like if he acknowledged how much they actually hurt he'd be screaming.

"There was just one crappy road in, one crappy road out," went on Mike, breaking the bud up between his fingers over the Chicago cover. "So at some point, we had to decide as a town whether or not to pave the road. If you leave the road be, you can keep paradise to yourself, if you can afford it. But if you fix it, the masses will come, the silver lining being that hopefully you can make enough money off them to stay."

"What do you down here?" asked Jack, as if bells were going off in his head.

"I bought a boat, soon as we arrived, before I could blow my money on anything else."

"*Blow* being the operative word," said Kenny.

"Funny." Mike took a swig of beer. "I take tourists fishing. Kenny, when he's not being a comedian, teaches them how to surf."

"My mom's a tattoo artist, does some henna too," Kenny said. "And she just sold her first painting."

"Yes, Sam is amazing," agreed Mike, "but she sold that painting to someone new in town, which, yeah, is great for us but as the town grows you gotta think about things, like how to get rid of all the waste those people create."

"And bring in enough fresh water," added Kenny.

"Then, as you guys discovered," continued Mike, "where there's a lot of money changing hands, there's the potential for shit to go down."

"Man, did it," sighed Darryl.

"I've run into this Ivan character on several occasions," Mike told them, filling the bong again. "Once when he was still living on the Caribbean side." He shook his head. "I don't trust that cat for nothin'."

"So what should we do?" Brian asked. "Go to the police?"

"No, not yet," said Mike. "You don't know if Ivan told them anything."

"Besides a lie," said Darryl.

"At some point the police will be looking for that Italian couple," started Jack, as Mike handed him the bong. "And considering we took off with all the jewels and money, Ivan could easily blame whatever happened to them on us."

"How much money do you guys have?" asked Mike. "Cash. Show me."

The guys emptied their pockets on the table, Jack tallying, "a little over two million colones."

"That's about thirty-five hundred bucks," said Brian, still able to do math in his foggy state. "Plus whatever dollars any of us have."

"I have a hundy," said Jack. "It's in my passport."

"Keep it," Mike told him. "That's a good place for it."

"All the money from the cooler is in dollars too," said Darryl.

"Lita has it," said Jack. "And there's a lot of it."

"Yeah, I wouldn't try to spend that just yet," Mike told them. "Might make it easier for the police to track you down. This is a win-win for Ivan. I can see an end game where he gets to keep the jewels, maybe even the money, that house you were talking about too. He'd tell the judge that Brian was blinded by love, tricked, then got greedy. And if Ivan catches up to you first, he won't give you a chance to prove otherwise."

"How'd this all happen?" asked Brian, before taking his turn on the bong. "To me?"

"It's too late for that." Mike tossed some colones onto the pile, then lit the bong for him. "Kenny says you're making a run for the airport in San Jose."

Brian coughed up his hit, unable to reply.

"That's the plan," Darryl confirmed.

"By all means," agreed Mike. "Get your asses on a plane home."

Brian passed the bong to Darryl who skipped it this time and handed it to Kenny.

But Kenny waved it off too. "Oh, I don't smoke."

"You mean that was an option?" asked Brian, still coughing.

"My dad smokes enough for the two of us," said Kenny.

Mike laughed. "Sounds like quite the feat if you ask me."

"How're we gonna get through an airport?" asked Brian, failing to suppress another series of coughs. "They'll be looking for us."

"The question remains who though, the police or Ivan, maybe both." Mike took a big hit, held it, then blew a parade of smoke into the jungle. "As you know, Oz never did give nothin' to the Tin Man."

The guys all looked at each other, confused, while Kenny just rolled his eyes.

"Oz never did give nothin' to the Tin Man," began Mike again, "that he didn't already have."

"Seals and Crofts?" tried Brian, recognizing the song.

"No, America," laughed Mike, rocking back on forth on his pillow. "The band not the country."

Brian shrugged his shoulders. "I don't get it."

"It means you can figure this shit out. It's in you." Mike made sure it was still just the guys, then spoke under the music. "Sounds like you just defended yourselves, so if you really want to go home, cut the girl loose. Sam and I will help her any way we can."

"We're engaged," said Brian, not doubting his sincerity or his libido. "That isn't an option."

"Okay, I get it." Mike rested a hand on Brian's shoulder.

"But if you're with the girl, you're gonna be the fall guy, so let your friends try and clear your name before anyone finds you. That way, if it doesn't look like you'll get a fair trial, at least you've still got a shot to escape."

"Brian's right though," said Jack. "We can't just get on a plane. That'd be the first place they'd look."

"It takes resources," said Kenny. "They'll check Liberia first. And they have to watch the borders in case you try to leave by land."

"Depends how much of a priority they consider you," added Mike.

"I didn't say anything about you guys to the police in Tamarindo," Kenny told them. "I just said there was a problem at the Bamboo House."

"But if they are looking for us, we're talking about a country that's smaller than, what, West Virginia," said Brian. "That's not much ground to cover."

Sam walked in looking worried. "Qué mala nota."

"Go on," Mike told her, "in English."

"Alfie phoned from town," she continued. "Said a Jeep full of men was headed here. With beards. Don't know why he mentioned that but—"

Darryl snapped his fingers, regrettably. "Roxy had a Jeep."

"And the Canadian had a hairy entourage," said Jack. "We've met them."

"Fuck." Brian jumped to his feet, while Darryl helped Jack scoop up the money, then he rummaged through his suitcase until he found his running shoes (and the condoms), socks, a clean polo, and a backup pair of beige khakis.

And though chafing badly, he kept his new swimsuit on, aware that he most likely hadn't completed the water hazard portion of his trip.

Beside him, Sam pulled a worn, hand-knit poncho over her husband's head, like it was a suit of armor. "It's time for your friends to go."

Mike turned to Kenny. "Take them down the hill the back way. Whoever it is, I'll stall them for as long as possible."

Lita ran out onto the porch in fresh jeans and a blouse, the sack strung over her shoulders.

Meanwhile, Jack removed Ivan's gun from his trackpants, followed by Mike, who dislodged a .44 Magnum from underneath the coffee table.

"Is everyone packing down here?" asked Brian, stuffing what he could from his kit into his pockets.

"No different than Chicago," replied Mike.

Does anybody really know what time it is? (I don't)
Does anybody really care? (care about time)
If so I can't imagine why (no, no)
We've all got time enough to die

--Chicago

Brian took Lita by the hand, following Kenny and the guys through the kitchen and up a ladder to the roof, where they found themselves at the top of the trees in a jungle without end.

Kenny walked over to the far side of the roof and tugged on a rope, which was attached to a branch hanging over the house. "Watch."

"Watch what?" asked Brian, fearing what he had in mind.

Kenny didn't hesitate. He just held onto the rope at the edge of the roof and swung himself over . . . a ravine . . . to a neighboring tree, maybe twenty feet away, landing feet first on one branch while grabbing the branch above it with his hands.

"Christ," sighed Brian, sizing up the task unfavorably.

"What about your heart, Jack?"

Kenny swung the rope back to the roof.

"What about it?" Jack grabbed the rope and followed suit, swinging across . . . and though he lost his hat, landing successfully next to Kenny.

"Your friend is crazy," said Lita, shaking her head.

Brian caught the rope this time but nervous as shit, deferred to Lita, as if a gentleman. "Ladies first."

Lita took the rope, then kissed him smack on the lips before taking off . . . and nailing the landing beside Jack and Kenny.

Brian didn't know what was more unsettling; the kiss or the ravine dropping a good thirty or forty feet below him. His response was to stall, taking longer than necessary to tie his shoes.

Darryl caught the rope and held it out to him. "I'm heavier than you."

"I know, I know," started Brian, but then the music stopped from the porch, replaced by Mike talking to someone, several someones, testily.

"Doesn't sound good," said Darryl.

"Damnit." Brian squeezed the rope and ran off the side of roof over . . . the ravine and to the tree where the rest of them were waiting—face first into the trunk.

Realizing too late that there wasn't any room left on the branch, Kenny motioned for everyone to start climbing down the tree, as Brian tried to hold his bent and bloodied nose in place.

Brian alternated his hands from nose to branch, frustrated at miscalculating the jump as well as in a lot of fucking pain. "On a scale of one to ten," he said to himself, "that sucked."

Finally, it was Darryl's turn but, "I'll only get us caught," he said, from the edge of the roof. "I probably already did."

Brian stopped and looked back up through the branches.

"No," he called out. "If this is anyone's fault, it's mine."

Darryl was already headed to the ladder though. "I need to get to a real doctor. And I'm hungry as shit. If anyone asks, I'll say you went to the airport in Liberia. It'll buy you some time."

"Come on, don't fuck around." Brian didn't like the sound of that, even if it made sense. "What if it's Ivan at the door?"

"Then I'll beat the shit out of him." Darryl held firm. "Seriously, I got this. I'll get Carmela working on a lawyer."

"Hold it," said Brian, trying to come up with an alternate plan. "Wait."

But Darryl was gone, just like that, back down the hole in the roof.

"What the fuck?" Brian was stunned, not to mention still stoned.

Kenny passed him going down the tree, lowering himself from branch to branch. "You need to keep moving, mae."

"Yeah." Once more Brian started down, determined to see Darryl again, though well aware that sacrificing Lita to save himself, even his friends, wasn't an option. He was all in, which meant he could no longer play the passenger.

15

On The Road Again

Take action. Go for it. He'd begged himself to a thousand times. However, Brian prided himself on being a thinker, so it was only appropriate for him to weigh his options, kind of a checks and balances then tended to veer toward check and double-check. Therefore, though he had committed to taking charge countless times before, he still left some wiggle room to talk himself out of it and fade into the pack.

What he couldn't refute, however, was that tree climbing was one of his favorite things to do growing up. Easy for him. A skill, in this instance, impossible to ignore, even with his nose hurting like hell. Besides, she'd kissed him! Of course, she might've thought she was about to die, but still.

So, even though it required a more difficult descent, Brian reached the bottom branch before the others, already judging the final leap to the jungle floor to be a good ten, eleven feet through the thick bush.

Unfortunately, it was much less than that, which meant Brian didn't have a chance to bend his knees before landing and hit the ground hard, surprised his kneecaps didn't pop out of their sockets.

Jack and Lita lowered themselves off the last branch and rushed over to Brian, one more concerned than the other.

"Quit fucking around," barked Jack, helping him to his feet.

While Lita brushed off his back, more gesture than need, then dabbed at the blood still spilling out of Brian's nose with his shirt. "Estás bien?"

"No, not really." Brian bent over and held each knee in place, seeing if they still could function.

"Where's Darryl?" Jack asked him. "And Kenny?"

"I've got to help my family," came his voice from up in the tree. "I'll try to get Darryl to a hospital."

"Thanks!" Brian called out to him. "He's our best friend. And thank your dad."

Climbing back up, Kenny was already a blur amongst the branches. "Suerte!"

"Fuck." Jack wasn't happy. "I knew Darryl wasn't getting on that rope."

The three of them were digesting the news, when Brian felt the first few raindrops falling from the sky, leaf to leaf to him. "It's raining," he announced, as if he had a knack for such discoveries.

The rain began to drum the ground, at first slow and deliberate, then building to a consistent pitter-patter. "What do we do now?" asked Jack.

"We get wet," replied Brian.

"I get that part," he said, "but—"

Lita put a finger to her lips for the guys to be quiet and then, without an obvious path to follow, began to lead them through a web of seemingly impenetrable jungle. Brian made a mental note; escaping slowly, not as satisfying as escaping quickly.

He paused and looked back, the path they'd forged past jumbo leaves and pesky vines already closing off again, making it hard for Brian to discern if anyone was following them, man or beast.

"Um, Lita, what about snakes?" he asked. "Should we be worried, I mean, are there any snakes out here?"

"Yes, there are snakes," said Lita. "Many snakes."

Jack gave Brian a dirty look. "Why'd you have to ask her that?"

"I believe she's making a point," replied Brian.

"You don't have to worry," she told them.

Brian looked over at Jack. "See, it's better to ask."

"Unless," said Lita, "we meet big snake, then it is okay to worry."

"That's not funny," Brian told her. "You shouldn't joke about snakes."

She stopped walking, motioning for Brian to go first. "Who say I was joking?"

Brian reluctantly forged ahead. "Aren't you?"

"Maybe we should be keep it down," said Jack. "They might hear us."

"Snakes don't hear, not like we do," Brian told him. "They feel."

"I was talking about whoever came knocking on Kenny's door." Jack brushed Brian aside and took up the lead, trying to clear some resemblance of a path with the butt of the Walther.

Brian let Jack do his thing and eventually the rain let up but after an hour or so of getting nowhere, he had to ask, "Do you know where you're going by any chance?"

Jack was curt. "Same way she was."

"To the beach." Lita pointed toward a break in the clouds, where the sun was already shining down at an afternoon angle. "We can find help there."

Brian felt the need to make sure they were all on the same page. "A car to the airport would be very helpful."

"Dos carros," said Lita, seemingly sniffing out an exit from the jungle.

"What?" asked Jack. "Why dos?"

"Cabuya Road will take us to other side of peninsula," she replied. "But from there it is faster to mainland by boat."

"And then to San Jose?" asked Brian.

"Sí, car number two." She pushed aside the brush to reveal a gravel parking lot in the back of a roadside market. "Estamos aquí."

Brian had a look at the few cars in the lot, then to Jack. "I don't see any red Jeeps."

"Not at the moment." Jack reached on top of his head for— "Damnit, you know I lost my hat back there."

Wanting to keep him as calm as possible, Brian made sure to strike a sympathetic chord. "Yeah, sucks."

"Just because I had it for a short time doesn't mean I didn't care about it." Jack pulled a soggy crumpled cigarette from behind his ear. "Sorry, I need to think."

"A cigarette helps?" asked Brian, delicately.

"Sure fucking does," said Jack, hell-bent on lighting it.

Brian didn't see how that was possible but for Jack's sake remained positive. "Okay."

Once he got his water-logged lighter working, Jack ran the flame from one end of the cigarette to other, trying to dry it out and straighten it, then made several frustratingly unsuccessful attempts to light it, followed by several more.

Just when Brian thought it was taking too long, Jack somehow succeeded in getting it lit. And a few fidgety puffs later, his eyes went big, his interest sparked by a man in a University of Iowa tank-top.

He was around fifty, in decent shape, with a carefree mop of salt and pepper hair and a deep dark tan, like he was on permanent vacation.

Organizing his groceries in a leather shoulder-bag, he was

headed for the road, unaware that Jack was hustling after him, cigarette clinging to his lips.

"What're you doing?" Brian called out to Jack. "Stop!"

But Jack kept going, pointing to a tattoo on the man's back, which Brian recognized right away:

The familiar blue circle.

The red *C* inside it.

The *ubs* inside that.

The man crossed the road, joining a beautiful brunette, similar in age and almost as tan. She was in cut-off jeans and a Cheap Trick t-shirt, leaning against a motorcycle with a helmet under her arm.

She took a drink from a hole in the top of a green coconut, then held it out to the man, offering him some, "Pipa?"

"No straw?"

"Don't need it."

He gave her a kiss, "Nice one, honey," and took the coconut from her.

Brian turned his attention back to Jack, suddenly aware of what he was up to, while the couple put on matching red helmets, vintage ones with the number *74* emblazoned across the side in white.

Jack approached them. "Excuse me, I don't mean to interrupt but I saw your tattoo." He held his cigarette behind his back. "Your Cub tattoo. World Champions. Can you believe it? A rain delay of all things."

"Yeah," smiled the man, the boy in him bubbling to the surface. "One hundred and eight years of drought ended by seventeen minutes of rain."

The brunette took off her helmet, then spoke to the stranger, a note of skepticism in her voice. "You're from Chicago?"

"Sorry." He reached out to shake her hand. "I'm Jack."

"Angie." She looked at Jack's hand for a moment before

deciding to shake it, then nodded to, "Doug."

"Doug, Angie, nice to meet you," said Jack. "Yes, we're from Chicago."

Doug gave him the thumbs up. "Right on."

"To be straight with you," continued Jack, "we're in a bit of a jam, a big jam actually, in a hurry too, and we could really use a motorcycle."

Angie took the keys out of the ignition. "Our motorcycle?"

Jack shifted his approach. "You didn't just come from Mike's place, did you? We're friends of his, Kenny too."

"We know Mike and Sam," was all she would give him.

"I knew it," said Jack, snapping his fingers. "We'd get a bike ourselves if we had time but we need to keep a low profile. Seriously, this is life, death, code red, a real emergency. My buddy and his girlfriend, fiancé really, they're in trouble." Jack waved over Brian and Lita.

"It's not ours to just give away," Angie told him, eying Brian's mangled nose. "We rented it."

"We're heading up the coast," added Doug, "all the way to the border."

"Did you get it here in town?" asked Jack.

"Uh. . ." Doug removed his helmet, hesitant to respond. "Yeah."

"Great, rent another one. Please." Jack put a pile of cash in Doug's hand. "That should be more than enough for a rental."

"I'm sure it's close," said Doug, casually sorting the money. "But I don't get the feeling you're going to return the bike."

"And it's on my Chase card," said Angie.

"Okay, well thanks, worth a try," mumbled Brian, ready to walk away.

But Jack stopped him. "Give her your plastic."

"Really?" Brian wiped his bloody nose with the back of his

hand.

"Trust me, I got an idea," Jack told him. "And your nose. Can't you do something about that?"

"It's broken." Brian took his one and only credit card out of his wallet and handed it to Angie. "I don't feel any better having done that."

Jack ignored him. "Give me the money back and put the bike on his card, switch it over," he told the couple, "and then use it to rent yourself another one."

"What do we do with your card?" asked Angie, as Doug returned the cash. "Just leave it there?"

"No, for your inconvenience, take it wherever you're going," replied Jack. "Buy dinner, get a place to stay, whatever you like."

"Um, Jack." Brian took off his polo and held it against his nose to soak up the blood. "Are you sure about this? Won't we need it?"

"Use the card until Sunday," Jack continued with them, "and then tear it up and throw it away."

"Why Sunday?" asked Angie.

Jack took a quick drag off his cigarette. "Because if we're not home by then we might never be."

"You sound desperate," said Doug.

Brian blew his bloody nose into his shirt, as much for cause as effect. "We are."

But Angie still wasn't sold. "You didn't kill anyone, did you?"

"Not exactly," said Brian.

"She was kidding," Doug told him. "Kind of."

Brian thought they'd lost them but Jack persisted. "We're innocent. We just don't wanna spend the rest of our lives trying to prove it."

"Brian is good man," said Lita, soft but with conviction, prompting Angie to ask her a couple of questions in Spanish.

Then, apparently satisfied, Angie turned back to the guys. "You're really from Chicago?"

"Suburbs," admitted Brian.

"And die-hard Cub fans?" asked Doug.

"Yeah, of course," said Jack. "Let's play two, try not to suck, fly the W."

"Tinker to Evers to Chance," threw in Brian for good measure.

Angie took it upon herself to have a closer look at Brian's nose and, clearly concerned, handed him several tissues from Doug's bag. "I take it you're in love with her?"

"Um. . ." All eyes on him, Brian surprised himself with his ease of admission. "Yes, definitely, but I'm new at it."

Angie put the motorcycle keys in his hand. "If you're lucky enough to find true love, you hold on to it. Tight."

"Thanks." Brian started to shake Angie's hand but hugged her instead, Doug too. "Thank you. Really."

"We're keeping the helmets, though," said Doug. "They were a present."

Angie kissed Doug and the two of them set off on foot toward the beach, arm in arm, like it was just another night in Costa Rica. . .

Jack took a final drag and tossed his cigarette to the ground. "He shoots, he scores!"

"I appreciate your enthusiasm," said Brian, stamping out the butt, "but how is not having a credit card going to help us get home?"

"Those two are heading north," said Jack. "If Ivan gets the police involved, your bank records will have them thinking you're making a run for Nicaragua."

"I guess."

"And with Darryl on his way to a hospital, that's two reasons for San Jose not to be at the top of their list."

"Okay." Brian threw his blood soaked polo in a garbage

can.

Meanwhile, Jack squatted like a baseball catcher, looking over the Honda as if he knew it from a Suzuki. “When’s the last time you rode something like this, Bri?”

“Can’t remember.” Brian straddled the motorcycle. “Jamaica?” He turned the key in the ignition and spun the throttle, revving the engine. “You’re not coming, are you?”

“I’ve got a better chance of helping us if we split up.” He gave Brian his cellphone. “Give me yours. Charger too. Same idea as the credit card. Throw off the scent.”

Brian ceded his phone and charger, not completely comfortable to take possession of a flip-phone. “What about our passports?”

Jack reached into his pants, “Sorry,” and removed Brian and Lita’s, the marriage documents too, “Just in case,” and handed all of it over.

Brian started to give Lita her passport but she shook her head, so he stuffed everything in his shirt, then realized that like Darryl he might not see Jack for a while, maybe ever. “This sucks.”

“Majorly.” Jack handed him the cash they’d rounded up, keeping as little as possible for himself. “Just know me and Darryl love you.”

“Find him,” said Brian. “Get him home.”

“We’ll be drinking a cold one by sundown,” Jack told him. “Anything happens to you, just pretend you’re on a TV show.”

“I knew it,” said Brian. “You’re channeling Magnum again.”

“Of course, I am,” said Jack. “Look at the dude, he got to catch bad guys in Hawaii.”

Brian revved the engine again. “I guess we should go.”

Lita kissed Jack on the cheek, “Adios, crazy man,” and got on back of the motorcycle.

"Wait." Jack handed him the Walther.

But Brian wouldn't take it. "You never told me how you and Darryl got away from those bearded guys, I mean, did you have to . . . kill anyone?"

"No, but I can't say I didn't try." Jack held the gun out to him again. "Now take it."

"I don't know. Sounds dangerous."

"That's the point," said Jack. "There's only one bullet left anyway."

Lita took the gun from Jack and tucked it in her blouse, muzzle first, held firm between her breasts. "Vamos."

"Take care of that heart of yours," Brian told him. "You promise?"

"Of course," smiled Jack, shifting his eyes toward Lita. "And you take care of yours."

Rattled, Brian turned the throttle too hard while kicking the bike into gear and took off unexpectedly with a jolt; tires spinning, treads spitting out dirt.

The motorcycle felt like a wild animal beneath him, bucking and fighting, and Brian unintentionally popped a wheelie, Lita almost falling off the back.

Luckily, and that's all it was, he regained control of the bike before he could do something really foolish and settled into a comfortable, albeit slow clip, leaving Jack behind as the two of them ventured down the lumpy, bumpy, jungle road. . . .

First Darryl. Now Jack. It all seemed so abrupt to Brian. No last suppers. No final toasts. Not even a farewell fist bump. He was on his own now with Lita, hoping to make it from one side of the peninsula to the other, as a team of stars took their rightful positions in the evening sky.

Brian drove them down a narrow road, one that cut through a long deep valley, lush in jungle, like a cocoon, allowing him to focus on keeping the motorcycle upright, which he'd tell you was easier said than done.

Except for the stars, it was dark, street lights being few and far between. And having recently rained, the road was a mess, making it hard to distinguish between puddle and pothole. Plus, he just so happened to be carrying the most precious cargo of his life—Lita!

And even though he felt like he'd unearthed some of his manly side for her, where action supposedly took precedence over words, he knew he should say something about what he admitted to Doug and Angie.

Several rounds of internal deliberations later, Brian turned his head to the side, so she could hear him. "About what I. . . Uh. . . About how long will it take us to reach the coast?"

It sure looked like she was moving her lips but Brian still couldn't hear a thing out of his left ear, so he turned his head the other way for a response to his question.

"Tus ojos," she said, pointing ahead of them. "Eyes with road."

He did as he was told. "How long?"

"Siempre, forever."

"No, I mean, how long until we hit water?"

"With you driving. . ." She paused, as if giving it genuine thought. "Todo el día."

Brian looked over his shoulder to see if she was just teasing him.

"All day," she translated.

"I got it the first time." He pulled the motorcycle over to the side of the road and got off, more wary of the time than embarrassed. "I take it you've ridden before?"

She ignored the question and, hands on her hips, asked one of her own. "Love?"

"I didn't know what to say."

"You say, *love*."

"Before you jumped off the roof, you kissed me."

"Sí, I think maybe I die."

"Hmmm, I figured that was the case."

She handed Brian the sack and scooched up on the motorcycle, patting the seat behind her.

And Brian got on. "By the way, I meant to pop a wheelie back there."

"Papa who?"

"Forget it."

"You are confusing for me."

Brian thought he detected a smile. "Where do I hold on?"

Lita hit the clutch, quick but under control. "Where would you like?" Then, without waiting for an answer, she took off down the road at breakneck speed. . .

Brian held her tight, he had to, locking his hands around her waist. This woman, this unbelievably divine woman set his world on fire. His brain. His body. *Down boy*!

He thought about pulling a safety before the trip, to clean the tanks, since he doubted he'd find any privacy with the guys around. Even at forty, Brian did the five-knuckle shuffle two or three times a week, for medicinal reasons he would tell you rather than youthful lust; basically, so he could concentrate at work.

However, he wasn't sure if he could keep up with the guys without clips in the barrel, so like a prize fighter, he abstained.

And now, brimming with passion, Brian found himself right behind Lita with an engine humming between their legs, trying desperately to suppress any burgeoning feelings by steering his thoughts elsewhere, like small rooms with bars over the windows.

It was hard to ignore her though, especially with her windblown hair slapping his face, as if demanding his attention.

She began talking in rapid fashion about Ivan, and how she suspected that he wasn't paying the taxes on the Bamboo House with the money she'd given him.

Cruising that fast along the road, it was difficult for Brian to pick up everything she said, but the gist of it was that without her permission Ivan spent her husband's money on several bad business deals; namely buying beachfront land for a hotel, only to find out that he couldn't get a concession to build within 150 meters of the water.

Ivan, she claimed, was why the Bamboo House fell into debt, though he lied to the court, saying that though he felt the house was justly his, he would bail her out and take over the property—with a small loan.

She said Ivan owed some bad people a lot of money, that they may have been responsible for her husband's death.

Then, seemingly out of nowhere, she started in on Brian, telling him that *no*, she wasn't in love with him. Nor did she really know him. But she reiterated that he was kind and handsome and even used the word sexy.

Unfortunately, before Brian could properly bask in her words, Lita was theorizing that whoever showed up at Mike's house, whether it be Ivan or the police, no one would expect them to head for the outskirts of Cabo Blanco.

If you were in a hurry, you'd go through bigger towns, she said, with better roads, like Cobano to Tambor, where they'd have the option of a boat to Puntarenas or a short flight to San Jose, not the extra time it took them to cover the miles of rolling hills bordering the national park.

Still, it was peaceful, he thought. And the weather, Brian loved it, because as in his dream there wasn't any; not cold enough to catch a chill or hot enough to break into a sweat, just an impartial breeze shielded by Lita's soft warm body.

He found his balance on the back of the bike, letting go of

Lita long enough to raise his arms above his head in celebration. An all-out victory, no, but certainly a win.

With Lita at the helm, they made up time, the rugged dirt road eventually leveling out and taking them into Cabuya, a remote village on the southeast coast of the peninsula.

They drove past the usual suspects; Lita pointing out *la bomba* (a gas station), *la panadería* (a bakery), and *la soda* (a small restaurant), with the compulsory Imperial sign hanging outside.

Brian spotted a couple of kids drinking orange sodas outside the market and a shadowy path promising a hotel. There were also signs for a yoga retreat and a guide company offering horseback rides.

But that was about it. They were in and out of town in under a minute, Lita riding them right up to the beach, where they were alone, except for a few fishermen cleaning out their nets.

Lita got off the motorcycle. "Now we wait."

"For what?"

"For the tide to go out." Lita pointed to a tiny plot of land about a hundred yards off shore, just visible in the dark. "Then we can walk to island, find a place to sleep."

"Walk?" He took a second look. "To an island?"

"Sí."

"Oh." He wasn't exactly sold. "What's it called?"

"Isle de Cabuya." Lita took off her sandals, digging her toes into the sand, like she missed it. "But some name it Cemetery Island."

"That's not very inviting," said Brian. "Why'd they name it that?"

"Because it is cemetery."

16

Go On Take The Money And Run

Shortly after they arrived in Cabuya, Lita went back into town to get them something to eat and drink. Meanwhile, Brian, if he was being totally honest, was thinking about leaving, about bailing on her. What if Ivan was right? What if Lita really was a hurricane, destroying everyone in her path?

Brian imagined running over to the fishermen, confessing everything. He'd tell them he was confused. Something cultural. That he was a good guy. Meant no harm.

He held fast though. And true. To her. He was just testing himself. Putting his feelings for Lita on trial—yet again. He took a deep breath, then tried to expel any unwanted ramblings from his head.

And here she was, walking down the beach. To him. Holding a bottle of water and some kind of green, football-shaped fruit that looked more like a dinosaur egg.

Brian knew she could've just as easily taken off on the motorcycle, accused him of everything. She even had an out:

Jack had harassed her on Instagram, then showed up at Nogui's. Where Brian stalked her and followed her to Monkey Bar. They got kicked out of one place. Pressured her to find another. Wouldn't pay their bill. Robbed her beloved father-in-law. Killed her amiga Roxy. And kidnapped her!

Brian was good at digressing, too good, so he was distracted when he let Lita walk past when surely a hug from him was in order.

She sat in the sand under the evening shadow of a palm tree and took a sip of water. "Nobody say anything to me."

He sat down next to her. "Pardon?"

She handed him the bottle, then got up and sat on the opposite side of him to speak into his good ear. "In town, no problema."

"Oh." He flipped the cover on Jack's phone, trying to make it look cool, and discovered it was at 11%, good for a few texts, maybe an emergency call. He showed it to Lita. "Of course Jack gives me a phone that isn't charged. Can I use yours?"

"Maybe police use phone to find us."

"It's possible."

"Who do you want to call?"

He let the question linger, though Darryl would've been at the top of his list. He didn't mind her being paranoid though, not a bad trait to have when your life's at stake.

Brian told her if they ever got caught, he was going to blame everything on Trump. Seriously. The insanity plea, also known as *Cheat, Lie, Deny*. "The guy's loco," said Brian. "Moo-wee."

Lita laughed, bashfully placing her hand over her mouth, as if it wasn't appropriate given the dire circumstances. Of course, he wasn't sure how much she was just humoring him.

Didn't matter though. He'd made her smile, which made him proud in a way, like he had really accomplished something worthwhile.

Lita pulled out a pocketknife he didn't know she had and cut into the fruit's soft white flesh. "Guanabana," she called it, giving him a chunk.

He had no idea what he was in for but its insides smelled like a pineapple, its texture looked like a banana, and its taste he likened to a mix of sour apples and strawberries . . . and damn good, which didn't surprise Lita, who was already handing him another piece.

However, knowing their faces were probably plastered all over the TV and internet, he could barely eat.

She motioned to the sky. "Osa Major y Osa Pequeño."

Brian looked up and found what she was talking about. "Ahh. . . Big Dipper and Little Dipper."

She pointed to the Little Dipper, to its brightest star. "Estrella del norte."

"Yes, the North Star, or sometimes we just call it Polaris."

"Does it shine brighter in Chicago," asked Lita, "because you are closer?"

"I don't know." He took her hand and kept it in his. "We'll have to take a look someday, um, from my backyard."

"I would like that." Her voice tapered off and she put the future on hold, recounting how she made it to town, that she had no idea where she was going when she ran into Kenny.

Brian mentioned the fire dancer, he felt he had to, and Lita was clearly bothered when he did, not like she was mad at him but because it weighed on her so heavily, even though she said she'd do it again to save him.

She was determined to clear her name though, or at least justify her actions, for her daughters, so they could have a normal life, without shame. The house was one thing, she admitted, but Lucia and Ariana were everything.

"Mi corazón." Lita placed her hand over her chest, which Brian was intrigued by, before realizing that she was referring to her heart.

The girls were fathered back in Nicaragua by her first husband, who she said was a good man, just not the man for her. He was older, settled, and she was just nineteen. Anyway, he also died, not long after Ariana was born, though she once again omitted the all-important how.

She said men were, “mala suerte, bad luck.”

Brian made his *huh?* face, unsure if she meant men were bad luck or she had bad luck with men.

So she made herself clear: “I do not need a man. I need husband.”

“But I’m not a citizen. How can I help you with the Bamboo House?”

“I want to sell it, take my daughters to America. With Ivan aquí, they are no safe.”

“Oh.”

“I want to start over with them, somewhere they have chance.”

Brian couldn’t get a word out; too many of them were competing for his attention.

“Are you mad at me?” she asked.

“No, I’m just, I appreciate you being straight with me.” Still, it hurt, like maybe he was just a pawn, but then she scooted closer, so that they were almost touching, and looked at him with those big brown eyes.

It wasn’t until after midnight that the tide began to recede, gradually revealing a walkway of rock and coral straight out to the island. However, it was slippery and full of holes, so Brian extended his hand, as much for his sake as hers, and she took it with the kind of natural ease that warmed his soul.

A white stone archway, a dozen feet high, greeted them ashore, the word *cementerio* carved across the top. Then, beyond that, a dirt path led them through a garden of agave plants, palm trees, and graves.

The island was empty, except for the dead, some buried in

coffin size tombs adorned with shells, others laid to rest with just a cross in the sand.

Lita took the lead, turning one way and another until she found a place to her liking. “I am tired,” she told him.

“Me too.” Brian knew he couldn’t sleep though. He was exhausted, of course, but he was too stressed out about their next move, assuming they had one.

So, he just watched as Lita got down on her hands and knees and smoothed out a bed of sand, removing a few twigs and leaves. “Are you coming?” she asked.

“Uh, where? To sleep?”

She laid down on her side.

He was nervous. “I’ll watch.”

“Me?”

“No, I mean, yes, but I was thinking about whoever may be after us.”

“Gracias, Brian.” She patted the sand behind her, like she’d done the motorcycle seat. “Come.”

Brian relented and spooned her, less than an inch from her. However, Lita scratched her ankle like she’d been bit, slightly altering her position, and he had contact.

Ahh, the simple things in life. I’ll rest when I’m dead, he told himself. Then again, that would be a rest he couldn’t wake up from.

That’s how his heroes lived though, big screen idols like Willis and Schwarzenegger, or even The Flu Game when a feverish Jordan put up 38 points in a pivotal playoff win at Utah.

Brian remembered the guys packed in his garage to watch the game, the last time it was all seven of them, playing basketball in the driveway during the commercials.

He wanted badly to go back home. Was that too much to ask? Though, even if they did make it to the States, wouldn't Costa Rica just ask for them back?

Across the water, he could see a sprinkle of lights in Cabuya, mostly homes, he figured, as the town shut down for the night, free of any commotion; for example, a manhunt.

He wondered, hoped really, that he was worrying for nothing. That whoever showed up at Kenny's was merely relaying good news. Even no news. Maybe no one was after them. Maybe they were in the clear.

But then what? If they weren't being chased, there was no need to run. However, it would really suck to mistakenly give up, especially if they had a lead. Yet, if they did keep running, even as a precaution, didn't that imply some level of guilt?

Brian woke up, surprised that he'd fallen asleep, and reacquainted himself with the island, the cemetery, the death all around him.

He imagined his own grave, suddenly concerned with where he'd be buried. Sue would want to bring his body home and lay him to rest with their mom. And dad, not wanting to upset her, would back her up on this.

Jack, of course, would tack the other way. His idea of honoring Brian would be to bury him where he was finally living out his dreams—in Costa Rica.

Brian thought Jack's idea was perfect. Romantic even. He'd be a legend in Evanston. Tourists would seek out his headstone, like Jim Morrison in Paris.

Why such adulation, you ask? Well, Brian was becoming more and more determined to go down in a blaze of glory. Yes, he saw *Young Guns* in his formative years, age eleven to be precise, so he had to ask himself, why take one lethal bullet when he could take a hundred?

Besides, at least three other people were possibly dead, which meant he had to come to terms with there being more to come, percentage-wise. Meanwhile, his head was aching, the pain emanating from three distinct sources.

He touched the bridge of his nose, reluctantly acknowledging the new and probably permanent bump on it, then felt for the knob on the back of his head, which owed its existence to gravity and, of course, the coconut. Finally, he reached for his ear but was unable to get to it under the make-shift bandage, which was matted to his scalp.

And that's when it him. *Fuck.* Lita was gone. He jumped to his feet in a defensive stance, probing a darkness just hinting at dawn, and looked around. She'd left him. With nothing. Sack. Gun. Everything. Gone. Even Jack's phone. Only the ring remained.

He promptly followed their footsteps in the sand back to the entrance at the arch, the mainland waiting for him a football field away, though without any trace of a path leading back to it.

The tide was in. He'd have to swim. But was he going after her? Or going on his own? He didn't have to answer that question though, seeing as he heard someone just past a row of ferns.

Brian pulled back a giant leaf to find Lita kneeling in the sand beside a headstone, speaking softly in Spanish.

When she saw him she made the sign of the cross and stood up, explaining, "I could not sleep last night."

"Oh."

"I was talking to mi abuela."

"That's her, uh, this is where she's buried?"

"Sí."

"I'm sorry."

"Do not be sorry."

"My family, we go to my mother's grave every Thanksgiving, you know, leave flowers. I don't know why I said mother. I mean, my mom. She was definitely the mom type."

Lita picked up the sack, brushing white sand off the black

velvet with the back of her hand. "When we move to Montezuma, we live with mi abuela and she help me with the girls when I am working. Before they leave for school, she want the girls in her room to see that their hair is combed and their clothes are clean. But when she become sick, she get angry and do not want anyone in her room. The girls would not listen. Todo las dias, they go in and help her change into clean clothes and comb her hair. And then, one day, she just smile at them . . . and die."

"That's, that's beautiful." Brian knew right then and there that he'd be buried on Cemetery Island, because he was planning to spend the rest of his life with this woman—or die trying.

Lita would insist that he be buried next to her grandmother. And when she came to visit, she'd leave him a cold beer, perhaps say something endearing to him in Spanish about how he was her heart, her hero.

Then again, she was the one who saved his life back at the Bamboo House. He should be thanking her, but when he started to do so—

She interrupted him, almost like she knew what he was going to say. "We can wait for the tide to go out this morning or we can get wet."

Brian knew there was plenty of living to do, so prior to the town waking up and wondering who spent the night out on the island, the answer was to swim to shore.

"Cuidado." She gave Brian the sack. "Be careful."

"Um, yeah, by the way, have you seen Jack's phone?"

The flip-phone was in the sack with the rest of the stuff. Lita said she checked it to see if someone had tried to reach them. At some point, Brian knew he'd have to quit doubting her. She'd gone into his pocket to get the phone. She could've easily taken the diamond ring.

Maybe she left it because she still wanted him to give it to her. Or, his doubts proposed, maybe the ring was a fake, not worth the trouble.

Fed up with his utter lack of faith, he put her ring on his pinky and raised the sack over his head and without removing his shoes and socks or even his pants, walked straight into the ocean. . .

So, in dawn's earliest light, Lita followed him for a change, perhaps mistaking his frustration for courage. . .

The water was deep enough that they had to swim, forcing Brian to hold the sack on his head with one hand and paddle with the other. The current was being quite pushy too, giving Brian got a scare, and it took over ten minutes before they were able to touch their feet to the bottom and trudge the rest of the way to the beach.

When they reached the road, Lita went to give him what looked like a congratulatory kiss on the cheek, however, Brian instinctively turned his head, giving her a quick but proper kiss on the lips. "Sorry, I think maybe I die."

Proud of himself, he was still smiling when they took off on the bike, continuing north along the coast. But they hadn't gone very far when she pulled over to admire a tree, easily the most enormous tree Brian had ever seen, at least width-wise.

"Higuerón de Cabuya," said Lita. "That is what the locals call it."

Though he felt more like a fugitive than a tourist, Brian nodded his head, taking in the tree's multiple trunks and interwoven branches. He figured it had to be close to seventy feet around and almost twice that in height.

"Some people say it is banyan tree, or Matapalo," she continued, "but I think you say fig."

"I guess, probably a strangler fig."

"Mi abuela told me it is biggest tree in all of Costa Rica."

"Cool."

"The tree means we are close."

"To where?"

"To Montezuma," she said, getting back on the motorcycle. "There, we will look for boat to Jacó."

"You don't think we should keep riding?"

"No, yesterday, because we go long way, we can go short way now."

"Okay, yeah." Brian got back on the bike and wrapped his arms around her, this time before she'd even turned on the engine. "I, uh, just wanted you to know that I appreciate what you said about me last night. And what you didn't. It was honest and flattering and well. . ." Brian was caught off guard by his own candor but decided to keep going. "Just so you know, I really do think I love you."

I love you. It felt fantastic to get those three words out. And mean it. It'd been years. Since Jenny. Sure, he could have thought it through a little longer before making such a bold proclamation but it wasn't necessary. He felt it.

As for Lita, she may have felt something for him too, but she said nothing. Perhaps, she was screaming for joy on the inside, thought Brian, or she'd heard it all before.

She had turned away before he finished speaking, focusing instead on starting the bike, as if not seeing him say those words made it less necessary to reply.

And Brian was fine with that. He said what he wanted to say. And they were moving again, even if questionable road conditions were slowing them down.

Meanwhile, the sun was rising over the water, forcing Brian to cup his hands above his eyes to get a glimpse of the mainland, which proved too far to see.

He knew from the map he had googled on the plane that they could keep going by land to San Jose, up and around the bay, but Lita seemed fixated on going by boat.

And since the shortest distance between two points was still a straight line, Brian had no reason to argue with her. He realized, however, that Montezuma was located toward the bottom of the peninsula, at the entrance to the bay, so crossing to Jacó would mean getting out on the open ocean.

Not long after the fig tree, they crossed a river, Rio Lajas, then ten minutes later Rio Montezuma, where Lita stopped the motorcycle once more to play guide.

She pointed up river into the jungle, describing a series of beautiful waterfalls where she took her daughters when they were little.

Interested, Brian got off the bike to have a better look. "Must've been fun." But Lita was already heading back across the road, where several bungalows were tucked into a garden of orchids, just off the ocean.

Brian realized it was a hotel and read the sign out front: "Amor de Mar." Easy as it sounded, he didn't dare translate it out loud and risk screwing things up with her. He just knew it had something to do with love and the ocean, a winning combo as far as he was concerned.

Lita smiled as if she understood what he was thinking, at least that was Brian's interpretation, then led him around the side of the first bungalow so he could get a look at the view.

She stopped on a well-manicured lawn, the grass full and green, like a football field; one sideline the orchids, the other a battlefield of lava rocks rising out of the ocean.

Hmmm. . . Brian marveled at the setting, romantic dreams in his head, beginning with a hammock strung between two palm trees.

There was even a swing by the water's edge, practically beckoning them. Pushing your girlfriend on a swing was a rite of passage for lovers, thought Brian, the whole of the twentieth century. Now what? Showing each other how the latest app works?

“We will get a room,” Lita told him, abruptly heading back to the front of the hotel.

“What?” Brian was right behind her, “Great, I mean—”

“But no stay.”

“Huh? No stay. Why?”

“We can stay with my friend.”

“Then why are we. . .” started Brian. “Oh, I get it. I think.”

“We will leave the motorcycle.”

“Right, so if someone comes looking for us, we’re making it easy for them. They’ll think we’re in the room. All we have to do is stay away from the hotel, then call reception and ask if we’ve had any visitors.”

Lita stopped outside the lobby door. “You have done this before?”

“No, of course not, just, it’s a good move. Usually you don’t know if someone’s found you until you get caught.”

Lita nodded her head in agreement, though appeared to be still processing the idea as they walked inside.

Behind the front desk was a young Tica in a comfy chair, reading a book by Bonnie Jo Campbell, one apparently so good that she didn’t bother stopping when they came in, the words, “Bienvenida,” barely escaping her mouth.

Lita spoke to her with a sense of urgency in Spanish, to which the girl dog-eared the page she was on and welcomed them again, this time with a smile.

Whether that smile was forced or not, Brian wasn’t sure, so he tried to pick off a couple of words from the back and forth that followed.

Brian could only hope that ten years from now he’d know everything they were saying, maybe even chime in, hopefully because he was living with Lita in Chicago, not bunking with a Tico at the lockdown hotel.

As for now, he got relatively nothing from the

conversation, however, he did learn the word for key, *llave (ya-vay),* which, attached to a rope, the girl placed around Brian's neck, as if she suspected he might lose it.

Lita told him it was ninety dollars for the room, that he should pay for three nights, which the girl used a calculator to show them was about ₡160,000.00 colones.

"I've got dollars if that's okay," said Brian, paying her straight from the sack without much discretion. He didn't feel it was necessary to be overly covert with the girl, that they'd rather she was on to them in case she heard something, so that she could warn them, whether she meant to help them or not.

17

Montezuma's Revenge

Brian wouldn't have known it at the time but Montezuma was one of Costa Rica's original tourist hot spots, coming of age in the 1980s with backpackers, nature lovers, retirees, rock stars, and a famous actor or two.

In addition, it had gained a coveted spot on the western hemisphere's version of the Hippy Trail; a must-do destination for any seasoned traveler looking to get off the beaten track for an extended period of time, joining the likes of Kathmandu, Bangkok, and Goa on the other side of the world.

Brian and Lita were in the room long enough to put out the Do Not Disturb sign, then snuck across the road and picked up a path, crisscrossing the river several times over rocky, ankle-deep water.

However, just as he was getting comfortable with the terrain, the water grew stronger, the path steeper, giving Lita reason to stop and assess their next move.

He thought it might be a good time to take her hand again, but she calmly removed her sandals and took off; deftly maneuvering over the rocks barefoot, leaping from one to the other, a regular Tarzan to Brian's Jane.

Brian was impressed. Downright besotted, in fact, and he wanted to take a picture of her. So, disregarding the low battery, he reached into the sack for the phone—then recoiled, like he'd frightened himself.

He didn't need to take pictures when they went swimsuit shopping. Or surfing. And he hadn't even thought about it at the wedding. He was beginning to realize that the only way to truly capture a moment was to be completely in it.

He knew that, of course, and was quite good at it when he was younger; able to totally immerse himself in a game of cards or wiffle ball, thinking about nothing but wiffle ball: *Strike three! See ya! Take a seat!*

Therefore, with the morning sun warming his back, Brian ran after her, up into the jungle, jumping from rock to rock, busy being present, and as Jack promised, being rewarded for his efforts.

Not how he imagined it but living life to the fullest nonetheless. Just how long that life was expected to last, he wasn't sure, though he realized that was most likely part of the bargain.

She stopped just ahead of him, rather abruptly pretended Brian, so he could wrap his arms around her waist from behind. "Excuse me. I didn't see you there."

She squirmed playfully, then rested her hands on his over her stomach, nodding in front of them. "Mira."

Brian tore his eyes from her, getting a load of the waterfall up ahead. Tall. Beautiful. It was stunning, really. Que the music.

Though while Brian was dreaming of the perfect John Williams score, Lita wriggled free of his grasp, which worried him, less so when she began removing her blouse one anxious button at a time.

She stopped halfway to take off her jeans, lowering them

over the curve in her hips, a bit of a struggle to it, as if she didn't already have his attention.

Transfixed, he watched as she stood before a palatial pool of water in just her bra and panties; white lace ones, each with a tiny bow front and center to greet him.

And though covering more skin than her bikini, he somehow found this ensemble sexier, like being out of place made it more risqué.

Eyes closed, Lita lifted her chin to the sky, praying to the Sun Gods, thought Brian, who got down to his swimsuit in mere seconds and joined her at the water's edge.

Lita smiled at him, as if pleased that he was keeping up, then walked into the water until it was deep enough and dove in. . .

He wanted to swim after her, to hold her and squeeze her and kiss her but instead lowered himself underwater, allowing his tired head to soak.

The bandage unraveled on its own beneath the surface, liberating his damaged ear, and the cool water soothed his wounds, but he had to come up for air rather quickly when he realized he couldn't breathe through his nose anymore.

That was worrisome but spotting Lita, he swam after her, fast as he could. . .

And she caught him, a mesh of arms and legs.

He thought he should say something witty or romantic but couldn't come up with the right words, so he kissed her instead, hard on the mouth.

And she kissed him back, her tongue finding his for several hot seconds before she pulled away, as if coming to a revelation. "Tengo hambre."

Brian wasn't sure but it sounded like, "You have a man?"

"No," she said, heading for shore. "I am hungry."

They got dressed and climbed the far side of the waterfall, up high into the jungle, which was becoming wet and muddy. Along the way, Lita pointed out a couple of cock-shaped mushrooms, as if Brian might learn something from them, though she never slowed down, using her toes like talons to grip the earth, while he slipped again and again.

Then, out of nowhere as far as he was concerned, they came upon a utopian compound complete with butterfly sanctuary, micro-brewery, restaurant, and bed & breakfast; officially the Mariposario Montezuma Gardens.

Lita went straight for the restaurant, Cocina Clandestina, finding a table just out of reach of the sun, across from a few backpackers talking in morning mumbles.

When an earthy young woman with a pixie blond hair-do came over, Lita wasted little time ordering, "Tacos Callejeros."

"Does that have meat in it?" asked Brian, taking the waitress for an English speaker.

She smiled sympathetically. "Usually, but if you like, we can do a veggie one."

Brian wanted desperately to confide in her, tell her that he once ate meat, gain her trust, then reveal their deep dark secret in the hope that she could fix it for them:

Don't worry about it, she'd say, *my dad works for the State Department.*

And he's got his own plane.

He could have you home in a day, sitting at the counter at Sarkis.

She never could've known about Sarkis though, how the guys ate breakfast there before school senior year. Brian had gone too far, taking his fantasy about getting out of the country and ruining it.

"Which one is your favorite?" he asked her.

"The pork," replied the waitress, practically licking her lips.

He thought about that movie, the one where the plane full of soccer players crashes in the mountains and they have to eat each other to stay alive. If he couldn't eat a pig or a cow now, how was he going to eat the elderly lady in the window seat?

Fed up with the confusion. . . the ridicule. . . "Fuck it, I mean, yeah, sorry, the pork would be fantastic." In an instant, Brian was no longer a vegetarian and, of equal importance, no longer cared.

Lita ordered them two beers; Sunset Amber (a red lager) and Luna Azul (an ale), which the waitress pointed out were brewed on site.

Beer for breakfast, thought Brian. "Cool."

"Tuanis," said Lita, apparently translating for him.

"Twa-nees," he tried. "I heard Kenny say that. It means cool?"

"Sí, from too nice, but some say it is from bueno."

"Like slang?"

"Más un código."

"A code?"

"Sí, a Salvadoran general use código when he invade Nicaragua. This mi abuela told me many times. Because everyone is speaking Spanish, he change the words by switching letters, the same way we say, *brete for trabajo*, for work."

"Interesting."

The waitress returned, her smile warm, the beers she served them cold. She also gave Brian a paper towel with some ice in it, which Brian thought was odd until he realized it was meant for his nose.

He thanked the waitress and raised his pint to Lita's, "To another day," clinking his beer into hers, then added, "with you."

Lita smiled, almost blushed, and drank her beer, at a loss

for words again, he noted, like she was used to such flattery but not honesty.

Brian never could've gotten those last two words out of his mouth if he didn't mean them. Pleased, he held the ice to his nose and smiled back at her, then took another drink from his beer, which appeased his tender throat.

Soon, the pork tacos were on their way and they found themselves in a conversation with the owners; one a Tico, the other from the gist of it, Oregon.

Lita asked about a boat to Jacó but the woman suggested the ferry to Puntarenas. However, that wouldn't do, Lita told them, too slow, as they were meeting friends and traveling down the coast to Drake Bay for a week's holiday.

Brian wondered if perhaps they were drawing too much attention to themselves, especially when Lita ordered shots of rum for everyone within shouting distance and then paid for them from a sloppy pile of $50 bills.

He couldn't tell if the alcohol was responsible for Lita's good mood or just burying her fear, since either way it was affecting her better judgment.

It was one thing to leave bait at the hotel, he reasoned, seeing as they weren't there, and another to implicate themselves in murder—in person.

Then again, as the morning wore on, Lita began to speak mostly in Spanish to people at the restaurant, so he really didn't know what she was talking about, only that he didn't notice anyone call the police.

Meanwhile, she reached under the table and placed her hand on Brian's thigh, as if for balance, smiling at him like she was admitting that the booze was getting to her, though he was almost certain she was flirting with him.

And despite being more than game to kiss her again, he was distracted to say the least; escape already seeming like a longshot to him, without pausing to swap saliva.

Twenty years ago he figured they'd have a chance to make it out, maybe disappear in another country. But that was pre-internet, before technology could swallow you whole.

He imagined them at the airport, walking toward the entrance. He'd look for security cameras as soon as they went through the main doors and, in doing so, stare right into the lens of one.

An iris recognition program later and he's popping up on a backroom monitor, an eager young employee notifying their superior that they've spotted the bloodthirsty American.

That would be it.

Ballgame.

The end.

No mas.

His life would become a constant shuffle between courtrooms and jail cells and, well, communal, no mixto showers, though he had to admit that since his time had become finite, it was a lot easier to focus.

Make or break, he had a day, day and a half max. 36 hours and counting. Roughly 2,000 minutes. And if that was all the free will Brian had left in this world then he was determined to—

Lita cursed angrily, taking him out of his head, and he looked around to see if anyone had noticed, but the backpackers had all cleared out and their waitress was over by the kitchen. "What's wrong?"

"Nada," she replied, scrolling through her phone. Then she stopped and faced him, a hand on each of his thighs now. "Mis hijas, they are with Vincent and Cecilia. They text me. They are safe."

"That's good, right?"

"But I do not know when I see them again."

"Soon, I hope, they, uh, seem like great kids."

She smiled, though she didn't look happy. "They go to school. Try very hard." Brian could see the tension growing in her eyes, as if debating how forthright she should be. "They do not make problem for me." She looked away, past him. "It is me, I am problem."

"I doubt that." Brian lifted his hands, palms up, like he was making a point, then rested them on top of hers, like he wasn't. "Raising kids isn't easy."

"You have?"

"Me? No. I always thought I would. Now I don't know, I mean, I would if, you know."

Lita pulled her hands free of his and started to look through her phone again but quickly grew frustrated and slammed it against the table.

Brian watched in slow-motion as her phone did a triple-axel in the air and landed on the ground a few feet away. "I understand. I do. Really." Then realizing, she wasn't going to get it, he calmly picked it up and handed it back to her, as if he didn't notice the newly cracked screen. "We should lay low."

"What is lay low?" She scooted her chair even closer to Brian's and looked deep into his eyes, drunkenly swaying from side to side. "You think I am easy? I am puta?"

Brian couldn't tell if she was joking or not, not with more than one language at play. "Poo-da? What?"

She lowered her voice to a whisper. "You want to lay low?"

"Yes, but no, not that, that's something, you're thinking of something else, I am not, I mean, sure, a little bit."

Her hands found his thighs again, this time higher up his leg. "You want to take me someplace, sí or no?"

Brian raised his hand, looking for the waitress. "La cuenta por favor!"

Brian and Lita left the restaurant and began walking again,

this time with a good buzz going, a walk which was gradually becoming more of a hike; back into the jungle, farther up to the second waterfall and finally the third and last one, behind which the land plateaued, revealing a dirt clearing that was fenced off in either direction.

The fence was about Brian's height, made from cut tree branches that had been stuck back in the ground and, to his surprise, were sprouting fresh leaves. Strange, considering that he assumed they were dead. Anyway, it was easily climbable but, like any fence, he knew it was put there for a reason.

Either to keep unwanted company out.

Or those with questionable judgment in.

Better safe than sorry.

For both sides.

Brian figured they'd hit a dead-end, however, Lita found a wire latch on the fence where there didn't appear to be one and opened a small gate, motioning for him to go first.

And he did, apprehensively, wondering what kind of animals were roaming this—

"Rancho," she told him, as if reading his mind. She followed him onto the property, pointing ahead to a stable, one end of it covered with a thatched roof, where a dozen or so horses were appreciating the shade from the harsh, unapologetic sun. "Caballos."

"Ka-bye-yos." repeated Brian. "The horses?"

"Sí, do you ride?"

"Jack's dad used to tell us: Never sweat anything petty or pet anything sweaty."

"I do not understand."

"Me or what I said?"

"Both." Lita closed the gate behind her and secured the latch.

"I've never ridden a horse, no."

"And you are American? Hmm." She shrugged and walked ahead of him toward a white one-story stucco house.

The first thing Brian noticed out front was the red bougainvillea, trained to cover a patio that gave shade to a large castle-like double door.

Beside the door, there was a man rolling a cigarette in a rocking chair, head down, as if he didn't notice them approaching, which Brian didn't necessarily believe.

Short, round, close to sixty but with a healthy crop of black hair; his jeans were tucked into rubber work boots that went up to his knees.

Aware that Costa Rica's Most Wanted list might have updated overnight, Brian was hesitant, nervous, wondering if anyone in the house had heard something.

Lita, on the other hand, walked right up and hugged the man, who happily stood to greet her, but then spotting Brian over her shoulder, his smile quickly faded to a frown.

Brian wasn't sure if bad news had arrived from Tamarindo or the man just didn't like the look of him:

A tourist.

A white one.

A gringo.

He took in Brian's beat-up condition, then sniffed at the air. "Has estado bebiendo?"

"Un poco, pero. . ." Lita continued in Spanish; Brian picking up on words like *dinero* and *muerta* and *policía* and finally *Ivan*.

That name got the man's attention and he pointed at Brian, motioning to his disfigured nose. "Quien es este?"

"Mi amigo."

"I'm Brian." He reached his hand out.

"Paco," he said, firmly taking it.

Lita turned to Brian. "He is like father to me."

"Oh." Brian felt some kind of apology was in order. "Sorry

to—"

"Estamos cansados," said Lita, cutting him off.

"What's that?" Brian looked over at her. "What did you say to him?"

"I say, we are tired."

"Oh. Okay."

"We are going bed now," she told him, in a way that suggested it wasn't up for debate.

"Wait. Bed? We're tired? In the middle of the day? Are you sure?"

"Sí." She took the sack from Brian and walked into the house. . .

Paco went after her, raising his voice, "Rosalita, Rosalita!" He gave up rather soon though, like he knew better, then returned to the patio and sat back down in his chair. "What are you going to do?" he asked Brian.

Brian didn't realize he could speak English. "You mean right now?"

"Brian!" Lita called out from inside the house.

Paco shook his head, "Stay," then sealed his cigarette with one final lick across the rolling paper. "You pistolero?"

Brian wasn't sure if he was genuinely asking him if he was a gunfighter or just teasing him because he already knew the answer, though it led him to check for the Walther in the back of his pants.

Paco held out his hand, as if he knew the gun was there the whole time, and Brian handed it to him. "This is Ivan's," said Paco, looking it over. "He tried to sell it to me when Lita married his son but he wanted too much for it."

"Ven!" Lita called louder.

"What about Ivan?" Paco took a drag on his cigarette. "Have you considered killing him?"

"Joel Campbell," blurted out Brian. "Did Lita tell you that my friend sat next to him, well not right next to him, but across the aisle from him on the plane here? That guy, let me tell you, he's got some moves. I don't know why Arsenal keep sending him out on loan."

Paco looked confused but curious. "You know Joel Campbell?"

"I, uh, don't actually know him but he's a heck of a soccer player, I mean football player. I don't know why we call our sport that. You guys are the ones using your feet."

"It is true," said Paco, seemingly impressed with Brian's take.

"And your national team, La Sele? Is that right? The goalie, Navas," continued Brian. "Who's he play for? Real Madrid? That's as good as it gets, right?"

"Sí, they are a very good club, one of the best in the world." Paco held up his tobacco pouch. "Would you like a smoke?"

"I, uh. . ."

Lita called out again, shouted really, from a window down the side of the house. "Ven, Brian! Ven ahora!"

"Go," Paco told him, returning the Walther. Then he nodded to the door, where an old but apparently still functioning shotgun stood at attention against the wall.

"Sure, of course, I. . ." Unable to look Paco in the eye, and not because both of his own were swollen, he just stared at his boots. "I should see what she wants. I, uh, excuse me."

Brian left his muddy shoes by the front door and went inside the house, following a long tiled hallway before he found Lita in a room, already in bed.

"Take off your clothes," she ordered, as soon as he entered. "I do not want you to get everything dirty."

"What about the boat? Shouldn't we—"

"Shhh. . ." Lita told him that she used to work on the rancho, with the horses, that Paco's family took her and her daughters in when her abuela died. "This is my old bedroom," she said, as if they had all the time in the world. "My girls were across the hall."

"We're losing daylight."

"I cannot think anymore. I need to sleep." She practically pouted. "Veinte minutos. Then we go."

"Okay, but Paco didn't exactly give me the green light here."

"Are you going to listen to him?" She let the sheet slip, exposing the top of her breasts. "Or me?"

He sighed, truly torn. "I already have one man trying to kill me, I don't need two."

"So much talking." Disappointed, Lita rolled away from him, toward the wall.

Wellallrightythen. Brian did what the moment called for and set the gun down on the nightstand, then took all his clothes off and joined her underneath the covers.

They didn't fool around if that's what you were thinking. Not with Paco outside, a shotgun within his reach. At least that was Brian's excuse. Besides, they both dozed off rather quickly, sleeping soundly for twenty minutes just like Lita wanted, the twenty minutes after that too . . . and so on.

When Brian woke up it was getting dark out. Or worse, light again. He wasn't sure, but a sick, panicky feeling consumed him.

Like he'd overslept the SATs.

Or drank too much and blacked out.

Or, in this case, missed his last chance flight out of San Jose.

He wasn't sure what had awakened him until he heard the second gunshot, BANG, then two more, BANG BANG, louder if not closer.

Lita jumped out of bed and ran over to the window, grabbing her clothes along the way, while Brian went straight for her bedroom door. “Someone named Paco is gonna kill me!” He put the whole of his weight against it, despite not wearing a stitch of clothing. “Does this thing lock?!”

“Get dressed.” Lita had what Brian perceived to be a healthy glance at his manhood, then turned back to the window and pushed the curtain aside, just enough to have a peek outside. “We must go.”

She started for the door but Brian was still leaning against it, his hands covering his private parts.

“Paco loves me,” said Lita, throwing the sack over her shoulder. “He will not hurt you.”

Brian grabbed his swimsuit off the floor and put it on. “That’s easy for you to say.”

“Yes, it is.” She put the gun in the sack.

“Won’t we need that?”

“One bullet will not help us now.”

Brian relented, trusting Lita enough to lead him back to the patio, where Paco was busy loading shells into his shotgun.

“Qué pasa?” Lita wanted to know.

With a calm determination, he nodded for them to take cover behind the doors, then aimed his gun across the ranch and fired two quick shots, *BANG BANG*, into the dim light.

“Twelve gauge,” Paco told Brian. “Remington. A friend gave it to me when he moved back to the States. He told me he had many problems getting it in the country and didn’t want to risk losing it on the way out.”

“Does every gun come with a story down here,” asked Brian, putting his shoes back on.

“No,” said Lita. “He is proud of it. You are not being very kind today.”

Paco separated a tangle of prickly vines with the barrel, giving Brian and Lita a look at a red Jeep parked just outside the main gate, about fifty yards away, several men positioned behind it, one that looked like Ivan with a gun.

"Fuck." Brian began pacing. "What's wrong with that guy?"

"He is crazy," said Lita.

"Where is he from anyway?" asked Brian.

"No one knows," said Paco. "Some say Russia, some say Poland. He'll tell you both, depending on the day."

"Who is caring where he was born?" asked Lita.

Brian was. He was counting on it. A conversation piece. "You mean this isn't one of those situations where we drink a few beers with Ivan and work this out like adults?"

"Go," Paco told them. He put another shell in the gun's chamber and cocked it.

"Go?" questioned Brian, from behind the door. "Where?"

He fired again at the Jeep, then nodded to the stable. "They are ready for you."

"Who's they?" asked Brian.

"Los rucos," replied Lita, before kissing Paco goodbye on the forehead. Then she grabbed Brian's hand and scrambled around the side of the house to the stable, where two horses were tied to a post, stirring uneasily. "This is Manchas," she said, rubbing the spotted one's nose. "You can ride the mare."

"I told you, I don't ride," said Brian, dreading not just the thought of getting on another animal's back but for the first time actually needing to. "I don't even know how."

Another BANG rang through the ranch, "Fuck," causing Brian to duck instinctively. "Can't we go back inside the house?"

"No." She unbuckled a leather strap underneath Manchas' belly and removed the saddle.

"You're riding bareback?"

She shook her head and handed him the sack, then climbed the stable fence so she could lower herself on the horse's back. "Pretend he is motorcycle and hold on."

Brian climbed the fence as she did and got on behind her, just as a series of shots—

BANG, BANG, BANG

Echoed throughout the ranch in both directions.

Lita snapped the reigns, heading straight across the property in a sprint, as Brian tried to make himself smaller behind her, then realized that was a cowardly if not heartless move and sat up straight, shielding her as best he could.

While Brian was getting accustomed to hero mode, Lita was urging Manchas to run, "*Carré! Carré!*" And to his credit, the horse did just that, until they reached a dirt road.

Once again surrounded by jungle, it got quiet, too quiet, thought Brian, just the clip-clopping of Manchas' hoofs on the road. They were heading to the ocean though, which was great considering they needed a boat.

They had to go slow, however, due to the downward slope, which unnerved him, more so when Lita stopped and dismounted, holding her hand out for Brian to do the same.

"Are we too heavy?" he asked.

"No, the sky is dark now. Ivan will stay with road."

"Do you think they're following us?" Brian managed to get off the horse without looking like a complete idiot, barely. "What about Paco?"

"He will be fine. They will not get close to house." She pointed Manchas back up the hill with a smack to his hindquarters, "Halé, halé," and the horse took off. . .

Brian watched Manchas go, jealous he'd been relieved of further duty, that he was going to live. "What now?"

"Back to the waterfall." She tugged on his hand and led him into the thick of the jungle.

"Maybe those were just warning shots," he said, trying to keep up with her. "Maybe they just want the money back."

"I need money to leave country."

"I've got money. Not on me but. . . We could split the cash with Ivan. Give him some of the jewels. Call it a day. No harm, no foul."

"Qué?"

"It means we can fix this."

"Roxy is dead. I killed her." Tears were flooding her eyes. "No one can fix this."

"It was an accident, kind of, you'll, we'll, together, we'll have to explain it. Either now or someday."

"I want to go to Chicago with you."

That, well, hit home with him. Wait until he showed her the city; the lakefront, Wrigley Field, Cook County Jail! *Damnit.* His festering head wounds were beginning to worry him, like maybe they were affecting his ability to think clearly.

Meanwhile, the moon was beginning to shed a little light on the situation, and though the view was spectacular, even at night, he wasn't sure why Lita lingered at the top of the first waterfall. "Why're we stopping?"

Lita carefully walked over the wet rocks to reach the very the edge of the fall, a good 80 or 90 feet in Brian's estimation to the bottom. "I want to look one last time," she told him.

"No rush," came a woman's voice from behind them.

Brian and Lita turned to find the Canadian woman, pointing a shiny silver handgun at them, which despite its diminutive size shook in her hand. "Ivan wants his money."

Lita didn't flinch. "It is not his, Anna. You know this."

Anna ignored her and motioned to the sack on Brian's back. "Is that it?"

"Yes." Brian took it off. "It's all yours. Would that do it? Would that make everything go away?"

"Do not give it to her," Lita told him.

"Why?" His eyes pleaded with hers. "We can be done with this."

“What about the jewels?” asked Anna. “Are they in there too?”

“He stole from me.” Lita gritted her teeth. “All of it is mine.”

“It doesn’t matter.” Anna looked past them. “I brought a friend.”

Brian and Lita glanced back to where one of the beards stood a few feet away; eager, like he was anxious to inflict pain.

“Qué dicha,” said Lita.

Though he picked up on her sarcasm, Brian wasn’t sure what she meant. Still, he held up the sack. “It’s all there,” he told Anna. “Do you want me to count it for you? His gun’s inside too.”

“Give her nada,” ordered Lita. “Ivan es el caco.”

“He is. You’re right,” said Anna. “But he’s my thief.” Then she turned back to Brian. “Show me the Walther.”

Brian reached into the sack and removed the gun, then handed it to Anna as she slipped her own gun into her back pocket.

“Now give me the sack,” continued Anna.

But Lita yanked the sack out of Brian’s hands and held it defiantly to her stomach.

Anna sighed and spoke directly to Lita, while pointing the Walther at Brian’s head. “This is your first and last warning.”

Lita dropped the bag at their feet, between them.

Whether scared, fed up, or just plain ruthless, Brian wasn’t sure, but Anna fired the gun, just as he bent over to pick up the sack for her—shooting the bearded man behind him straight in the chest.

It didn’t kill him though, not right away. He just dropped to his knees, a confused look in his eyes before he face-planted into a rock.

Brian stood back up, stunned. “Shit. Sorry. I, uh. . .”

Anna looked frightened to the point of giving up but instead raised the Walther at Brian a second time, shaking but sure.

And she pulled the trigger; once, twice, three times before realizing the chamber was empty. “Shit.” She reached for her own gun.

But Lita lunged for it, wrapping her fingers around the barrel. Still, Anna held tight to her gun, so much so that when Lita let go, Anna stumbled backwards and lost her footing, falling over the edge of the waterfall. . .

Lita turned away, unable to watch. But Brian did, his eyes following Anna all the way down, smacking into one rock after another before crashing into the water below.

18

Free Fallin'

When they reached the bottom of the waterfall, Kenny ran over and gave them a big hug. Definitely a warm feeling, thought Brian. You're alive, other people are glad you're alive. Still, he couldn't help but notice how downright surprised Kenny looked to see them.

The feeling was mutual; Kenny explaining that he remembered a friend Lita had spoken of from time to time. And how she lived on his ranch, the one above a waterfall in Montezuma. And since it was on the way to San Jose, he thought he'd give it a try. He had to.

He warned them it was Ivan who came knocking in Mal Pais and that his dad admitted they had just bailed, which was hard to deny since Darryl was there. Then, as if by mistake, his dad steered Ivan back north, telling him the plan was to make their regularly scheduled flight from Liberia.

"Though Ivan must know of this place too," Kenny continued. "So we still gotta be careful."

Brian stopped him, "You need to see something," and led him into the shallow water beneath the waterfall. . .

But it was dark and he couldn't figure out what Brian was talking about until he almost bumped into her. "What the fuck, mae?"

It was Anna, splayed out awkwardly, like a tortured starfish.

"Ivan está aquí," Lita told him.

"Somewhere," added Brian, "close."

Kenny looked at Anna again and then back at Brian, as if his opinion of him had changed. Whether that was some newfound respect or even fear, Brian wasn't sure, though normally he would shun the spotlight and profess his innocence, mostly worried about getting caught in a lie.

However, if it meant protecting Lita, he was glad to take the heat and stay silent, especially since she had just saved his life—again.

Brian spotted Anna's gun a few feet away in the mud and picked it up, telling Kenny that they left the Walther up top, that it was out of bullets.

However, Kenny never asked where those bullets went. He just shook his head like he'd heard enough and hustled them past the Amor de Mar to the first beach out of sight of downtown Montezuma.

And that's where they found a boat anchored just off shore, Mike balancing on the bow with a beer in his hand. "W'sup people?"

Mike's boat was an old Boston Whaler, 14-feet long, 16 tops, when Brian was expecting, hoping really, for something much bigger. But what choice did he have? None.

So, he put his new gun in the sack and held it over his head, then walked into the water up to his armpits, reading the name written across the back of the boat out loud: "*Blood, Sugar, Sex, Magik.*"

"That album came out when I was in India." Mike reached down and helped Lita aboard, leaving Brian to fend for himself, then motioned for the two of them to sit in the front. "We need some weight up there."

Brian thought maybe an explanation as to why the boat required balancing was forthcoming, but Mike was still talking about music. "Sam got me a bootleg from Bangkok on cassette. Remember that video they did in the desert?"

Brian was interested, kind of, not really, maybe under better circumstances, but he wanted to get going. He sensed all of this was a game to Mike. Some kind of adventure. Or, as in India, a misadventure. "Who doesn't love the Chili Peppers?"

Lita gave Brian a dirty look, like she wanted to get going too. And yet, Mike went on. "Did you know that album came out the same day, September 24, 1991, as *Nevermind*?" He switched on the green and red bow lights. "And get this, also same day, *Badmotorfinger*."

Brian knew the band, but when he hesitated Kenny spoke up. "Soundgarden."

Seemingly pleased that his son had nailed the answer, Mike put the boat in gear, forward, just enough speed for them to creep quietly out of town over the water. . . .

Once clear of the coast, the wind picked up and the ocean became choppy, waves beginning to crash over the bow. Mike's response was to drive faster, to ride the swells, which wasn't exactly working out, mostly for Brian and Lita who were getting bounced around up front.

And since they were already wet, Brian pulling a canvas cover over them was less a chivalrous move and more a survival one designed to keep them from being launched out of the boat.

This was not how Brian imagined dying. Not in a boating accident, a small fortune attached to his back as he came to rest for eternity on the ocean floor.

Good story, he told himself. *Stop it.* He didn't want good stories. Or even great ones. He wanted boring. He wanted to live.

And though Lita snuggled into him, wrapping her arms and legs in his, she hadn't said a word since the waterfall.

Brian felt he should say something about what happened with Anna, that he hadn't given up. He just gave up briefly, while a gun was pointed at him.

It was too chaotic, however, to have that conversation in the boat, so he didn't say a word. He just tried to make his body as soft and giving as he could and shelter her from the high seas; a swashbuckler to Lita's pirate princess.

It was an hour or so before Mike finally slowed down, flipping the cover off of them to announce their arrival at, "Herradura Bay."

Brian got up, relieved they were approaching land, which Kenny said was just a two hour car ride to the airport.

Then, as a marina came into view up ahead, Mike flicked off the lights in the bow and stern. "Spend the night here in Jacó," he told them. "You won't make a flight this late."

Kenny grabbed a rope. "The less time you spend at the airport the better."

"Hire a van with everyone else going to San Jose," continued Mike. "Tourists, locals, try to mix in. Anything you do on your own you'll be marking yourself as two, as a couple, the Tica and the American everyone's looking for."

"Thanks, I get it," said Brian. "Thank you for everything. If you're ever in Chicago—"

"I will," Mike assured him, pulling up to the first of several piers, away from a row of overhead lights.

"Cuidado," said Kenny, helping Brian and Lita onto the pier.

"Aren't you going to tie up?" asked Brian.

"Nope." Mike pointed the bow back out to sea. "Gotta

check on Sam."

And as Kenny once again called out, "Suerte," his dad and him were already fading from view. . . .

Tomorrow, thought Brian. If they could just make it to tomorrow. To San Jose. And liftoff. That's all he wanted. A plane. A chance. He didn't care what happened after that. If the Feds were waiting for him when he landed, so be it. He'd find a great lawyer. Cop a plea.

Meanwhile, thinking they would play the innocent card in court, he felt they might as well play it in Jacó too.

First thing off the boat, he took Lita to a boutique just off the beach for a fresh set of clothes, even better (though Brian had to convince her), his and hers outfits consisting of white jeans and matching floral tops; Lita's a soft blouse, Brian's a stiff collared shirt.

He was fully aware that this could be their last night together. Getting caught meant getting separated. So did getting killed for that matter.

Still, he feared jail more than death. With that in mind, Brian ran across the street and had an ice cold Bavaria waiting for Lita when she came out of the changing room.

She thanked him and did a little twirl on her toes to show off the ensemble, prompting him to go for the flip-phone, even on its deathbed, to take a photo.

He managed to stop himself though and check for a text from the guys instead—but there was nothing. Worrisome, yes, moreso when Lita told him she'd lost her phone.

"Where?" Brian asked her, then realizing that was a stupid question, he bought two more Bavarias for a walk, finding Jacó about twice the size of Tamarindo and just as busy.

By their fourth beer they were standing in the lobby of a fancy hotel in the hills above town, where Lita told the manager they were on their honeymoon, all the way from

Chee-kaw-go, while Brian requested a top floor suite with a view of the ocean and a charger for the flip-phone, unsure if one even existed.

All of this, Brian would want you to know was fairly accurate, could be googled, like splurging on the room. Even so, it wasn't a coincidence that the hotel was located off the beach, north toward the highway leading to San Jose.

Blending in, he figured, also meant staying somewhere decent, not a hostel hideaway in the jungle but something suitable to their age and supposed lifestyle.

Lita wrapped her arm in his and laughed all the way to the suite, then wasted little time taking her clothes off and getting into the shower.

Brian thought about following her into the bathroom, all nonchalant, like he needed to brush his teeth, when what he really wanted was to get caught staring at her, perhaps in the mirror.

She would pretend to be offended, Brian apologizing profusely as he turned to go. But before he could reach the door, she would invite him to join her in the shower, telling him that there wouldn't be much hot water left if he waited his turn.

Brian didn't push his luck, though, thinking he could use some later, and hung back in the room. Not that he wanted to. Just, assuming they were still in charge of their own destiny, he thought he better come up with a plan first, starting with a ride to the airport.

He went outside on the balcony to get a better signal and checked the phone again, but the battery was officially dead.

He missed Darryl's laugh, *Damnit,* he missed Jack's mustache. But, more importantly, he wanted to know if they were okay, and if they were, was he okay too?

Lita joined him on the balcony in a fluffy pink bathrobe with a few thoughts of her own. "I think we should not spend so much money."

"That's not a bad idea, I mean, we could do that, yes." He pointed to a cluster of lights along the coast. "Beautiful, isn't it?"

"You are thinking of la vista?"

"And you're thinking of money? Now? I bet they're going to charge us for that robe."

"Should I take it off?"

"No, keep it, sorry, everyone's expecting us to go straight to San Jose, not go on a shopping spree." He leaned over the balcony railing. "I mean, we weren't exactly careful in Montezuma. What if we threw money around everywhere we went? Where would they start? Give the police a hundred leads, we might have time to slip out a back door or two."

Brian thought he was on to something but Lita put her hands on hips, practically pouting. "You are talking mucho again."

"Come on, let's go out to dinner, spend some of this loot."

"Loot?"

"The money."

"Ah, in Costa Rica, we say la harina."

"Oh, cool, I don't know why I said loot. That's something my grandpa would say. Hmmm. I don't know if that makes me old or wise or none of the above. Unless—"

Lita stomped her foot. "You do not want to kiss me?"

"No, yes, I do want to . . . kiss you."

"Bueno."

Brian shuttered, then placed his hand on the back of her neck and guided his face to hers; one kiss, two kiss, and he was lost in her; lips smacking, tongues tangling, their mouths sealed tight.

But his nose was so clogged with blood that he eventually had to come up for air. "Does this mean we're skipping dinner?"

She leaned her forehead against his, “No,” and kissed him hard, her two front teeth stabbing his lower lip. Then she walked back into the room, prematurely dropping her bathrobe on the floor along the way. . .

He wondered if that was a *Come and get it or a Be patient, Grasshopper?* Either way, in a rare move, he followed her inside. Of course, being a gentleman, Brian would never tell anyone what happened next.

Actually, they got dressed, though they held hands the entire taxi ride down the hill into town, an act in past circumstances that Brian might've taken as a defeat but with Lita was almost as thrilling as making love to her, a simple yet intimate gesture of trust and affection and sweaty palms; after which they walked along the shore until they found a restaurant to their liking on the beach, complete with pillowed lounge chairs and tiki torches.

Lita ordered *margaritas y langosta,* Brian a *shrimp cocktail and French fries.* He told her stories about the guys and him, which had her laughing, and he got lost in her smile. But when they were done eating, they turned their attention to a young couple in their late teens at the table opposite them.

Brian had been watching them, pegging them, really. Tan, skinny, even a bit dirty, like they'd been on the road a while, stretching their money, maybe nearing the end of their trip.

Brian excused himself for interrupting their dinner, explaining that his phone was dead and he'd be grateful if they could look up flights to America, that he just found out his great-aunt had died and he really wanted to make the funeral.

They stared quizzically at Brian, until he offered to pay for their dinner, after which they took to their phones, the girl finding a flight on Spirit Airlines to Fort Lauderdale the next afternoon, the boy, one on Avianca to Los Angeles through San Salvador. And though it was considerably more expensive, he also found a nonstop to Chicago on United.

The Chicago flight turned out to be full but Brian and Lita had options now. Plus, Lita had previously sorted out her visa for the States (something Brian wasn't necessarily thrilled about but understood). They didn't book a ticket though, Brian figuring it best to minimize the time they were on a flight manifest.

The next move was to go back to the hotel and organize a ride to the airport in the morning. But first, Brian had an idea; convincing Lita to check into two more hotels and a hostel before they got a taxi back to their suite.

That way, if anyone was sniffing around they'd have several leads to follow up on in town before checking out a hotel in the hills.

Lita liked this idea too, a lot, and by the time they got back to their place they were kissing and hugging each other all the way to the room.

Brian tossed the sack on the bed and turned on the TV to a music channel, then took a bottle of champagne out of the mini-fridge and had a glass waiting for Lita when she emerged from the bathroom. "Salud."

"You are very good at getting me drunk." She laughed and took a sip, then got serious, holding his gaze. "Gracias. Gracias por todo."

"My pleasure." He kissed her softly on the lips, then stepped back. "And thank you for, you know, what happened in Montezuma."

"I did not mean for her to fall but she was going to shoot you."

"I know."

Lita crawled onto the bed and turned the sack upside down, smiling, a tinge of naughty, spilling diamonds and pearls, dollars and colones, from one end of the mattress to the other.

Then she sat on the edge of the bed and pulled Brian between her legs, so she could unbutton his shirt.

Meanwhile, Brian was thinking about what article of his clothing was coming off next, when she laid back on the bed and rested her feet on Brian's shoulders. "Take my pants."

Brian tugged on her jeans until they came off, surprised to find her underwear never made it beyond Paco's, "Oh," and eager for his next instruction. "Now what do I do?"

"Your pants."

Brian did as he was told. "Swimsuit too?"

She nodded.

He stepped out of his swimsuit, sneaking in a quick ball adjustment. "Now what?"

"You stop talking." She pushed his head between her legs rather aggressively, practically suffocating him before he realized what was expected of him and his tongue.

However, just as Lita was beginning to squirm with delight, Brian noticed that the song coming from the TV had changed:

I was working part time in a five-and-dime
My boss was Mr. McGee

--Prince

It was Prince! The Purple One! Again! An absolute favorite, but Brian feared the third time couldn't possibly be the charm. He tried to keep busy but knew it would go all wrong and sure enough there was a *knock* at the door.

Brian stopped what he was doing, much to Lita's disappointment, and waited to see if whoever was outside their room would go away.

But again, *knock knock*.

He apologized to Lita and tip-toed over to the door, sticking his less swollen eye up to the peephole, where he spotted a young boy in the hallway, maybe eleven or twelve.

The boy was holding up a phone charger. "Disculpeme, señor."

Brian threw on Lita's new pink bathrobe and swung open the door, two Tico men barging past the boy straight into the room, one wearing a police uniform, his gun drawn.

Lita held the blanket up to her chin, as Brian took refuge on the floor, face down, hands voluntarily clasping behind his neck.

The older man, the one not in uniform, walked up to him, his shiny black shoes just inches from Brian's face.

He braced himself for a kick to the head, but the man merely bent over to look at him, his eyebrows like bird sanctuaries, then flashed a card from his wallet, saying that he was a private detective bestowed with some kind of government authority that Brian didn't fully understand.

Brian thought about checking his credentials more thoroughly but didn't want to risk insulting him, though he was already second guessing himself as the detective gravitated toward the bed. . .

Brian sprang to his feet, ready to defend Lita, but the officer leveled his gun at him. *Fuck*, just minutes ago, he was convinced that he knew the meaning of life.

But as the detective snatched the blanket out of Lita's hands to reveal not only her but all the money and jewels, he was suddenly unsure any meaning ever existed.

"A cachete," said the detective, amazed by his discovery. He picked up the grill and tossed it to the officer.

Who seemed quite pleased to be receiving such a gift. "Al chile?" He put his gun down to try and fit it in his mouth, which it did, almost.

Next, the detective picked up a string of pearls, “Para me esposa,” and let them slowly slip through his fingers, then scooped up a handful of $50 bills, “Para mi.”

Lita took the blanket back and wrapped it around her. “Qué deseas?” she asked him, scared but clearly irate.

He had a question of his own, though. “A dónde vas?”

“We are flying to America tomorrow,” she told him, sticking to the honeymoon story. “I am meeting his parents. Is that problem?”

“You have a lot of money and valuables in your possession,” said the detective.

“Sí,” she agreed. “It was not safe to leave it behind.”

He said something privately to the officer in Spanish, who in turn removed a set of keys from his front pocket, then turned back to Brian and Lita. “Why don’t you let us drive you to the airport. It will be safer that way.”

“We’ve already booked a ride,” Brian told him. “Thanks anyway. Very kind of you.”

“Come,” he said, as if he hadn’t heard him, then held out his hand. “Passports please.”

Never give up your passport, thought Brian. He contemplated making a run for the balcony and hurtling himself into the jungle. Instead, he just turned to the boy, who was still standing in the doorway. “Can I get that charger now?”

19

Been Caught Stealing

Brian figured the police would give him one phone call, which he'd use on one of the guys, to make sure they were okay and tell them that whatever lawyer Carmela finds needs to get on a plane to Costa Rica, *pronto*.

Meanwhile, he was determined to stick to the story that they took what was rightfully Lita's and were only running out of fear of being chased. Bottom line, they were innocent. Final answer. Any admission of guilt could mean serious jail time, especially with a body count.

The fire dancer, bless her heart, fell on the sharpened end of a long piece of bamboo; one she was in the process of attacking them with. Horrible. But an accident.

Then there was the first beard, your honor, and the crocodile. Isn't there supposed to be a sign warning tourists about swimming in the river? Poor fella.

As for the Canadian woman, she shot the second beard by mistake, bad luck really, then freaked out, lost her balance, and fell over the edge of the waterfall. A tragedy.

What was with all the beards, by the way? Even Brian knew that massive amounts of facial hair was transitioning from radical . . . to trendy . . . to ridicule, so it was hard to tell if lumberjack face was a coincidence or a requirement for that lot of thugs.

Lita had made it clear that the cash and jewels were just a start to what Ivan owed her. In the end though, Brian knew it would be that asshole's word against hers. If, that is, they could get to the end.

"Murió la flor," said Lita, under her breath.

Brian scooted closer to her across the backseat. "What?"

She whispered in his ear, "Murió la flor. It means, the flower has died." Lita took his hand, squeezed it. "It is over."

"Us? This? No, no way, they're doing us a favor."

"This is favor?" Lita nodded to the two men up front; the same one in uniform driving, the detective sitting opposite him, sack across his lap, stroking it like a favorite pet.

Unable to deny just how bleak a picture they were looking at, Brian slid back over to his side and leaned his head out the window, where he ran into a cool morning mist.

A spell of relief for his tired sweaty face but thick enough to slow traffic, made worse by an old, one-lane bridge that forced them to take turns crossing with oncoming cars.

For the life of him, and yes, he considered it life and death, he couldn't come up with a reason why they didn't build a two-lane bridge, (his best bet was that before cars, the bridge was perfectly suitable for horses to cross simultaneously).

Regardless, they waited half an hour to get to the other side; thirty additional minutes to ponder his fate, maybe even miss the flight to Ft. Lauderdale, when what he really wanted was to get this whole ordeal over with.

He spotted a sign for highway 34, *Costanero Sur*, and several for an *Iguana* crossing, no joke, plus another one pointing out that they were 60 kilometers from San Jose, which Brian converted to less than forty miles and hopefully, as promised, the airport.

In their brief interrogation, the detective never asked questions about Ivan or Roxy and Anna or any of what had gone down. And he let Brian charge his phone, while Lita explained her side of things in English, purposefully as far Brian could tell, so they could stick to the same story.

She told him the jewels were hers and the cash a repayment of a loan she'd made to her father-in-law, that they were planning to put it in a bank near the airport before leaving the country. She even showed him her visa, to prove the trip had been planned for months.

And though nodding along, Brian didn't get the idea that the detective was really listening, especially when he didn't follow up on their flight plans, or make any phone calls, or even explain how he found them at the hotel.

Instead, the detective really did give himself a parting gift, perhaps, Brian thought, taking what he felt was owed to him after so many years of dutiful service.

He didn't get greedy, though, keeping just the pearls for himself and only pocketing about a quarter of the cash, reluctantly, like he was tempted to take more. Plus, he confiscated their new gun, which Brian stated wasn't theirs to begin with.

Despacio/Slow. That was another sign that Brian kept seeing on the side of the road, which he found totally annoying considering what a hurry Lita and him were in. Between those two words were drawings of *a person, a dog, a sloth, and a monkey* crossing the road. He felt compelled to pick one, his spirit animal, Oprah would.

He chose person and forced a smile, draping himself over the seat to admire the sack. "Have you ever seen that much money?"

But neither man could be bothered to look at him.

"Harina," tried Brian, remembering Lita's word for

money, and sure enough, it got their attention. "We should get a picture of you two with it."

The officer turned hopefully to his superior, the grill already in place, but his green smile was shot down by just a disinterested glance.

Brian persisted, though. "I could take one right now to show the guys at the station. Or your grandchildren. No one's going to believe you had all this money on you. And the jewelry, my god. It'll be one of those stories that's much better with a picture."

Brian wasn't sure if the detective was hesitating because he was intending to keep the sack or turn them in, or both, until the man looked in the side-view mirror and pushed what little hair he had behind his ears. "Bien," he said, handing his phone to Brian.

But Brian held up his flip-phone. "Takes much better pictures."

The detective shrugged and turned in his seat to face Brian, sack held open, his smile all cheese, while the officer drove on, clearly upset he wasn't in the frame.

"Got it," said Brian, taking the shot. "Who should I send it to?"

"Me." The detective took the phone from Brian and entered his number.

Thank you, thought, Brian. He had a plan for that photo, what exactly, he wasn't sure. But if the detective attempted to double-cross them, he'd use it against him, whether he still had the phone in his possession or not.

In his head, Brian was already delivering a lengthy monologue on the pluses and minuses of the internet, politely advising the detective that if he were to be arrested, authorities from the United States would look at his text messages and emails and photos, deleted or not, thanks to the wonderful and wicked Cloud.

Consequently, Brian would conclude, the detective will have captured two high-profile fugitives with nothing to show for it but a possible government reprimand for attempting to confiscate and benefit from *valuable* evidence.

They arrived in San Jose, however, without any such discussion, only to become embroiled in more traffic, driving so slow that Brian thought about throwing open the door and making a run for it with Lita, convinced they could disappear in the crowd of cars within seconds, even though that would surely eliminate flying home.

Then, just as Brian was beginning to see signs for Juan Santamaría International, the detective handed their passports over the seat. “Go directly to the ticket counter.”

“Yes, of course,” said Brian, still trying to play it light and breezy, as the car pulled up to the terminal.

The detective returned the sack to Lita. “Adios, mi belleza.”

“That’s it?” Brian got out of the car. “You’re not coming with us?”

But the detective either didn’t hear him or didn’t care. He was already gone, the officer driving away as soon as Brian and Lita exited the backseat.

Maybe they’d done their job, thought Brian, worked both sides. Maybe there were bigger fish waiting for them at the airport.

Lita, on the other hand, didn’t appear to have any such worries, heading right through the terminal doors before realizing Brian hadn’t left the curb.

He folded his arms over his chest. No way. Unwilling to give up or just not wanting to get caught, he wasn’t certain. But it was far too late to concede so easily, to just walk right up to some airline counter and show them their passports.

This was an all or nothing proposition for him. Either he

was sleeping like a puppy in his own bed tomorrow night or tossing and turning in a jail cell. Great win. Excruciating loss. In Brian's mind, it was better to have less of a chance to get away than more of a chance to get caught. "We have to. . ." He waved her back over to him, like he meant it. "We have to get out of here."

Lita didn't say a word. Nor did she budge.

"The airport," said Brian. "It's a trap."

She put the back of her hands on her hips, defiant.

"Think about it, Lita. The detective didn't ask a ton of questions or threaten us or even accuse us of anything. He just gave us a ride to the airport. For some pearls and a few grand? Maybe. But he also delivered us to the capital in perfect working condition for someone else to arrest us, without risking his cut." He held out his hand to her. "Venga."

She glared at him, then reluctantly allowed him to lead her past Restaurante Malinche, where a row of colored mini-vans lined the curb, waiting to escort tourists to beaches and rainforests and volcanoes and—

She knew what to do and spoke to one of the drivers, who in turn pointed out a blue van with a large toucan painted on its side, idling at the front of the line, just a couple of open seats left.

As soon as they got in the van, Brian called Darryl, not worried if anyone could trace the phone back to the airport, since they were leaving.

Jack would be too much for him right now. He needed Darryl to sort this out. He knew both of them were okay, though. They had to be.

Everything's cool, Darryl would tell him, cracking open a beer: Ivan is in custody, though he didn't admit to knowing who might have killed his son. Regardless, all the guys were booked on the same flight to the States tomorrow, Lita and her daughters too.

Unfortunately, Darryl's phone rang . . . and rang . . . So did Jack's. He tried texting them, cryptically, not revealing where he was going, not that he knew, just that it was away from the airport and the potential for handcuffs.

Later, Lita told Brian they were heading toward Puerto Limón, which was the place he remembered Darryl talking about, east to the Caribbean.

Meanwhile, their driver, a Tico man of about thirty, had the look of someone who wanted to get there in a hurry, like his girlfriend was waiting impatiently for him.

He put his foot to the petal and cranked up the air conditioning, much to everyone's relief, and fought his way free of urban congestion, the ride becoming straight and green; a fast pace on a two-lane highway, lush with coffee farms and banana plantations and endless wild jungle.

None of the other passengers talked very much, a few even settling into sleep, including Lita. Brian, however, just stared out the window as the van flew down the road, as fast as the cars ahead of them would allow, picking out the odd home or barn, a few roadside vendors selling pineapples by the cartload.

After a few hours, the space between cars tightened up again, so that there was no chance to pass, which was good, thought Brian, since it wouldn't allow anyone following them to catch up.

He knew bailing on the airport was either expert intuition or the bonehead move of a lifetime. Yet, being wrong about the airport was good; it meant no one was after them. Being right was bad; it meant someone was.

They needed a new plan, taking geography into consideration. Brian figured Lita would want to head north once they reached the coast, home to Nicaragua. She even talked about friends in Bluefields, a Caribbean port named after a Dutch pirate.

Forget boring, thought Brian, this was good for the story. If he was going to talk about the next twenty-four hours for the rest of his life, or someone else was should that no longer be an option, hiding out in a pirate town fit the bill.

The van let everyone out for a breather near the cruise ship terminal in Limón, where Brian and Lita found an open table on the sidewalk at a busy cafe. He turned his chair to face the afternoon sun, a blessing after five hours in a chilly van, but he also wanted to keep an eye on the street to see if they were being watched.

He was trying to get a signal on Jack's stupid phone, when Lita ordered a *capirotada* to share.

"And dos cervezas," said Brian, "bien fria, por favor."

Lita winked at him, approvingly, the slightest affirmation of pleasing her and it felt so good to him, like getting a gold star from his first grade teacher.

Normally, Brian wouldn't request that his beer be *fria*, especially in a foreign country, fearing that it could be construed as an insult. Back home, sure, a cold beer seemed obvious, but he was aware that Europeans had been confusing the rest of the world for years with their indifference.

Christ, he thought, get your head straight. Back to the bad man. To the madman! If he saw Ivan right now, he'd . . . run. But Lita. He'd have to stay and protect her. Fight Ivan. Hurt him. He owed him for the first bout. Someone might film it on their phone, though, cement Brian's guilt.

He didn't notice the capirotada had arrived at the table until Lita held out a bite for him on the end of her fork. What he saw looked like some kind of chocolate bread pudding and he swallowed it whole, rewarded, he figured, for his imminent bravery.

They took turns with the dessert, while watching a ship navigate the terminal's tight quarters; Brian, in particular, was impressed with the deft maneuvering. Then, when the waiter returned, he got the cafe's WiFi password and tried to reach Darryl again. And did!

Darryl said he was in a hospital, afraid someone would send him to jail when he got better. "Better," he repeated, "isn't jail."

"I get it but are you okay, Darryl, are you going to be all right?"

"Yeah, I'm fine but no one's seen Ivan. Have you?"

"Yeah, well, almost." Brian lowered his voice to a whisper. "But the Canadian woman, uh. . ."

"Uh, what?"

"We're gonna need a bigger lawyer."

"Carmela's on it. She's already got Neal involved. Where the hell are you and Jack?"

"Jack? I don't know. He left us in Mal Pais to go back for you but Lita and I are in Puerto Limón." Brian surveyed his surroundings for Ivan and the police and big ugly men with beards. "What the fuck am I supposed to do?"

"Hold on, Kenny just showed up. You and Lita are in Limón?"

"Yeah."

"Kenny says go to Angler's Lair. You got that? Angler's Lair. Say you know Kenny but if anyone has a problem with his dad just agree with them. Oh, shit, cops are here." And that was it. Darryl hung up, like he had to.

Brian quickly googled *Angler's Lair*, finding a vacation rental on Airbnb. "Where's Puerto Viejo?"

"Not far," said Lita. "South."

"Is he pointing us to Panama?" wondered Brian. Sounded good to him, so long as they kept moving. "How do we get there?"

"We get back in the van."

About an hour later, Brian and Lita were in Puerto Viejo, yet another Costa Rican party town, this time on the Caribbean; famous for its world class surf break, *Salsa Brava* and, as Darryl pointed out, its cultural diversity.

They were barely out of the van when Brian declared he wanted a haircut. Immediately. Time to change his look. Mix it up a bit. Why make it easy for someone to pick him out of a crowd?

Lita told him she understood, even while her eyes lingered on his nose and, with a curious tilt of her head, his ear.

He got the message but when he spotted a salon across the street, he decided to let fate have its way. And within minutes, he was settling into a chair under the guidance of a woman name Cookie, who was poised to lop off his curls.

Brian took her for about his age, though with her supple coffee-colored complexion, he easily could've been off by ten years in either direction.

She wore a yellow tunic that might've been designed to downplay a woman's figure but failed miserably to hide her curves, while beads, baubles and feathers adorned her long brown braids, which were tied up on her head in a bouquet.

Right away, Cookie saw the bruise on his scalp and used her scissors to carefully cut around it. "Don warry," she said, in an English creole, "I won ask what appin."

"Thank you," said Brian.

She took a bottle of alcohol off the shelf and held it up to him. "You wanna drink?"

"No, thanks, I'm good."

Then she turned the bottle upside down on a cotton ball, which she used to dab at his assorted wounds.

"Ouch." Brian felt the need to vocalize his pain, so as not to invite more.

Cookie smiled, wider when Brian kept grimacing. "Dis jus shooga cane." She showed him the label on the bottle. "Guaro."

"Burning water," said Brian, turning to Lita, not for approval but help.

But Lita was busy by the door, keeping guard, while Cookie got out an electric shaver and gave him a buzz cut; even turning his week without shaving into a fashionable goatee, though with his bumps and bruises Brian looked more like a hoodlum.

"Be still." Holding a razor blade between her thumb and forefinger, she groomed his sideburns, while chipping off dead pieces of flesh and dried blood. "Someone not happy wit chu."

"I thought you weren't going to ask."

"I dint," she laughed.

"There's probably a list of people who aren't happy with me," he admitted, "though it's, uh . . . getting shorter, I suppose." He shrugged, then reached into his front pocket for his Neosporin. "The guaro's great but could you try this when you're done? Please. Thank you."

But Lita objected. "You do not trust her?"

"No, I do, I just—"

Cookie laughed even louder, then gave Brian a break and started talking about her husband and kids, pictures of them framing the mirror, mostly on surfboards.

When she asked what they were doing in town, Lita went with the honeymoon story again and Cookie soaked it up, even got teary when Lita changed it from meeting Brian's parents to just his dad.

Lita glanced over at him, then told Cookie, "I will never know his mother but I am thankful to her . . . for bringing this man into the world . . . and sharing him with me."

That was, *gulp*, a wonderful thing to say, thought Brian;

the two most important women in his life—bonding.

When Cookie was done, Brian took a long look at himself in the mirror and rubbed his prickly head. He was probably born with more hair, but it felt good.

His nose, on the other hand, shaped like the letter *Z*, didn't feel good. And his ear hurt so much he could barely feel it, yet alone hear with it. Plus, his eyes were still puffy and purple and his face, burnt red by the sun, was already blistering.

Lita approached him from behind the chair, checking him out in the mirror, while trying not to look worried. "Your hair is very short but it is cute. I like it."

"Thanks."

"It will grow back, yes?"

Brian laughed. She was very dry, he thought. Or was she serious? "Why wouldn't my hair grow back? Is that a thing?"

Lita laughed, despite everything, inspiring Brian to ask Cookie about a place to get a beer. And she came up with Hot Rocks, where a band she knew was playing.

Angler's Lair, of course, remained the goal but Brian was uncertain how much, if anything, could get done before tomorrow.

Besides, it was decided. He loved Lita. He loved everything about her. And though love instantly gave him a feeling of dread, of losing that love, he wanted to celebrate. . . or get drunk and forget everything.

They found Hot Rocks on a busy corner in the center of town, just across the street from the beach. It was big, open-air, except for a thin plastic roof which lit up yellow in the lights. The main floor was lined with picnic tables, packed with people eating dinner, as a couple of men went about setting up a stage with instruments and microphones and speakers.

Deciding to play the part, Brian ordered a couple of Bavarias before they even sat down at the bar. This was his story. He had first dibs on the hero role.

"What was up with that song?" he asked Lita, as their beers came. "The one from Playa Grande, when you danced for us."

"I did not dance for anybody."

"Of course not."

"I dance for myself."

"Me too. . . Siempre."

She smiled, as if she couldn't help it. "The song is by Maná," she told him, "y Shakira, you know her?"

"Shakira?" repeated Brian, an image of the Colombian singer shaking her tail feather in a video, flashing before his eyes. "I don't know. Maybe."

"It is called, 'Mi Verdad.' " She flicked her hand at the bartender and suddenly he was pouring them each a shot. Lita took hers, held it up. "It mean, *my truth*."

"What is your truth?" Brian picked up his shot too. "If you don't mind me asking."

"I do not mind." But before she could explain, a 5-piece band took the stage led by a black man in a beret, who introduced them as, "*Plan B!*"

Lita downed her shot, then dragged Brian up front as he drank his; the band kicking straight into a hard reggae beat with Spanish flavors, a groove Brian wasn't sure he could find without looking like a complete idiot.

He tried anyway, bouncing to the bass, as if in slow motion, shoulders hunched, elbows up, like a monkey. Another couple smiled and laughed at him, giving their approval, or so he imagined.

Getting into it, he found that he enjoyed being the star of his own show, at least until he spotted a police officer at the door, giving the place the once-over, like a sheriff from an old western.

The officer was young, good-looking, an Erik Estrada type, thought Brian, with a clean honest face that would garner great praise for his role in capturing Lita and him.

Brian turned his head so he wouldn't be recognized, only to see a second officer walking toward him from the opposite side of the bar. . .

His heart sunk.

It was truly over.

And it wasn't Ivan.

There was no point in putting up a fight or running.

Brian grabbed ahold of Lita and pulled her close to him, but the second officer walked right by them, out to the street with the other one. . .

Brian couldn't believe it. He took a glass of water from the nearest table and chugged the whole thing, then apologized to his fellow tourists for his lack of manners, forgetting just how scary he looked.

Maybe, he thought (or rather wished), Jack and Darryl had sorted things out. Maybe Lita and him were home free.

She never saw the officers and playfully grabbed Brian back, then led him closer to the band, where she stared into his eyes and shook various body parts until he started dancing with her again.

Song after song.

Until they were completely wiped out.

And somehow raring for more.

By midnight, however, they both knew it was time to call it quits; Brian suggesting they phone Angler's Lair to see if it was available, while Lita already had her head in a taxi, negotiating a ride.

The taxi took them south, out of town along the coast toward Playa Chiquita, not far, maybe ten minutes before the restaurants and bars became fewer and far between and it was just jungle and beach and quiet.

The driver pulled over and let them out opposite the ocean; a single light bulb hanging from the branch of a tree in charge of illuminating two paths.

They took the one to the right, walking only twenty yards or so when they spotted a long wooden gate. Brian walked right up to it. “Think this—”

RUFF!

A dog lunged at him, a very big dog, from the other side of the gate, where a white man stood; thick, strong, middle-aged, and seemingly indifferent to the situation.

By the time Brian found his breath again, a woman, equally white, had stepped out of the shadows, joining the man, her voice warm but wary. “What can we do for you?”

“Hi,” began Brian, with an eye on the dog. “We’re looking for Angler’s Lair.”

“This is it,” she said. “Didn’t you see the sign?”

“Uh.”

“Most people book online,” said the man.

“We got into town late,” he told them. “We were, uh, trying to be spontaneous.” He checked the time on his phone. “Sorry.”

The dog sniffed at Brian and Lita through the gate. “Don’t worry about Zuri,” the man said. “She loves everyone.”

“How long were you looking to stay?” asked the woman.

“Just the night,” replied Brian. “We could pay for Saturday too but we might not be here.”

The woman looked over at the man, like she wanted his opinion, but he didn’t say anything as if he knew she didn’t.

Lita spoke up though and said a few words to her in Spanish.

To which she gave the man a second look, not much more, prompting him to swing open the gate, allowing Brian and

Lita to step through before he locked it again behind them. They followed the woman through a tropical garden, wild but tended to, Brian looking for an opening to drop Kenny's name, as if it could somehow lead to them getting out of the country.

Or, as they came upon a house on stilts, was Kenny just recommending a totally cool place to spend their last night of freedom?

The woman introduced herself as Janet, telling them she was from the States, her husband too, that they lived on the second floor and rented out the bottom to travelers.

She flipped on a light and showed them the ground floor unit; the kitchen and living room open to the jungle, only the bedroom had four walls around it. There was also an outdoor shower, two bicycles, a swimming pool, and a hot tub.

Hanging from the rafters, Brian noticed a piece of driftwood, the shape and size of a surfboard. He read the words carved into its side: *Like First Time.*

He liked that, its meaning resonating with him in unexpected ways; Lita being not only his second chance at love but a breath of fresh air that made everything feel new again. He handed Janet several hundred dollars. "Will this cover it?"

"I'll bring down your change," she said. "There should be a few eggs in the fridge, oh, and the last guests left some whiskey."

"Thanks, thank you, that's very kind of you," said Brian. "Sorry if we woke you."

"If you need anything, let us know." Janet pointed at the man who was now waiting for her by the stairs, half in the dark. "That's my husband Nick."

Janet turned to go with him but Brian wasn't done. "Do you by any chance know someone named Kenny? Early twenties. Long blond hair."

“Kenny?” She gave it thought. “No, can’t say that I do?”

“Or his dad Mike?” continued Brian. “From Chicago.”

“I don’t think so.” She looked at Nick. “Do you?” But he shook his head no.

“They live on the Pacific side,” said Brian.

“Mal Pais,” added Lita.

“Sorry,” said Nick, though he didn’t appear to be. “Don’t know many people on that side.”

“Oh,” continued Brian, “Kenny was the one who recommended your place.”

“That was nice,” said Janet.

Nick glanced at her, then back at Brian. “What did he say?”

“Just Angler’s Lair,” Brian told them. “It was over the phone. A quick call. Kenny just said, Angler’s Lair.”

“Well, you made it,” said Nick. “Good night.”

The couple went upstairs, Zuri too, leaving Brian and Lita grateful for a place to sleep but disappointed not to get more.

“What do we do?” asked Lita.

“There’s only one thing we can do,” said Brian. “Hot tub.”

“You are not funny.”

“You’re right.” Brian began unbuttoning his shirt. “But tonight, it’s all we got, and well, it’s a hot tub.”

20

Ain't Supposed To Die On A Saturday Night

On his seventh and what he hoped would be his final morning in Costa Rica, Brian heard the faint rustling of leaves, up high, far away, followed by a succession of ghostly *howls*, growing closer and closer until passing right over him; awakening him from a dream, a pipe dream, one in which he went to work on Monday and bragged to all his co-workers about the beautiful woman waiting for him at home, cooking gallo pinto.

Those were Howlers, he thought, meaning he was still thousands of miles from Chicago. He was, however, beginning to appreciate their wake-up call; a step up from the roosters on the Jamaica trip, which just so happened to be the last time the guys settled for affordable accommodations in favor of a good night's, and more importantly, a good morning's sleep.

Case in point, roosters tended to linger, *get up*, *get up*, whereas the monkeys were already gone, meaning Lita was still curled up against him, sound asleep, holding him, not a stitch of clothing or even a sheet covering either of them.

He couldn't believe he might spend the rest of his life with this woman . . . or just a few desperate hours. About to wake her, he stopped himself, pausing to admire her beauty, something he was aware of but continually amazed by.

He gently ran his hand along her thigh to the curve in her waist, paused, and traced it back down again, then took a timeout to count the freckles on her nose. He gravitated to her eyelashes. Long. Thick. Black. And all hers. The kind most women take ten minutes to paint on. Brian knew. He'd waited those ten minutes. Cost him the opening sequence to *Saving Private Ryan.*

As Brian watched her sleep, he tried to imagine all the hardships Lita had endured in her life; her husbands and their deaths and now Ivan the Terrible.

How does one deal with all that, wondered Brian? How does it shape them? He thought about his mom. How slow her death was. And painful. He never forgave god for such cruelty, especially her hair falling out.

Her funeral was on a bitterly cold December morning, the ground so hard they had to wait until spring to bury her. After the service, Brian, though just a young boy, told his dad he wasn't going to church on Christmas Eve, or any time, ever again.

He told him he'd been praying for his mom ever since she got sick, and she only got worse. And though his dad started going to church almost every Sunday, he never ragged on Brian for not coming with him.

When their mom first got diagnosed, she told her kids: "Don't worry about me. We're all dying. Either too soon. Or too late."

Morbid tidings from his mom, thought Brian, and it haunted him for years. However, it flipped the switch that morning on Lincoln's quote, the one his therapist reminded him of, about willing yourself happy: *Just make up your mind!*

After all those years, he realized his mom was actually giving him words of encouragement—*Go for it!*

As for last night, he remembered very little. They'd hit the whiskey. And the hot tub. Made it to bed. Barely. And . . . passed out.

Rested, Brian shifted gears, faster, one bordering on an almost frantic energy that required him to be on top of his game at all times.

Gotta keep moving. That was going to be the answer to just about any question. But because of Lita, Nicaragua was too obvious. Better south to Panama, of which he knew only about the canal (without Trump's help) and the Van Halen song, which was currently rattling around in his head:

Don't you know she's coming home with me,
You'll lose her in the turn,
I'll get her,
Panama!

--Van Halen

What?! That was the first time those lyrics made sense to him. Before, it was just Diamond Dave madness. So, he followed through on an urge to kiss Lita on her forehead. "Buenos dias."

Slowly opening her eyes, she found Brian and smiled, like she was happy it was him. "Good morning, guapo."

"About last night. . ."

Lita sat up in bed, folding her arms over her breasts. "Qué? Que pasó?"

"Nothing . . . much, I mean, when we were talking at the bar you never told me what your truth was."

Lita turned away from him. "We should go."

"Okay."

"My head is hurting."

"Sorry." Brian started to stand. . .

But Lita grabbed his hand, bringing him back down on the bed with her. "Mi verdad," she started, taking a deep breath. "My daughters are mi verdad, my truth."

"That's great."

"But I do not know if my truth makes me strong . . . or weak." She paused, then looked up at him. "I know I can protect mis hijas but I also know I cannot. Not always."

"That's uh. . ."

"Hard work." She snuggled up close to him again. "Y usted?"

"My truth? Hmm. I guess I'm still trying to find it."

She tenderly rubbed the end of her nose along his shoulder. "You do not know?"

Given time, he knew he could explain how important she had become to him but for now he inched closer to her and began kissing her neck.

And in turn, she nibbled on his good ear.

He ran his hands up her legs.

She pushed him back down on the bed.

And he pulled her on top of him.

Bodies pressed together, heart pounding against heart.

Their lips met, their––

Knock, Knock, Knock at the door. "Hey, good morning," came a man's voice from outside their room. "I've got something for ya."

Brian knew it was the owner but kept kissing Lita, hoping he'd go away.

"I think I know what you're looking for," he continued.

Uh, yeah, thought Brian.

Nick spoke louder. "Angler's Lair."

Covering his midsection with a pillow, Brian begrudgingly

left Lita and opened the door. “Isn’t this place Angler’s Lair?”

“Come with me.”

Minutes later they were riding in Nick’s truck along the coast, back to Puerto Viejo, when he stopped at a beach, rich with black sand, called Playa Negro. Brian assumed the dark color was the result of an oil spill. “That’s too bad.”

“The sand comes from a volcano,” explained Nick.

And though Brian thought that was cool, he hoped that wasn’t what Nick had brought them there for.

“See that?” Nick pointed toward an old abandoned barge, grounded just off shore.

Brian noticed a tree rising from its rusty deck, which was partially overgrown in grass. And there were kids of all colors climbing up and down a ladder, jumping into the shallow water, even a couple of men fishing off the deep end.

“The barge?” asked Brian.

“No.” He nodded farther out, past the swell, about a hundred yards offshore.

“The sailboat?” Brian had a better look at it; roughly forty feet long, two tall masts, no sign of anyone aboard. “What about it?”

“A buddy called me this morning,” said Nick. “Thought it funny that a boat was anchored off shore called Angler’s Lair.”

“Funny,” said Brian, “and perhaps interesting.”

“There’s more,” went on Nick. “Apparently, the guy who owns it has already overstayed his welcome in town.”

“He give you a name?”

“No.”

“Thank you, it’s a start.” Brian shook his hand. “You’ve been very helpful.”

“No worries.” Nick got back in his truck and said, “Take care,” like he meant it, then drove off. . .

Brian turned to Lita, who was still staring out at the sailboat, and used her words. "Tengo hambre."

"Sí." She reached for his hand. "Yo también."

Brian needed some food in his stomach, something to settle his nerves. And though he was convinced the menu at the soda was limited, it was merely limited to things he could understand.

Lita ordered the, "Tortilla con natilla," for them to share.

"And dos," said Brian, employing his Spanish, "Dos café con leches, por favor."

The older Tica woman behind the counter smiled warmly, seemingly pleased with his effort, and Brian knew asking around about the sailboat would be easy. And though a transparent strategy was fine before, he didn't see a need to make their presence known this late in the game.

A young boy, no more than six or seven, brought them their coffee with a plate of homemade tortillas, warm off a little counter-top stove, and a cup of thick cream.

Lita spread the cream on her tortilla. "Natilla," she said, taking a bite. "Es todo natural."

Brian followed suit, willing to try anything for her. "Not bad."

"Not bad?" She moved the plate closer to herself.

"Okay," laughed Brian. "It's bueno. Can I have some more?"

"I will think about it."

Brian took a sip of his coffee, then laughed again.

"What is so funny?"

"Nothing." He was beginning to find the way she spoke in long form not just cute but elegant, then realized that must be love.

When they were done with their snack they ventured down to the water, Brian beginning to appreciate the sand, which changed on a fine line from a creamy white to the blackest black.

"The lava," she told him, letting the black sand run through her fingers. "It is floating, just a little."

"But how does the sand stay separate?"

"The white sand is coral, it travels in the water, but the black sand stays above it, so the waves push the sand one way and the currents another."

"Smart and beautiful." Brian kissed her. "Lucky me."

"No, I am lucky." She kissed him back. "You see that in me."

Brian wrapped his arms around her and whispered sweet-nothings in her ear, which they truly were, since he was just mumbling, teasing her.

She laughed and kissed him again, then stopped when she realized they were surrounded by a swarm of kids, the ones they'd seen on the barge.

An older boy, or at the least the tallest of the bunch, quieted the rest of them down, asking Brian and Lita if they wanted surf lessons.

But Brian politely declined, before realizing the boy was on to something. "But can we just get boards off you, maybe with some paddles?"

"We don't rent boards, we give lessons," the boy said.

"Can we talk in the shade?" asked Brian, heading for a palm tree.

"You pay for the board and the lesson together," said the boy, following after him, his minions in tow. "One price."

"But—"

"Fifty dollars each."

And that was the status quo amongst the kids until a girl squeezed her way to the front of the pack. She couldn't have been more than eleven or twelve, figured Brian, with a reddish-brown afro, almost bigger than she was, and freckles from head to toe to match.

"You don't want lesson?" she asked, like she wanted to set the record straight.

"No," Lita told her, nicely. "No los necesitamos."

"Solo the boards," said Brian.

"Por quánto tiempo?" the girl asked.

"Dos, tres horas," said Lita.

"There're no waves," the older boy felt the need to point out. "Not until later."

But the girl shot him down. "They just want boards."

"With paddles," confirmed Brian.

She nodded her head, coming to a conclusion. "I can do. No lesson, thirty dollars each."

"Perfect." Brian handed her a $100 bill.

Her eyes lit up. "Pero no tengo cambio," she said. "I don't have change."

"Keep it," said Brian.

The girl looked like she wanted to burst with joy but maintained her composure, holding the bill up to the sun, trying to see through it, then flicking at it with her finger.

Once certain of its authenticity, she handed two of the younger boys some coins from her pocket and sent them off to fetch the boards, much to the annoyance of their former leader.

By the time the boys returned with boards and paddles, Lita had bought a new bikini, a teeny tiny bikini; not a thong but not very businesslike either, thought Brian. Meanwhile, knowing they might not return the boards, he put $2,000 dollars in the pocket to his jeans and asked the girl if she would look after their clothes.

Brian was on the water within minutes, sooner than he expected, paddling after Lita with his legs out in front of him like he was in a kayak, the sack on his lap, already halfway out to the sailboat.

"What's our plan?" he asked, catching up to her.

"It has not changed," she said, paddling ahead of him again from her knees. "We are leaving country."

"Yeah, okay, but then what's our plan right now?"

"I do not have a plan because I do not know who is on boat."

"Good point," conceded Brian, though he was hardly satisfied.

As they paddled on, Brian began to notice a change in the wind; not only switching direction but picking up in intensity, so much so that by the time they reached the boat, the sun had been pushed into the background by a milky gray sky.

Lita didn't waste any time calling out, "Hola! Buenos tardes! Hola!"

Brian was half expecting a *No trespassing* or *Fuck off* in return, but there wasn't a response. Just silence. "Maybe they're below deck. We should give them a minute."

A flash in the sky and they both turned in time to see a bolt of lightning crash into the ocean, far enough that it didn't make a sound but big enough to know it was on its way.

Lita stood up on her board and paddled hard to where a fishing net dangled like a giant spider web over the boat's hull, which rose a good seven or eight feet above her.

Then she looked back at Brian as if to say, *this is the plan*, and nimbly climbed up the netting with only her paddle for protection before disappearing over the side of the boat.

"Lita!" he shouted, as quietly as he could.

An anxious moment or two passed before she popped up on deck, staring down at him. "Shhh. . ."

"Why, shhh?" Brian was having a hard time steadying his board in the rough water, which was beginning to lap against the hull. “Someone’s either here or they’re not.”

“The boat is empty,” she said. “Venga.”

“What about the boards?”

“They will live,” she said, “and I saw you leave her money.”

“But what if we need to get back to the beach?”

When she didn’t answer him, Brian labored to his feet, then almost fell in, so he grabbed the sack, Lita’s hand already reaching down to take it from him.

She took the sack and went away again, leaving Brian below in the water. So, he put his foot in the bottom rung of the netting to test if it could hold his weight.

Satisfied, he started climbing, with difficulty, one rung at a time, until he fell over the railing, plopping down at Lita’s feet.

Out of breath, Brian rolled over on his stomach, pretending to have a closer look at the deck. “Yeah, that looks about right?”

“What does?”

“The boat, of course.” Heeding his own words, he paused to take it in. With its copper casting and ornate wood finish, it was beautiful, even if years in the sun had given it a washed-out look.

And thankfully it dwarfed Mike’s boat, though with multiple sails he knew they’d be utterly challenged to manage it on their own without use of its engine. Still, whoever left it was surely coming back for it.

When the rain came, they decided to wait below deck, Lita gravitating to the master suite and a stereo CD player straight out of the ’80s, a subtle reminder to Brian of how dated his youth had become.

Lita rifled through the CDs. “I like dancing with you last night.”

“The Monkey Bar was fun too.”

“I am drinking too much that night.” She found a CD to

her liking and put it in the tray, already tapping her foot.

"You don't remember me kissing you on the dance floor?" tried Brian.

"No. You did not kiss me." She pressed play and turned her full attention to Brian. "But you want to."

"I did?" he teased.

"You did not?"

He sat down on the edge of the bed, unable to lie to her. "I did."

She smiled, caressing his cheek with the back of her hand. "You must learn to salsa."

"Okay." Brian took that as a sign they had a future together, and he vowed to follow along as best as he could. "Lay it on me."

She reached her hand out to him, nodding over her shoulder to the stereo. "This is Lalo Rodriguez."

He stood up, facing her, ready to dance.

She moved her feet back, "One, two, three," and then forward, "Five, six, seven."

"What happened to four?" he asked, trying to mimic her steps.

"Four, you rest." Thunder accompanied the lightning this time and Brian thought the dance lesson might be over, but Lita only turned up the volume on the stereo. "Es el primero salsa song I am dancing."

Brian felt like the room was spinning, which he attributed to how he felt about Lita, then realized it was more of a pulling sensation, as if the boat was straining to go. . .

"The anchor," he said, pleased to have solved the puzzle but worried what it might imply. "Do you think the anchor will hold?"

Folding her arms around his neck, she stared deep into his eyes. "The song is called, 'Ven, Devórame Otra Vez.' It means, come devour me again. "

He forgot about the anchor. “Really?”

“Sí.”

“Are you trying to seduce me?”

“You are talking too much.” She backed away, then turned the music up even more. “Uno, dos, tres.” She put one hand across her stomach, the other palm up, signaling for him to do the same. “Cinco, seis, siete.”

Ay Ven devórame otra vez
Ven devórame otra vez
Que la boca me sabe a tu cuerpo
Desesperan mis ganas por ti

--Lalo Rodriguez

Brian was struggling to keep time with her, especially when she placed her left hand on his shoulder, her right hand in his, stepping with him toward her and then back again.

She was into it, he thought, into him, not paying attention to how much the wind had kicked up. So, he tried his best to follow her moves and she rewarded his efforts with a kiss, one that started fast, then . . . lingered.

Meanwhile, Brian reached around her back, untying her bikini top, then surprised even himself and went to a knee to remove her bottoms.

While he was down there, he thought he should say something about the inclement weather but instead said the first thing that came to his head: “Take me, I’m yours. Because dreams are made of this.” He stood back up, but without his swimsuit, both of them completely naked. “Forever they’ll be a heaven in your kiss.”

“This is your poesía?”

"My poetry, no," he admitted. "Squeeze."

"Squeeze?"

"It's a band."

"Soy una mujer." Lita pushed him onto the bed. "So squeeze me."

Brian could feel the boat rise in the water, yanking hard on the anchor, but he was on top of her, so he held her close, kissing her wherever his lips took him, his hands racing up and down her body.

"I have protection," he said in her ear, before realizing where. "In my pants. Which are on the beach. Damnit."

"You are my protection." She rolled over on top of him.

"Oh."

"Do not move."

Brian obeyed orders, laying still on his back, as the cabin windows lit up, followed by a loud *CRACK* of thunder.

Oblivious, or perhaps determined, Lita slid her leg over his waist and found him, slow at first, until their hips fell in time together, while Brian arched his back, taking her in completely, moving with her as one, on fire with feelings of love and desire.

This woman, this moment, he wanted to hold on to it forever, so he rolled back on top of her, withdrawing to kiss every inch of her body until she was so overcome with pleasure that she grabbed his ass and pulled him back in to her for a few heated minutes before they finished together.

With thunder *CRACKING* all around them.

Or was that gunfire?

That was fucking gunfire, realized Brian, jumping out of bed so fast that he bumped his head on the ceiling, though he didn't think he was unconscious more than a second or two.

Yet, when he opened his eyes there was a thin black man with long dreadlocks standing beneath the open hatch at the foot of the bed.

In one hand, he was holding their sack, in the other, Anna's gun, like he was letting it cool off. "Who wanna meet Bob next?" he asked them, all Rasta like.

"Who's Bob?" asked Brian, standing before him, just skin and sweat. "Bob Marley?" His mind raced to the Chili Pepper video Mike had talked about, to the song's lyrics. " 'Bob Marley, poet and a prophet.' "

The man frowned, unimpressed.

" 'Bob Marley,' " continued Brian, " 'taught me how to off it.' "

"We con be cute bout dis, mon, but it steel gonna end bad for ya."

"I can explain. . . I, was—"

"Fokeen yor ladee nme bed."

"Lovely accent by the way." Brian didn't doubt its authenticity but thought he heard something else in his voice, the way he struggled to say, *fucking*, as if he spoke more French than English. "Had you from Jamaica but now I'm thinking perhaps Martinique."

"Ya smatare dan ya look."

"I was right?"

"No." He centered the gun on Brian's chest.

"Okay, but Bob, you meant Bob Marley, right?"

He cocked his gun.

"Kenny!" shouted Lita, getting out of bed.

He lowered the gun, clearly enamored with the naked woman. "You can call me any ting ya like—"

"Somos amigos de Kenny," said Lita.

"Foke." The man's expression turned sour. "Yor Lita?"

"Sí."

The boat tugged hard on the anchor again, but he looked back at Brian. "An yor dee stupeed Amareecane?"

"Probably."

"Whada ell eez wrong wit cha?" he snarled. "When deed

Kenny say to foke yor lady in Ringtone's bed?"

"Sorry about that, I'm Brian, your name's Ringtone?"

"To friends," he replied, still worked up. "Me wuz two second from puttin a bullet in ya. . . An me clean dee sheets in town yeztaday!"

"Um, yeah, we sensed that," said Brian, "about killing us, not the sheets, though come to think of it they did smell fresh."

"Jez get dressed," sighed Ringtone, "both aya," as a wave crashed over the side of the boat, water pouring into the cabin from the hatch.

"We're Kenny's amigos," reiterated Brian, struggling to get his swimsuit on standing up. "We're, um, cool with him. He must've told you that. Seriously, sorry about the bed." He nodded at Lita. "That was our first time."

And she nodded back in agreement.

Ringtone got soaked by yet another wave crashing over the boat. "Me geteet."

"Thanks, I, you know, didn't know if I was ever going to get there." Brian reached out to shake Ringtone's hand.

But he was already heading back up the steps. "Time to set sail."

"In this weather?" questioned Brian.

"No choice, mon." He looked back down at them. "Me juz shoot two men."

They found Ringtone on deck, his face a mix of confidence and caution as he busied himself with buttons and ropes and a wind so strong the rain was hitting them sideways. He did, however, take the time to give his vessel a proper introduction, raising his voice over the storm: "Welcome aboard Angler's Lair!"

He pushed a button on the console, starting the engine, then flicked a switch, causing a long thick chain to recoil at the bow. “Me raisin’ da anchor!” he shouted. He took ahold of the steering wheel. “Brace ya selves!”

Once free of the ocean floor, the boat drifted toward the beach and in mere seconds was on the wrong side of the break, where runaway waves were crashing toward shore.

Ringtone slammed the engine in gear and pointed the bow into the oncoming wave, climbing up . . . and over the crest, barely, only to have to climb the next one. . .

Brian gripped the center console, while Ringtone somehow maneuvered them over the next wave and the one after, until they were past the break and headed out to sea.

“Where’re we going?” Brian managed to ask him.

“Port-au-Prince!”

“That’s. . . Haiti.”

“So ya seen a map.” He reached for Brian’s hand and returned the gun.

And Brian took it, preferring that Ringtone keep two hands on the wheel. “Thanks.”

“Don worry,” said Ringtone. “Kenny’s ol man owe me five grand, said yud double it.”

“You got it.” Brian gave him the thumbs up. “Whatever you need.”

Ringtone smiled but quickly became frustrated after flicking the anchor switch again.

“You, um, you shot two men, like you . . . connected?” wondered Brian. “Or you just shot at them?”

“Me handle dem.”

“Quién?” asked Lita, joining them.

“Me dint see dem follow me to the boat in da storm.”

Lita took the gun from Brian with little protest and checked how many bullets were left, leaving Brian to wonder if he was the only one in the world who couldn’t handle a gun. When she was done, she repeated herself. “Quién?”

“Be cool,” Ringtone told her. “Eet was beeg mon, beeg

beard, dee udder one, he in charge, call heemself Ivan. Now me know who he wuz lookin for."

"Shit." Brian leaned into the console to absorb the next swell.

And they cleared it, but there was a hard *thud* at the bow. "Foke, eet's slammin gainst me boat." Ringtone flicked the anchor switch up and down again. "Eez jammed. Eet's no all deeway up."

Ringtone cut the engine, as Lita stuck the gun in the back of her bikini and went to have a look at the chain, even with the boat rocking up and down from swell to swell.

When she reached the bow, the boat's nose lifted up out of the water and with it, clinging to the anchor, was a bloodied but breathing Ivan, who snatched Lita over the railing with one arm.

Brian couldn't believe what he'd seen. Nor could he believe how he reacted, running and diving off the boat in one fluid if not macho motion. . .

He hit the water hard but kept his bearings, reaching for Lita underneath the surface, but he couldn't find her, and when he came up for air, he couldn't find the boat either.

A feeling of despair overwhelmed him, but when he rose up in the next swell, he spotted the boat again, not too far; Lita clinging to the boat's netting, Ivan clinging to her, half in the water, trying to drag her down with him.

Brian battled his way through the rough water to the boat as Lita was reaching for the gun in her bikini, but Ivan was quick to grab her arm, and now she was doing everything she could just to hold on to the boat, which was bucking wildly.

Brian managed to get ahold of the netting behind Lita and pulled himself out of the water, then stuck his hand in the back of her bikini, trying to find the gun, which he did, not hesitating to shoot Ivan multiple times before realizing the safety catch was still on.

Releasing the catch on the first try, Brian shot him for real—

But missed.

Ivan was enraged, desperate, clawing at Lita's grip on the rope, using every ounce of his being to pull her under water.

She was barely hanging on, just by her fingertips, when Brian leaned around her and pressed the gun up to Ivan's head, pulling the trigger a final time.

Ivan fell backwards into the water, the last light of the day finding his eyes as he sunk to his grave, one staring up at them, the other already dead. . .

Ringtone reached down over the railing with Lita's paddle and helped the two of them back into the boat, "Me towtee wuz dead," then took his place behind the wheel.

When the storm finally passed, he turned off the engine and stationed his guests on deck, pointing at ropes and levers and sails and shouting out instructions. "Watch for dee boom!"

Summers on a sunfish at camp gave Brian some sailing experience and he was up for the challenge, familiar with what to do, just not on such a grand scale. Soon though, they captured a crosswind and were going faster than when Ringtone had the engine on.

Brian looked over at Lita to make sure she was okay. And there she was, following orders, raising the jib like a pro, though he realized he might be biased.

He made eye contact with Ringtone to see if he could leave his post and got his approval, then joined Lita up front, as she secured a rope in a cleat.

He wrapped his arms around her and hugged her tight, catching a final Costa Rican sunset over her shoulder, wondering if their troubles were behind them or merely lying in wait.

"Lita. . ." He let go of her and took the diamond ring off

his pinky, grateful it was still there. "Let's call this a promise ring."

"A promise ring?"

"Yeah." He held her left hand and placed the ring on the proper finger.

Then she removed the wedding band from her thumb and slid it on his finger. "Brian. . ." She looked up at him, her eyes soft and sincere. "What do you promise me?"

He hesitated, giving the question great thought, then came to a resounding conclusion. "Everything."

About The Author

A native of Evanston, Illinois, DOUG E. JONES graduated from UCLA with a degree in English Literature and a minor in Creative Writing. His first novel, *Nowhere To Goa*, follows a 19-year-old American boy to India. His second novel *Disco Inferno!* takes place in 1979 Chicago, where a 16-year-old boy has to decide between rock n roll, disco, and a girl. Prior to getting into the book business, Doug wrote for the hit TV show *Charmed*. You can contact him at dougejones.com.

52025371R00183

Made in the USA
Columbia, SC
27 February 2019